Child Abuse

Child Abuse
UNDERSTANDING THE PROBLEM

PAUL JOHNSON

The Crowood Press

First published in 1990 by
The Crowood Press
Ramsbury
Marlborough
Wiltshire SN8 2HE

© Paul Johnson 1990

British Library Cataloguing in Publication Data

Johnson, Paul
  Child abuse: understanding the problem.
  1. Children. Abuse & neglect
  I. Title
  362.7′044

ISBN 1 85223 360 5

Line diagrams by Sharon Perks

Typeset by Hope Services (Abingdon) Ltd
Printed by Biddles Ltd, of Guildford and King's Lynn

For Gill, Mick, Dick and Paddy

Contents

	Acknowledgements	8
	Preface	9
1	Defining Child Abuse	11
2	Increasing Awareness of Child Abuse?	33
3	Case Examples	57
4	The Effects of Abuse	89
5	Why are Children Abused?	114
6	Legal Aspects of Child Protection	141
7	Local Authority Procedures	162
8	The Rights of Parents and Children	183
9	Investigation and Initial Assessment	199
10	Treatment Issues in Child Abuse	226
11	Future Developments	255
	Bibliography	266
	Index	269

Acknowledgements

I should like to thank the following people, without whose help this book would not have been possible: Alan Ashmore and his team, for seven years of social work practice and free training along the way (I also owe my thanks to them for allowing me to refresh my memory of past cases); professional colleagues who have been kind enough to offer their opinions on the text, in particular Denham Ridgway, Moira Vangrove and Caroline Ambery; friends and relations whose constructive criticisms have always been appreciated and occasionally acted upon. Special thanks are due to Mary and Kim, for permission to use their story in the text. I should like to express my gratitude to all the clients with whom I have been involved over the years, many of whom have helped me much more than I ever helped them. I should also like to record my thanks to Carole Smith for her enthusiasm and advice throughout the time when the book was being written, and for suggesting the project in the first place. Finally, special thanks are due to Jane Dawson for typing the original manuscript from my increasingly untidy handwriting.

Preface

The aim of this book is to describe, as clearly as possible, some of the main issues which surround the topic of child abuse, from the perspective of a local authority social worker. The reader will excuse this perspective. The only personal contact I have ever had with the subject has been through my work, which has always been as a social worker. I have used the term 'social worker' in parts of the book in a very general way, and in doing so I do not wish to minimise the efforts which voluntary organisations (the NSPCC, for example) make in this field.

I have been increasingly aware over the past five years of the extent to which child abuse features in the press, on television and in everyday conversation. When people find out what I do for a living, they often display very clear and firm views about the subject, ranging from disbelief, through to a desire to bring back capital punishment. Although this developing awareness is to be welcomed, it is a source of some concern on my part that, in the main, the general public receives its information about child abuse and the social work role from the media. It is usually passed on in the wake of the latest public inquiry into a child death, or in the aftermath of some other crisis. Using information gleaned in this way can be misleading. One can receive the impression that all cases are life and death struggles between incompetent social workers and adults whose sole intention is to kill children.

I hope to be able to encourage the reader to look in more detail at the whole subject, in an attempt to demonstrate the complexity of the social work task and to show how difficult it is to protect children. I have tried hard to avoid writing defensively, from a professional point of view; quite clearly, social workers make mistakes and will no doubt continue to do so. I have balanced the text between hard fact (of which there is little), and opinion (of which there is a great deal).

Although I have illustrated the text with examples of work from my own experiences, I have disguised case examples heavily in order to protect confidentiality.

The book is not written with a professional social work audience in mind. I have attempted to keep it free from jargon and have aimed for clarity and readability. A great deal of my own uncertainties and doubts about the subject are contained in the book, and to that extent it is likely to be a source of some frustration for the reader who wishes to find solutions and definitive statements.

Note The opinions contained in this book are those of the author alone, and do not necessarily reflect those of any local authority or organisation with which the author has been connected.

1 Defining Child Abuse

THE NEED FOR DEFINITIONS

Social workers have a responsibility to protect children from harm and to promote children's welfare. In order that they can carry out this role, some generally agreed notions about what is and is not acceptable behaviour towards children must be arrived at and written down. This must be the case, for how else would it be possible to differentiate between those situations which require intervention and those which do not? The local authority social worker has to exercise his authority on behalf of the community which employs him. Ideally, the social worker's opinion as to what constitutes the abuse of children would be shared by the community in general.

If no attempt were made to describe the abuse of children and to set out the parameters of 'good enough parenting', the social worker would be left to conduct his investigations in a vacuum, and would be ill informed about the level of care which the community would describe as being acceptable.

Very often in the past, notions about acceptable standards of child care have been debated in the wake of the latest child abuse tragedy to hit the headlines. Then, often for weeks afterwards, many commentators displaying varying degrees of insight and judgement flood the popular debate with their own versions of where to draw the elusive line between inaction and intervention. Sometimes it appears as if social workers cannot win in the eyes of the public, no matter what they do. If they adopt a so-called 'passive' approach and decide, after assessing the degree of risk, to allow a child to remain at home, they can be severely criticised for their inaction if a tragedy subsequently occurs. If social workers are seen to adopt a hard line approach and remove children from home without the benefit of indisputable evidence of actual abuse, they can be severely criticised at a later date for being

11

heavy handed if it transpires that the grounds for their concern were ill founded and that they made a genuine error of judgement.

I am not attempting to justify all actions by social workers in the field of child protection. Quite clearly, bad decisions are sometimes made with serious and occasionally tragic consequences for the children and families concerned. My point is that social workers can often be left feeling quite isolated, having to take on too much responsibility for making up the rules as they go along. In my view, this is not a legitimate role for social workers to play. Professional judgement will always play a part in making difficult decisions about child abuse, but this judgement must be seen to operate within commonly accepted boundaries.

A similar relationship between professional responsibility and the public expression of what is and is not acceptable operates within the law. Although this relationship is a complex one, there is a sense in which public debate informs the legislature about the need for laws and about how far individual freedoms should be allowed to extend before they need to be curtailed. Although it is the lawyers' function to interpret the rules in individual cases, the rules themselves are often based upon commonly shared principles. If they are not, the law can in some cases be changed in recognition of the fact that it no longer reflects public opinion. When sections of society feel that the law is unfair, pressure group activity plays a significant part in terms of legal reform.

It is in the area of commonly shared principles that some of the main problems regarding the establishment of definitions of child abuse occur. As we shall discover, the concept of child abuse is an extremely elusive one and means different things to different people. It is hard to imagine a time when social workers will be assisted by more than the most general statements aimed at defining abuse. They will always be placed in circumstances where they have to make their own judgements about a very wide range of issues, only marginally informed by public opinion.

Why is it that public debate tends to intensify when a child

12

abuse tragedy occurs, and what are the implications for social workers? The simple answer to the first question is that the detail of media reporting so horrifies the public that the subject is forced into public awareness to a degree which makes it a topic of intense conversation for a while. We all like to pride ourselves on the care which we lavish on our children, so, why is child abuse not an issue of popular debate, other than around the times of extensive media coverage? I think that the abuse of children is such an emotive and unsavoury activity to contemplate that we all have a need to minimise, or ignore it as much as we possibly can. Even today, when the extent of the problem is slowly becoming more apparent, the debate often seems to be conducted only after the latest incident. This has serious implications for the support which social workers can expect to receive from the general public. Firstly, many tragedies and crises reported by the media document errors of judgement and episodes of bad practice on the part of the 'caring professions'. As the local authority social worker is usually the professional with the main legal responsibility to protect children, the bulk of any criticism is aimed at him. The general public can be forgiven, therefore, for assuming that social workers are incapable of adequately carrying out their child protection duties. This creates a climate of unease and mistrust, leading social workers to be reticent about their role, allowing conjecture and assumption to play a leading part in any analysis of the social worker's job.

Another implication of the reactive nature of the popular child abuse debate is that it concentrates the public perception on the more obviously serious aspects of child abuse. This can be extremely misleading in terms of reflecting reality, and is another source of public disquiet about the social worker's role. The popular view of child abuse used to relate to the physical injury of young people. Visions of youngsters with severe bruising, broken limbs and battered bodies would be conjured up whenever this subject was mentioned. It is that much easier to ignore less dramatic injuries to children. The subject of sexual abuse, which has only very recently been brought to the public's attention, can be seen in the same way. For many, child sexual abuse would mean sexual intercourse with children; in fact, it has a much broader definition. Physical neglect of children, and in particular emotional abuse, are other forms of abuse that are more difficult to understand and define than physical assault. This means that the social worker will often have difficulty in putting over to the public his role in cases which do not fall towards the 'very serious' end of abusing situations. Social workers will argue, quite rightly, that it is extremely dangerous to ascribe degrees of severity to episodes of abuse. Some incidents, which at first glance might appear to be less potentially harmful, do carry implications for children that are just as damaging as other, more obviously serious cases.

Social workers need to be guided by the communities in which they work so that they reflect widely shared values of what is reasonable behaviour. Definitions are important, and need to reflect as accurately as possible the consensus of opinion about what constitutes abuse. As we begin to examine some of the commonly quoted definitions which are prevalent at the moment, I shall endeavour to refer back to the issues I have raised in order to emphasise the difficulties created by the task of defining child abuse.

PROBLEMS OF DEFINITION

Child abuse is without doubt a major issue of public debate. This must be welcomed because an increasing public awareness of the subject can only help the process of detection and prevention. However, the subject of child abuse is an extremely complicated one and the public debate is often confused and littered with myths, half truths and bits of knowledge (*see* Mayhall & Norgard – Bibliography). Although there are a variety of possible reasons for this confusion, a key factor is the problem of definition.

We all have a view about the acceptable limits of a relationship between an adult and a child. We could all distinguish between justifiable discipline and physical ill-treatment, between physical affection and sexual assault, but how would our 'boundaries' compare with those of other people. For example, if I were to say that, as part of my role as father to my children, I regularly slap them across the face if they refuse to do as I tell them, would that constitute physical abuse? Some readers might say 'yes', without question. Others may decide that it definitely was not abuse. I would guess that the majority would be unable to answer the question, given the limits of the information available. Other questions would need to be asked. How hard do I hit them? How often? How badly do the children have to behave before they are hit? Even if all these questions and more could be answered, I believe that it would be an impossible task to achieve complete agreement as to whether or not my children were being abused. Why are definitions so difficult?

Our Own Experiences

Undoubtedly, the experiences which we have in our own childhood, our interaction with our own parents or guardians, influence the way in which we view the world. If, for example, a person is brought up in a household where it is common practice for all the men and boys to have crew cut hairstyles, this might have implications for the way in which they would deal with their own family. The reaction might be to carry on the family tradition. It might appear odd or unusual to outsiders, but not to those who have been brought up in that way. Alternatively, they might rebel and become violently opposed to short hair, refusing to allow their children to get their hair cut. Again, this could be a perfectly valid reaction to past experiences, which could none the less seem strange to the outside world. Thirdly, the person could be unmoved by his early experiences, and his decisions as a parent not influenced at all.

Early experiences are significant across the whole range of human behaviour. When we examined the question of whether I was abusing my own children, we came to

15

conclusions based, in part at least, upon what had been our experiences of family discipline in the past. Given that we all have very different experiences, it is safe to assume that, for a whole range of subjects, our views will differ from those of friends and neighbours. All of this is true in relation to the topic of child abuse. An adult who has been abused, in whatever way, is likely to let that experience influence his or her own parenting practices, and the way in which the practices of other people are viewed. A female who has been sexually abused by babysitters is likely to have particular views about leaving her own children with babysitters. She might refuse to allow it, and never trust anyone with her children. She might have been so damaged by her own experiences that she is unable to think about protecting other children – 'No one protected me, so why should I care?'. Those who had parents who slapped their faces if they misbehaved would have been making judgements about my behaviour which were influenced by their own childhood memories. Perhaps for some, past experiences influenced their opinion more than an analysis of the behaviour in question.

I think you will agree that one of the reasons why it is difficult to formulate definitions of abuse is that our reactions toward human behaviour are influenced by elements other than the behaviour itself. Definitions cannot reflect a wide variety of experiences and personal perceptions.

Emotional Responses

Most of us try not to harm children deliberately. We share a responsibility for protecting vulnerable members of the community from harm, and we respond in a very deep-seated, perhaps subconscious way to children's vulnerability. Our senses are touched by the appealing nature of babies – their big eyes, soft skins and immediate reaction to affection give us pleasure. Our sensibilities are therefore shaken when we see photographs of young children with bruises, or when we read about youngsters having been appallingly neglected or sexually assaulted. In part, this normal reaction stems from our not wanting to think about fellow human beings coming to harm. In my view, however, there is an extra dimension to the emotional response we feel when children are involved. This extra layer of feeling, whilst being perfectly natural, and probably a very healthy response, can hinder rational debate and discussion of the issues. Language such as the following is often used in discussions about child abuse: 'They must be animals to do it to kids', 'They are sick', 'They ought to be hanged', 'I wish I could get hold of them'.

I have used language like this often. The problem is, of course, that it makes it much more difficult really to get to grips with the subject if we are forever struggling with the emotional issues which the topic raises in each of us. It is very difficult to be detached enough to examine each case on its merits. To think about basic definitions is hard. Definitions are cold, mechanical, static things, while child abuse is alive, charged with feeling and emotion. If we can't define it, and if we can't make attempts to reach basic agreements about what it is, we have very little chance to make a co-ordinated response to it.

Uncertain Situations

If a definition is too general it often serves no useful purpose; with a little imaginative manipulation, most situations can be made to 'fit'. If a definition is too rigid, the converse can be the case. This general problem with any type of definition is of particular significance in relation to child abuse. In my experience, many cases which involve social workers contain many areas of doubt, are not clear cut and can be open to interpretation. It is an impossible task to devise adequate working definitions of abuse which will cover every eventuality. This is a rather sweeping generalisation, but its implications for those professionally involved in the protection of children are immense.

All situations of abuse are to be found somewhere along a very blurred scale of severity. We may have little difficulty at the severe end, but we can have many significant problems at

17

the other end of the scale, when it comes to agreeing that abuse is taking place, and that it is of a degree which calls for action to be taken. It would make the world of social work infinitely simpler if we could always agree what did or did not constitute abuse in each case. Definitions cope with clear-cut situations but provide limited help otherwise. At worst, rigid and inflexible definitions can hinder the task of protecting children, by allowing us to ignore those situations which do not fall neatly into our labelled categories. Our desire for labels must be associated with the need to feel in control of our environment and our social relationships. We are rarely comfortable with an issue until we have been able to compartmentalise it, and perhaps oversimplify the subject. This often does not make it easier to understand, especially if those who have been labelled act in a way which is contrary to the rules of their particular pigeonhole.

We do not understand or control child abuse simply by labelling the constituent parts. This process can lead us into a false sense of security and can confuse rather than clarify. It is better to accept that some issues defy absolute definition, and are therefore exceptionally confusing areas in which to work, than to invent and impose a set of generalisations which do the subject matter no justice at all. I do not wish to imply here that definitions should be ignored. They are a necessary element in an understanding of a subject. However, they ought to be treated with circumspection and distrust, and then they can be very helpful.

Reflecting Changes in Attitude

This seems to be another inherent problem with definitions, particularly in the field of human interaction. A definition of what constitutes abuse is, to some extent, rather a static statement. It cannot reflect the changes in attitudes towards child care that continue to evolve over time. Until recently it was common practice for school teachers to beat recalcitrant pupils with canes – this is now not the case. Definitions of physical abuse of children would have been much more narrow fifty years ago than they are today.

It is only recently that the concept of sexual abuse has been openly discussed. I am sure that people were aware of its existence in the past, but, for a variety of reasons, it is deemed to be a 'new' problem. It has consequently been defined in a variety of different ways, in response to the prominence it now receives. Quite clearly, definitions of abuse must be seen to constantly evolve and develop, being informed by, and responsive to, the prevailing attitudes and advances in knowledge of the way in which adults relate to children.

Cultural Issues

Any definition of abuse would have to be based on the premise that there was a universally accepted agreement about how an adult should behave towards a child. Once this base line of conduct is established, it is presumably quite straightforward to write down where that line, between acceptable and unacceptable, is situated. This becomes the definition of abuse.

To complicate things even further, no only do individuals differ in their opinion of what constitutes abuse, but groups of individuals from different cultural backgrounds often differ from other groups of people about child care practices in general. For example, Jewish boys are circumcised as part of their religious initiation. More often than not, there is no medical reason why a piece of flesh should be cut from the child's body, but it is done nevertheless. This is not an activity to which people object; it would not be seen as physical abuse by most people, but is an accepted ritual practised by a large group. However, it does involve an act which some other cultures might consider to be wilful violence. Similarly, it is common practice for very small children, girls and boys, to have one or both ears pierced. Again, this activity could be said to involve some element of potential abuse and would find severe critics in other societies. Custom, tradition and in particular religion can impose elements of physical abuse upon its followers which are often condoned and usually encouraged by the community in general.

What about non-physical abuse? When I was at school, between the ages of seven and eleven, I and the rest of the school pupils who were Catholics didn't go into assembly with the rest of the children. Our parents objected to their offspring being a part of a non-Catholic religious experience. We had to congregate in a little room off the main hall where we were encouraged to read a Catholic prayer book by a teacher who shared the same faith as ourselves (or, rather, our parents!). At the appointed time, when all the Protestants had sung 'All Things Bright and Beautiful' and said the prayer for the day, a knock came on the door, and, with the eyes of the rest of the school following us rather accusingly, I and my fellow outcasts (for that is how it felt) filed in at the back of the hall to hear how many goals the school football team had lost by on Saturday morning. Was that mental cruelty on the part of our parents? I doubt it, but it felt a little like persecution at the time.

There has been a great deal of press coverage about the predicament of Jehovah's Witnesses who feel unable to give consent to potentially life-saving operations on their children. Presumably, they are simply following their honestly held convictions, and not setting out deliberately to harm their children. However, in the case of the preventable death of a child whose parents refused medical consent on religious grounds, would that constitute child abuse?

The point is that ethnic, cultural and religious groupings have certain ideas about how to care for their children which will differ to varying degrees. Definitions of abuse, which of necessity involve the need to make some kind of judgement about where to draw the line between acceptable and unacceptable behaviour, must take into account these differences and try to reflect any common ground.

CURRENT DEFINITIONS OF ABUSE

The DHSS published a document in 1988 which sets out descriptions of categories of abuse in an attempt to achieve a degree of agreement across all professional agencies working for the protection of children. I shall use the categories provided in the document, *Working Together* (*see* Bibliography), page 26, in order to discuss current attempts to define abuse (being mindful of the problems which such an excercise creates, some of which have already been mentioned).

Physical abuse

The description given for physical abuse is as follows:

'Physical abuse: Physical injury to a child, including deliberate poisoning, where there is definite knowledge, or a reasonable suspicion, that the injury was inflicted or knowingly not prevented.'

This category appears to be straightforward, and as it relates to the most obvious and the most widely investigated type of abuse, it ought perhaps to be the easiest to categorise. However, it poses problems for those empowered to protect children. How serious does a physical injury have to be before it is deemed to be an example of abuse?

For example, if a mother is in the kitchen preparing a meal and her two children are fighting in another room, she may raise her voice in an attempt to quieten them. If it persists, she may decide to send them to bed. The seven-year-old refuses to go and throws a toy across the room, shattering a vase on the sitting-room table in the process. At this point his mother becomes very cross and smacks the boy on the side of the head. She doesn't hit him particularly hard, but possibly harder than she intended to; she is exasperated at the end of a long, difficult day with the children. The next day at school the teacher might notice some marks on the child's cheek and ask how they got there. The boy will say, 'Mummy did it'. If at this point you were in the position of a social worker, called in to investigate a case of suspicious physical injury, what would you think about this scenario? You might decide to visit the home. The mother admits to having hit the child. She has never come to the attention of the authorities in the past, and is quite open about describing the circumstances leading up to the incident.

If you were the local authority social worker in the case described above, and were working to a set of procedures which compelled you to act on cases of physical abuse, would you feel it necessary to take any action in the situation described? Going back to the material provided by the DHSS, the case would quite clearly fall within the physical abuse category. Where does the dividing line between a reasonable degree of physical chastisement of children and physical abuse fall? This story is not at all untypical of the kinds of incidents with which social workers and others must deal on a daily basis, and it is in these cases that the use of common sense and professional judgement becomes important. As I have already said, there are no firm guide lines written down which answer these difficult questions.

Consider another case. A nine-year-old boy is noticed, again at school, with red, angry and sore marks across the back of his right hand. He is questioned by his teacher in the company of the school nurse. He says he was punished at home over the weekend for playing with fire, and his dad burned his hand. On investigation it becomes clear that the boy had been caught by his parents playing with a cigarette lighter in his bedroom, burning the corners of a few books and writing pads. His father, who had often had to tell him off for lighting pieces of paper from the fire, and stealing boxes of matches, had marched him down the stairs and held the boy's hand up to the lighted gas fire for long enough to burn the skin quite badly. He wanted to teach him, by example, of the dangers of fire. In this case, would you decide that this parent had overstepped the boundary between acceptable and unacceptable behaviour?

It is interesting to examine responses to these two incidents, both of which are based on the numerous actual cases with which I have been involved. I would guess that a majority of readers would agree that the father who burned his child had behaved wrongly, and that perhaps that little boy required some degree of supervision in order that his welfare could be protected in the future. There may be those who would have considered a firmer line and decided that it might even be appropriate to remove the boy from home, at least for a period of assessment. There may also be a majority of readers who would not have felt it to be appropriate to take any action at all in the first example. However, there are similarities in the two cases. Both parents would claim, as indeed they did, that they were acting in the best interests of the child. Both parents felt provoked into taking the course of action they took because of the behaviour of their child. Both parents accepted that they had gone too far in their chastisement of the children. The main and glaringly obvious difference in the two cases is the level of injury sustained by the children. One child had a very badly burned hand, whilst the other child had a slight amount of reddening around his cheek. This seems to be the most significant factor in distinguishing between our initial responses to the two cases in question.

Further decisions about what course of action to take in these, or any other, case cannot be made unless much more is known about the background. At some stage, an assessment of the situation will be made, including a review of family relationships, development of the children, previous incidents, and so on. On the basis of this, a decision as to the seriousness of each case is made. This is an important point to bear in mind, because it is the decision-making process which follows on from a deeper look into each situation that sometimes creates a point of tension between social work and the general public. Often, brief pieces of information will be heard concerning a family about whom no action seems to be being taken, in comparison with other families ostensibly in the same situation, perhaps appearing to be equally negligent or harmful to their children, whose lives are disrupted fundamentally by the social services and other agencies. Although we all equate physical abuse and the level of future risk to the extent of injuries inflicted, this gives only an outline of the nature of the problem which any particular family might be experiencing. The point is that physical abuse cannot simply be categorised in terms of a straightforward 'league table' of injuries sustained, but must be examined along with a range of other matters. If, for example, we knew that the mother who had hit her child's face had previously ill-treated children, then our opinion about the current incident might change.

Neglect

Referring back to the guide lines contained in *Working Together* (*see* Bibliography) we will move on to an examination of the brief description which it gives of neglect. It suggests the following:

'**Neglect:** The persistent or severe neglect of a child (for example, by exposure to any kind of danger, including cold and starvation) which results in serious impairment of the child's health or development, including non-organic failure to thrive.'

This category contains many more terms and phrases which are open to individual interpretation than did the previous one related to physical abuse. This accurately reflects the serious problems encountered when attempting to encapsulate such a wide range of abusive and harmful activities which can fall within the term 'neglect'. In order to achieve any degree of common agreement about what actually constitutes a degree of neglect that requires the intervention of the local authority, we need to share some understanding about the needs of children. These needs are a mixture of physical, social and emotional, all of which will help the child to develop at an acceptable pace and to an acceptable level. Physical needs, if not met to the required degree, will result in neglect. What is the difference between physical abuse and neglect? As we have seen, physical abuse relates to deliberate acts of violence towards children, which may or may not result in injury. Neglect implies a failure on the part of the care giver adequately to safeguard the health, safety and physical well-being of the child. Again, though, the question of degree provides all manner of difficulties. If parents send young children to school without coats in winter, are they neglecting them? How much neglect is 'severe neglect', the term used in the DHSS material?

Consider the case of an unmarried mother living on welfare benefits. She has a three-year-old son and a newborn baby. She has numerous debts with finance companies, some of whom have very vigorous and persistent collection techniques. Her house is untidy and smells of urine. Soiled disposable nappies are strewn about the place and piles of clothing in various states of disarray. This woman, who is in her early twenties, has boyfriend trouble. The father of her son calls occasionally, convinces her that a reconciliation is a distinct possibility, steals her money, beats her up (but never harms the children), and leaves. Various friends and family members stay at the house from time to time but never help out financially. She dotes on the baby girl who is always well fed, clean and tidy. The boy receives less physical care than his sister. His bedroom is cold. The window is broken and badly boarded up so that the cold and damp easily get in. There is very little bedding on the broken bed which is supported by bricks underneath, stolen from an old building site across the street. Bedding is a mixture of tattered old sheets and items of outdoor clothing. The child looks thin and tired. He has dark rings under his eyes and long unwashed hair. There is usually no food in the house. His mother smokes about twenty cigarettes a day and goes out once a week with a group of friends and relatives. She assures those who visit that the boy is well cared for and fed, but she doesn't have the money to do what she would like to do for the family and, anyway, baby food takes up all her cash.

What should a social worker of this boy, whose circumstances typify those of innumerable children with whom he or she will come into contact on a regular basis? He is neglected, there is no doubt of that. He is not adequately fed, nor is he given enough protection from the cold at night. The household seems slightly chaotic, and one gets the impression that the mother's attention has been drawn away from her son to her daughter.This case is a very typical example of the kinds of situations within which social workers regularly have to make very difficult decisions. Do we make a distinction between deliberate acts of neglect (such as the parents who refuse to feed their children), and those cases where children may well be dangerously neglected as an almost inevitable by-product of a whole series of other problems? In the case under discussion, the child's mother is no doubt feeling very isolated, probably has little support and is suffering from a whole host of financial pressures. She is being systematically rejected and robbed by the child's father and is having to learn to cope with the demands of a new baby. The simple truth is that, whilst these factors may well have a significant bearing upon the extent to which this boy, and hundreds of others like him, are treated, the end result is still in some cases detrimental to the physical well-being of children, and requires action. Perhaps the distinction we can draw is between *deliberate* intent to harm and *understandable negligence*, although the end result may be just as tragic.

As has been demonstrated on many occasions, largely by way of public inquiries into child deaths, the effects of persistent neglect can be horrifying. There are cases in the press where children have been discovered in conditions of physical starvation, having been locked away by their carers in the house, and inadequately fed over many months. People may feel that cases of physical injury may not be as prevalent as neglect, but neglect certainly seems to have been neglected by research.

Considering our unmarried mother once again, to what extent can the treatment her son receives be excused and accepted because of her circumstances? Can she do no other than neglect him because she has no money? Perhaps the views of some readers on this point may have been different if she was a non-smoker who never had a night out. Again, we have the constant problem of where to draw the line between the acceptable and unacceptable. Is there a clearly understood baseline of care for children, and how do we measure when children aren't provided with this baseline?

If a child lives on a street where all the other families except his have three cars, and his family has only one, is this child being neglected? If it really upsets him that his parents don't seem as rich as the others, and this stigmatation is translated into behavioural difficulties at home and school, perhaps he is being neglected *relative* to the circumstances of those around him.

'Non-organic failure to thrive' is when a child fails to grow normally, and there is no medical explanation for this failure. There are a number of chronic conditions in children which lead them to be very small in stature, and appear thin and underfed. If a child is persistently underweight or even losing weight, or is not developing normally in terms of being able to walk and talk at the correct times, and there has been no indication of any medical reason why this should be, that child is failing to thrive. The degree to which this condition is the result of neglect on the part of his carers is sometimes impossible to determine, except by putting the child in an environment where his general care can be accurately monitored and any subsequent progress noted. Failure to thrive is discussed again later in this chapter with reference to emotional abuse.

Sexual Abuse

The DHSS guide, *Working Together* uses a definition for sexual abuse which has been much quoted in the literature:

'Sexual abuse: The involvement of dependent, developmentally immature children and adolescents in sexual activities they do not truly comprehend, to which they are unable to give informed consent, or that violate the social taboos of family roles.'

The definition of sexual abuse is a minefield of bias, preconception and misleading information. Sexual activities which occur between adults and children and are obviously abusive would include: rape, non-assaultative intercourse (implying that some forms of intercourse may not involve the use of physical threat or force), molestation and pornography. Most people would be in general agreement that these activities between adults and children are forms of abuse, but the potential list goes on: exhibitionism, talking to children in an erotic way, voyeurism (watching children in order to achieve sexual arousal and gratification), and so on. How many of the behaviours on the second list would be abusive? I was talking to a friend about this topic. He was anxious about all the newspaper headlines related to sex abuse following the Cleveland episode, feeling that he was becoming scared to allow his children out of the house in case they were abducted and raped. I think that there is a widely held misconception for many people that sexual abuse invariably means full sexual intercourse. This particular activity is not as common as some of the less obviously abusive behaviour I have just listed. Unfortunately, many children and adults who were abused as children will recount episodes from the past which involve having been spoken to in a very sexually explicit way by an adult, often a member of the family or someone whom they know, or will recall being 'flashed' at, and will describe this incident in a way which mirrors the horror and anguish of many children who experience full vaginal or anal sexual penetration. Again, as with physical abuse, it is a mistake to equate damage in emotional terms with the nature of the acts which took place; there is no simple scale of increased abuse.

I have talked to children who have been involved in vaginal intercourse, anal intercourse, oral sex, pornography, sex with animals, been forced to commit sexual acts with other children, and who have had contact with prostitution. I have met children who have been abused in foster homes and in local authority children's homes, as well as in their own homes. The horrific variety of cases to which many of us who

28

work in this field are exposed is never ending. Again, most of us would share equal concern and abhorrence about such activities, but there are as many blurred edges around definitions of sexual abuse as there are for the other types of abuse.

For example, what should you think of a father who, when bathing his three-year-old daughter, spends a little too much time rubbing his hands around the area of her genitals? He doesn't penetrate, but he achieves a sexual thrill from the activity. His daughter is not likely to be aware of her father's unusual behaviour, and may herself receive pleasurable sensations from the experience. No one is likely to find out. Is this behaviour acceptable? What about a father who always bathes the children, never touches them, but achieves a high state of sexual arousal simply from watching them? Is this man abusing his children? I would take the view that any activity, whether it involves touching or not, is an abuse of a child if it involves the expected sexual arousal and gratification of the adult. Many parents are in the habit of taking baths with their children. Some parents tell me that they get pleasure from physical contact with their children in this way. The perfectly normal and healthy rough-and-tumble which goes on in most households between fathers and their sons also involves the enjoyment of physical contact. The difference between this kind of activity and the bath-time scenarios is the motivation behind the adult's involvement. When sexual stimulation is the purpose, it is wrong, and constitutes sexual abuse. But what is the distinction between the pleasurable, sensual feelings we can achieve by hugging and kissing our children, and sexual stimulation? In my view the division is not entirely clear cut.

The problem for social workers, who are accountable to the public through the local councillors who employ them, is that it is usually only the sensational cases which hit the headlines. These are the ones where there can generally be no doubt that abuse has taken place. This gives a false impression to the public about the whole range of uncertain cases with which local authority social workers and others have to deal.

Emotional Abuse

'**Emotional abuse:** The severe adverse effect on the behaviour and emotional development of a child caused by persistent or severe emotional ill-treatment or rejection.'

This definition again comes from the DHSS publication *Working Together* (*see* Bibliography).

Emotional abuse remains possibly the least understood and least accepted of all the potential categories of abuse. This may partly be due to the fact that, as the DHSS document itself points out, emotional abuse is present to a greater or lesser extent in all other types of abuse.

Emotional neglect implies that some or all of the basic needs of a child are not being met. Neglect involves the basic physical needs which all children have for survival, but they also need less tangible means of support from their adult carers in order to mature into adulthood relatively unscathed. M. K. Pringle in *The Needs of Children* (*see* Bibliography) points out what these less easily identifiable needs are. They include the need for love and security, for new experiences and for praise and recognition. If children fail to receive these in reasonable amounts from their parents or carers, they can become withdrawn, isolated, acquire a whole range of behavioural problems, and grow up to be untrusting and unable to form lasting relationships with others. As can be imagined, the problems associated with deciding whether or not a household provides enough of these experiences to bring their children up successfully are immense. This explains why emotional abuse is not high on the agenda when child abuse in general is discussed.

Rejection implies a whole range of negative attitudes and practices. Children can be constantly shouted at, criticised or made to appear foolish in front of their friends. I have met parents who have punished children by not talking to them for weeks at a time. Parents may see their children as constant failures and refuse to praise them when they do something right.

I think that we can all see elements of at least the capacity to reject children in our own behaviour. If I am at home with my children and they are behaving well, this often implies that they are amusing themselves playing a game quietly. I reward this behaviour by ignoring them! If they are not behaving well, which means they are coming to my attention and forcing me to interact with them, I tend to become cross with them. (I would add that this isn't a constant feature of my brand of parenting, but I know I behave like this from time to time.) The children receive criticism for being boisterous and get totally ignored when they behave! I think many parents will be able to acknowledge that this is quite widespread. If this kind of interaction is taken to extremes so that the children never receive anything other than criticism from their parents, they begin to feel rejected and unwanted, and this will make them feel worthless, guilty and devastated.

It could also be argued that parents who become obsessively over-protective of their children are inflicting a form of emotional abuse. There are parents who refuse to allow their children out to play because they are excessively frightened about them hurting themselves or mixing with other children who might teach them bad habits. Children can perhaps be smothered with attention, as well as denied it.

I would wish to mention 'non-organic failure to thrive', again, because in the cases of severe emotional abuse which I have seen, the children have often caused concern to the medical profession because of their low weight, lack of height, and general ill health. Is there a case for saying that the withholding of love and affection from children is bad for their physical health? I have witnessed amazing improvements in the physical health of children who have been removed from situations in which they have been severely emotionally abused, so I would say that there can be a very definite connection.

Summary

This chapter has been about definitions. It may well have asked more questions than it has answered. For this I give no apology. Uncertainty and speculation represent the real world for most people working in the field of child protection at present.

The underlying cause of the uncertainty about definitions of abuse can be traced to one major problem. No one has been able to give the definitive description of what is 'good enough parenting'. We ought not to be in the business of insisting on unrealistic expectations of parents, all of whom have to contend with a variety of circumstances which will affect their ability to bring up their children adequately. We can all agree on the need to take steps to deal with the violent and sadistic end of the child abuse spectrum. In my experience it is the bit in the middle which creates all the headaches. You can easily test this. If a group of parents are asked 'What is a reasonable bed time for an eight-year-old who has to go to school the next day?', I would guess that earlier than about 6 p.m. or later than 10 p.m. would be agreed as being unreasonable. Between those times, though, it would be very hard to agree on a figure.

When society is agreed on the boundaries beyond which acceptable parenting becomes unacceptable and potentially abusive, the biggest advancement in the field of child protection will have been made. Until then, the role of the social worker, police, NSPCC, teacher, doctor, nurse, and so on, will involve the application of societal and professional values which, in all honesty, do not exist.

2 Increasing Awareness of Child Abuse?

HISTORICAL BACKGROUND

We often confuse a heightened awareness of the issue of child abuse with an increase in the actual amount of abuse which takes place. Rates of detection increase as general awareness levels rise, and this leads us to believe that abuse must be more prevalent now than in the past. Whether this is true is, as with many questions to do with human behaviour, difficult to determine. However, there is no doubt at all that an increasing concern about the way in which our children are treated has come about.

According to our knowledge of social history, what we would describe as abuse of children was being practised in a systematic way amongst all sections of society as recently as two hundred years ago in Britain. The current infant mortality rate is about 2 per cent, but this was in excess of 15 per cent in the mid-nineteenth century, and, during the early part of the eighteenth century, well over 50 per cent. There are many reasons for these statistics. Sanitation, housing, diet and general health care are all areas within which tremendous progress has been made over the past two centuries. The development of the medical sciences has also played a very significant part in improving the general level of care provided to children. There are, however, a great many other reasons why the standards of care afforded to youngsters in the past were relatively poor. A study of infant mortality rates alone provides only a very crude measure of overall welfare.

The history of the Labour movement is full of accounts of the way in which children were treated in the past. They were often forced to work extremely long hours, in physically demanding and dangerous occupations such as mill work and mining. Kingsley described the plight of the chimney sweep in his novel *The Water Babies* (1863). Our idea of Victorian England is suffused with images of poor waifs and strays begging in the streets, or being beaten mercilessly by villainous adult figures in authority, and there is no doubt that Charles Dickens (from whom many of these images come) did much to bring to the public's attention the problems of the poor in London. R. S. Kempe and C. H. Kempe in their book *Child Abuse* (*see* Bibliography) point out that in nineteenth-century London 80 per cent of illegitimate children who were put in foster care died soon afterwards. Apparently, the foster parents would take money from orphanages and private individuals to house abandoned babies, and then kill the babies. It was also common practice for children from poor families to be deliberately injured or permanently crippled in order that they might prove more productive as street beggars. The maxims 'spare the rod and spoil the child', and 'children must be seen and not heard' sum up the popular view in the not too distant past, of the way in which children ought to be brought up. These particular sayings are still commonly used now, but, as the former appears to condone physical abuse and the latter emotional neglect, perhaps they ought to be actively discouraged.

Sexual abuse has a long history too. Child prostitution has been practised for centuries and was rife in London not many years ago. The Bible has references to the sexual abuse of children, and particularly to the practice of incest, and recent history is peppered with scandals concerning prominent citizens being involved in sexual activity with children.

So far, I have painted an extremely depressing picture of life for children in the relatively recent past. I think it is fair to say that there is a significant amount of evidence for us to state that large numbers of children were systematically abused in the UK in the recent past, and that much of this abuse was both accepted and condoned by the community as part of the natural way of things. Why were people so apparently negligent about their children's welfare, and why is it that there are now many more minimum standards, rules and regulations which govern the way in which we deal with our offspring?

This can be traced back largely to the Victorian period, an epoch of tremendous contrast – wealth and poverty, industrial and agricultural lifestyles, aggressive patriotism and a thrust for progress (as evidenced by the rapid advances being made in the fields of science and technology). The reality of life for children in those times, especially the poor, was dire, yet there was a groundswell of popular opinion motivated to promote social change. The development of the popular debate on many social issues was probably fuelled by the rapid progress being made in science and technology, but, whatever the impetus, issues of social care were discussed as never before. As is pointed out by David N. Jones (Ed.) in *Understanding Child Abuse* (*see* Bibliography), numerous social crusaders seemed to become very active at around the same time. Lord Shaftesbury was spearheading a popular movement to begin to address the issue of working children and trying to improve their conditions and terms of labour. The increasing numbers of homeless and destitute children in London and elsewhere also became an issue which attracted significant public attention, no doubt assisted by the pioneering work of Dr Barnardo whose name is still linked with a whole range of child care provisions today. How did the particular problem of child abuse become linked into this growing agenda of worthy causes, because we have seen that Victorian society was well used to sending children out to work, beating them, using them as sexual objects, and generally behaving towards them in a way which would indicate that they were not worthy of serious consideration?

Just as Shaftesbury and his campaign responded to a pressing social phenomenon, the unsavoury elements of which were becoming more and more self-evident, so did Barnardo react to an issue which increasingly thrust itself into thè public eye. In other words, the social reforms which had their roots in the expression of a growing popular awareness came about at a time when the phenomena they addressed were also growing in size, and becoming impossible to ignore. The size of the problems, set side by side with ideas of progress and advancement brought about by the developments in the scientific world, created an atmosphere of potential change, which was ripe for mobilisation by energetic and public-spirited pressure groups. A similar link between an atmosphere of change and high-profile problems was occurring in the child abuse field.

The roots of many of the problems I have outlined which relate to the care of children in the past, lie in the way in which children were seen by adults. One can form a simplistic impression (which may well be founded on the truth), that, until fairly recently, children were seen to be the *property* of the adults with whom they lived, and that adults had every right to treat children in any way they saw fit. Children could be physically assaulted with almost complete impunity. They could be bought and sold for sex, and could be acquired or discarded without any great trouble. In real terms, children were little people with no rights. Some have the view that very little has changed, but there are now a great many legal provisions covering a wide range of child care issues which dissuade adults from ill-treating children, and which give youngsters certain rights – acknowledging that they are people too! This development of the legal recognition of children can, to a large extent, be traced back to the late nineteenth century. The increased awareness of child abuse as a social issue is worthy of study and reform must be seen within the context of the whole reformist movement of the Victorian period.

EARLY LEGAL RESPONSES

In New York in 1874 one particular case of child abuse, which is often quoted, created much national and international interest. It is reasonable to say, in fact, that much of our modern legislation can be traced back to the reverberations caused as a result of the New York case.

The case concerned a girl called Mary Ellen. She lived in a

tenement building in the city with her adoptive parents. A neighbour began to express her concern as to Mary's welfare, and eventually told voluntary workers who provided help to immigrant families in New York that she was concerned for the physical well-being of the child. Eventually, Mary was seen. She was found to be suffering from severe neglect, had been systematically beaten over a period of time, and had also been cut with a sharp implement. Her adoptive parents appeared not to be particularly dismayed that their treatment of Mary had at last come to the attention of the public. Indeed, there was little, if any, legal provision which prevented them from ill-treating her if they wished. However, Mary's plight came to the attention of a man called Henry Bergh, who was well known in New York as the man who had founded, some time earlier, the Society for the Prevention of Cruelty to Animals. According to R. H. Bremner in *Children and Youth in America: A documentary history Vol. II 1866–1932* (*see* Bibliography), Mr Bergh intervened in the case, and hired a lawyer who persuaded the court that Mary was an individual in her own right, worthy of protection from abuse. The case was proven against the adults, and Mary was removed from their care and placed in an orphanage.

There has been confusion about this case because of Henry Bergh's connection with the animal rights movement. The fact is that in 1874 in New York there existed more legislation with which to protect animals from abuse than there was to protect children. However, the case was not contested and won on the basis that Mary was a member of the animal kingdom (as is often believed), but because the lawyer hired by Henry Bergh was able successfully to convince the court of Mary Ellen's *human* rights, as C. Eugene Walker, Barbara L. Banner and Keith L. Kaufman point out in *The Physically and Sexually Abused Child. Evaluation and Treatment* (*see* Bibliography).

Due to the continued efforts of the lawyer hired by Bergh, the Society for the Prevention of Cruelty to Children was formed in New York in December 1874. Are animals better served in law than children now? As an ironic and sad postscript to the story of Mary Ellen, R. J. Light informs us in the article 'Abused and Neglected Children in America: a study of alternative policies', in the *Harvard Educational Review No. 43* (pages 556–598) that in 1970, the New York Society for the Prevention of Cruelty to Animals had more funds than the Society for the Prevention of Cruelty to Children!

In legal terms, the case of Mary Ellen proved to be the catalyst for major developments on both sides of the Atlantic. The very idea that children were not to be seen as the property of adults, to do with as they wished, was in itself quite revolutionary. In the UK, as a direct result of the formation of the New York SPCC, the National Society for the Prevention of Cruelty to Children (NSPCC) was established. The NSPCC in the UK was and still is a vociferous campaigner on the behalf of children. It was at the forefront of a growing movement which lobbied Parliament towards the end of the nineteenth century, seeking to establish increased protection for children in the law, illuminating their arguments using an abundance of case examples of physical abuse and severe neglect.

In 1889, this escalating public concern was acknowledged by the passing of the Prevention of Cruelty Act. Magistrates could now issue warrants which allowed private homes to be entered if there was a suspicion of abuse. Courts were empowered to take children away from the care of their parents if allegations of mistreatment were proven. Subsequent Acts were passed, in 1908, 1932 and 1933, which introduced separate juvenile courts and established the age limit of seventeen for child protection legislation.

In just over forty years, the status of children in society had been transformed, from almost nil to being recognised in law as special people by virtue of their vulnerability, and therefore deserving and in need of special rights. The work of eminent social reformers, a variety of voluntary agencies and especially the general groundswell of opinion pressing for social change, had borne fruit extremely rapidly. Except in some enlightened quarters of society, the very idea that children could be ill-treated to such a degree as to cause severe injury, mutilation or even death was not commonly accepted.

Physical abuse and severe neglect (the concepts of emotional abuse and sexual abuse were unheard of) were seen as being extremely isolated events, worthy of punishment when they came to the attention of the authorities, but not accepted as commonplace enough to warrant concerted public vigilance.

The origins of the modern social services departments can obviously be traced back to the voluntary organisations who first began to work with the poor, deprived and homeless in the nineteenth century. In 1948, the Children Act established Children's Departments which were the immediate forerunners of the departments we know today. Again, this action can be traced back to the concern expressed by the public after a child abuse tragedy. This case involved a young boy called Dennis O'Neill. He, along with large numbers of other children, was a war evacuee. He was subsequently murdered by his foster parents, who were duly convicted. This case had two key factors. Firstly, it reinforced the vulnerability of children who are always prone, to a large extent, to the negative aspects of those charged with the responsibility for their care. Secondly, it highlighted the practice of providing substitute homes for children. This has always occurred, but the particular experience of war-time evacuees emphasised this common practice. The government's response was to set up the Curtis Committee to look into the particular issues around the care of children by others than their parents. The 1948 Act was the result of their deliberations.

The Children's Departments were staffed by child care officers who were responsible for making sure that children living in the care of the local authority were being looked after properly. There was now in existence the basic framework of child care legislation, and a local authority department designed to promote the welfare of children.

MEDICAL AWARENESS

At about the same time as the Dennis O'Neill case was giving the popular conscience cause for concern, other developments were starting to have an impact upon the level of awareness of child abuse in the community. In 1946, a paediatric radiologist called John Caffey published a paper which subsequently became a landmark in the field of child abuse. Because of the developments in radiology during the early 1940s it had become possible to date fractures fairly accurately, according to the extent to which they had begun to heal. This meant that, for the first time, a fractured arm which had been previously broken on one or more occasions could (in the case of children at any rate) begin to raise suspicions – accidental causes could explain one or two old breaks, but three, four, five? Similarly, old injuries not properly treated could now be detected on parts of the anatomy not presented for treatment. Caffey described some cases of unexplained injury in children referred to him. These cases consisted of multiple breaks in arms and legs of youngsters which were discovered to be at different stages of healing. How could this be? At this stage no one was prepared to think the worst, or (with the wonderful benefit of hindsight) the obvious, and many possible explanations were offered. Perhaps rickets and brittle bones could explain why it was that these particular children seemed to be worryingly susceptible to multiple breaks? Caffey did suspect at the time that these injuries were caused by some kind of force, but he was unsure about the source of this force.

Silverman, in an article in 1953, suggested that these fractures may be the result of negligence by those who were caring for the children. According to Walker, Bonner and Kaufman, Silverman was careful to warn medical colleagues not to make the adults caring for the children feel too guilty about any responsibility they may have concerning the injured children, and actually described one of his child patients as being particularly accident-prone. It wasn't until 1955 that members of the medical profession were beginning to suggest that the injuries noted by Caffey, Silverman and their associates might possibly have been caused as a direct result of intent to cause harm on the part of the adults concerned. P. V. Woolley and W. A. Evans, who wrote the article 'The Significance of Skeletal Lesions in Infants Resembling those of Traumatic Origin', in the *Journal of the American Medical Association* (*see* Bibliography), were the doctors who were first able to suspend their disbelief about the things which adults could do to children in other than a few isolated cases.

Woolley and Evans opened the minds of the medical practitioners to the concept of child abuse on a significant scale. Dr C. Henry Kempe, an American paediatrician, helped to bring the issue more clearly into the public domain by presenting, with colleagues, a paper to the American Academy of Paediatrics which was subsequently published in 1962. 'The Battered Child Syndrome', by H. Kempe et al, in the *Journal of the American Medical Association* (*see* Bibliography) was the most influential paper yet published concerning the abuse of children. It openly acknowledged the topic as a matter for general concern, bringing home to a sceptical public the notion that the deliberate maltreatment of children was perhaps not as uncommon a phenomenon as was thought. Perhaps this last sentence is misleading. My view, although impossible to substantiate, is that it has always been known that adults do intentionally harm children. We prefer to fool ourselves that it isn't happening, perhaps because we are all aware of the potential within us to act violently and cruelly, especially towards the more vulnerable of our fellow human beings. To accept that one adult is capable of abusing a child may be to accept that it is a capacity which we ourselves share.

THE PROMINENCE OF PHYSICAL ABUSE

The reader will by this time have noted the marked absence of any discussion about types of abuse other than physical and, to a lesser degree neglect. What of sexual abuse or emotional abuse? The development of society's awareness of physical abuse has provided clues that help to answer many questions.

It seems as if society must develop through stages of awareness over a considerable period of time, before true acceptance of abuse is achieved. And it appears to be fairly self-evident that physical abuse is the easiest form of abuse to acknowledge and accept. We have over the years condoned a certain amount of physical abuse towards children. Many parents hit their children if they misbehave and many other adults would support parents' rights to do so. We seem to have a general acceptance of the fact that children will be physically punished if they misbehave. The accepted limits beyond which reasonable punishment becomes unreasonable assault are forever shifting, and perhaps modern society as a whole is less tolerant of physical force than used to be the case. However, most of us have been involved in situations during which physical punishment has been given and received. Whatever our personal views about it, the subject is not beyond the bounds of our comprehension. As mentioned previously, we appear to be more willing to contemplate physical acts against children which may do them harm, than to think about emotional ill-treatment or sexual abuse.

Physical abuse, when it occurs with any degree of severity, is often easily detectable. It is difficult to avoid coming to unpalatable conclusions if a little boy with a black eye comes to school and tells the teacher, 'My Dad got drunk last night, had an argument with Mum, and then hit me in the face with his shoe'. There is some substantial physical evidence to back up the story. We can't ignore this boy's problem or pretend it isn't there. We have to deal with it. Our senses are bullied into belief by the results of the abuse, in this case the bruised eye. Whatever we would like to think about the probability of our neighbour (whom we have known for many years) physically injuring his or her child on purpose, we would find it difficult to think of anything else if their daughter was seen walking to school one day with large weals across her face, complaining

that Mum had done it with a belt because she had refused to
tidy her bedroom.

Apart from the obvious fact that physical abuse, generally
speaking, is often easier to detect than other forms of abuse,
and that some form of physical punishment of children is
accepted as reasonable by large numbers of people, are there
any other reasons why it is this form of abuse which has, until
very recently, been most prominent?

Very severe cases of physical abuse and neglect (accepting
that these cases invariably involve some form of emotional
abuse as well) often lead to the tragedy of child death. This in
turn raises the general awareness level of the community, in a
way which seldom occurs with the less obviously damaging
effects of other forms of ill-treatment. It may be that it is the
most frequent form of child abuse, and therefore the most
likely to be acknowledged. Certainly there is evidence to
support the view that it is the type of abuse which is the most
commonly detected by the authorities. Physical abuse is also
the type of abuse which is easiest to process in court. Evidence
is easier to gather, more difficult to contest, and therefore
numbers of convictions are that much greater. Again, there
follows from that the assumption (which need not necessarily
be true) that more successful prosecutions mean that it is
more prevalent.

THE FAILURE TO ACKNOWLEDGE SEXUAL ABUSE

All I have said so far about our capacity to deny the existence
of abuse, and to fail to accept clear-cut evidence unless we
have to, appears to be even more true in the case of sexual
abuse. As we have seen, the sexual molestation of children is
by no means a new phenomenon, but, unfortunately, neither
is the practice of denial!

Sigmund Freud is a name which we all know. In many ways
his pioneering works paved the way for future psychiatric and
psychological practice, and in any analysis of the development

of modern thought, Freud would rank alongside Darwin, Marx and Einstein. However, in the field of sexual abuse, Freud has received extremely mixed reviews of late.

THE INFLUENCE OF FREUD

In 1896, Freud gave a lecture in which he spoke about patients he was treating for hysteria. Apparently there had been no indication from eighteen patients as to why they were suffering hysterical attacks over which they had no control. However, under deep analysis, these patients began to disclose to Freud experiences of having been sexually abused in childhood, either by an adult or an older brother or sister. Often, the patients had been unaware of this history themselves until Freud's psycho-analytical techniques were able to help them release the memory, which had no doubt been deliberately locked away for so long. When word of this lecture reached the academic community and the press, there was a great deal of debate, leading to a public outcry, in which Freud's ideas were denounced. How dare this man suggest that adults could do such things to children! There was an outbreak of self-righteous indignation and a denial of such strength that Freud changed his conclusions in the following year.

Before moving on to look at the alternative conclusions he reached, which I believe are very relevant today in the public debate about sexual abuse, let us compare 1896 and Freud with 1987 and Cleveland. Without wishing to be deliberately controversial, there seem to be certain parallels. A new, rather misunderstood medical technique claims to uncover significant numbers of sex abuse cases. There immediately follows a mass denial of the existence of abuse on a wide scale. Although we shall return later to the Cleveland affair, I think it is interesting to compare Freud's original reception in 1896 with events nearly a century later. We haven't learned much in between, have we?

Freud's way out of the controversy into which he had

landed was to develop the notion that his patients' recollections were, in reality, only fantasies and not real events at all. As part of human development, youngsters go through phases when they are sexually attracted to the parent of the opposite sex. These feelings can be so intense that they seem real enough to have been fulfilled for some people. Freud's eighteen patients were confusing reality with this perfectly normal stage of emotional development, which for them had got out of hand. This remains a very powerfully held belief in some professional quarters and can be dangerous. If a father is accused of molesting his five-year-old daughter, some deep-seated notion that this modern Lolita seduced the adult has some credibility as a direct result of the views expressed by Freud. This dubious theory, about which there remains a great deal of controversy, can in some cases be used as a way of nicely shifting the blame for sexual crimes against children from the offender to the victim. Denial, therefore, is not at work just with the layman, but also with the professionals. This is something which is particularly significant with regard to the impact of their work on social workers themselves.

REASONS FOR THE RECENT 'DISCOVERY' OF SEXUAL ABUSE

The sexual abuse of children is certainly an issue which has become very topical in recent years. Henry Kempe argues that society evolves its awareness of different types of abuse through specific stages. There may be some truth in the view that accepting that children can be deliberately injured and/or neglected by adults in some way sets the scene for acknowledging other types of abuse. America 'discovered' battered children in the early 1960s. Britain ˜ reluctantly followed suit some years later, unfortunately requiring the well-publicised deaths of some children, notably Maria Colwell, to speed the process up. During the 1970s a great deal of research was undertaken into sexual abuse in the USA.

Britain again lagged behind in any real acceptance of the size of the problem. It could be argued that events in Cleveland in 1987, and the subsequent publicity and vigorous public debate which followed, have done for sexual abuse what the Colwell case did for physical abuse.

In general terms, sex and sexuality are subjects about which people feel more comfortable now than in the past. The alleged sexual revolution of the 1960s, the women's movement and the massive growth in the establishment of the 'caring professions' have all helped to raise the level of consciousness about a whole range of sexual matters. The feminist movement, in particular, deserves special praise for developing notions about the oppressive aspects of sexuality, and the power of males over females. They are to be credited with putting the sexual exploitation of children firmly on the agenda of important social issues to consider. It may also be the case that women are less likely now than in the past to remain with men who sexually abuse them or their children, so that more cases are coming to light of abuse of all kinds, and in particular sexual abuse.

The idea that adults can be dangerous to children is a concept which is being implanted in the minds of youngsters by parents and schools. Training programmes pointing out this fact are becoming more common. Again, this is likely to increase the numbers of cases about which we hear. Doctors, police officers, social workers and other professionals are now being trained to be more aware of the signs of sexual abuse. Another significant factor in the increased awareness of sexual abuse is the fact that adults are becoming more able to recount previously hidden episodes of sexual encounters from their childhood. It is from retrospective studies that the potential extent of this form of abuse is becoming more clearly understood. Many children who are taken into care eventually begin either to make direct disclosures of sexual abuse, or else behave in such a way as to suggest that this may have been happening alongside the problems for which they were originally taken from their parents.

All these factors have a significant impact on the numbers

of cases uncovered and, by implication, on the extent to which the issue is forced into the minds of the general public.

EMOTIONAL ABUSE – THE UNDISCOVERED PROBLEM

Emotional abuse is a highly elusive phenomenon – *see* Chapter 4 for some of the potential indicators of this type of ill-treatment. I think it is fair to say that this form of abuse presents more challenges and difficulties for those charged with the responsibility of caring for children than any other form of ill-treatment, including sexual abuse. There is very little research material on the subject, yet all those who deal on a daily basis with troubled children know that it is an extremely widespread problem. The reasons why this knowledge has not translated into an expression of public awareness are unclear. This must obviously have something to do with the difficulty of quantifying the subject. I have met many children who have been, and who are still being, deprived of love and affection, many of whom, no doubt, will develop problems in later years as a result. How many generally unhappy and miserable children do you know? It is exceedingly difficult to obtain clear evidence that these children are being emotionally ill-treated. The fact that it is hard to bring a case to court makes it all the more difficult to gain public recognition of the scale of the problem.

A great deal of research needs to be conducted into the links between arrested healthy development and emotional deprivation before we will be able to talk about this subject with any degree of authority. The trouble with emotional abuse is that no one gets killed or badly injured so that we can all see the results. Our ever-present tendency to deny our faults and failings is therefore able to work that much more easily to put emotional abuse out of our minds. Perhaps fewer cases than we might otherwise think are missed because it may be that parents who systematically deprive their children of appropriate emotional support are also abusing them in

47

more obvious ways. Obviously, all cases of neglect, physical and sexual abuse are likely to involve some degree of emotional abuse, and so we may pick up on some emotionally ill-treated children by default, as it were. This seems to reflect common practice in terms of legal proceedings, where social workers and their legal advisers are much more likely to take a case to court on the basis of proving physical abuse or neglect, than they are to argue a case for civil or criminal proceedings using emotional ill-treatment as the sole basis for their submission.

HOW MUCH ABUSE IS THERE?

You could be forgiven for assuming that, coupled with a growing body of knowledge about child abuse, hard statistical data would be available which gave us extremely accurate assessments of the actual extent of the problem. Nothing could be further from the truth. Many commentators, most notably the authors of recent child abuse inquiries, have criticised the authorities for the lack of national statistics on the subject.

The Registrar General's figures for child murders over the past ten years have fluctuated from about 70 to about 105 per year. Research studies of child deaths where abuse is felt to have been a contributory factor in the final outcome push this figure up considerably. In 1987 the NSPCC published an estimate of child deaths based on a variety of source material and estimated that about 200 deaths a year are related to abuse or neglect, either directly or indirectly. In over 75 per cent of these cases, those who were most involved in the care of the children were considered to be responsible for the abuse. However, as is forcefully pointed out in *A Child In Mind*, the report of the commission of the inquiry into the circumstances surrounding the death of Kimberly Carlile (*see* Bibliography),

'By comparison, the number of children killed accidentally, whether in the home or on the roads or streets of this country, is about 1,000 a year. Compared to the widespread concern about child abuse deaths, the waste of children's lives due to avoidable accidents receives much less public, or even professional attention.'

Perhaps this helps to put the whole question of child homicide into some kind of perspective.

CHILD PROTECTION STATISTICS

In the mid-1970s local authorities were instructed to set up registers of children who were being abused or who were deemed to be at risk of abuse. These lists have been called by numerous titles: child abuse registers, non-accidental injury registers and, currently, child protection registers (by way of signalling a move away from simplistic notions that abuse involves physical injury only, and that lists of children at risk of abuse are about prevention in broader terms). Although I propose to examine the nature of child protection registers in more detail (*see* Chapter 7), a word of explanation is needed here before we go on to examine currently available figures.

Each local authority in England and Wales keeps a list of children about whose welfare it is especially concerned. Until very recently, no attempt had been made to collate the numbers of children appearing on these lists to provide an accurate national picture. In the past, the best that has been achieved has been an assessment of the national picture based on about 9 per cent of the population, with regard to whom the NSPCC carry the administrative responsibility for the register.

In 1988, the Department of Health collected information from child protection registers for the first time. Final results from this survey were published in May 1989, and these figures provide the most authoritative picture to date of the numbers of children on the registers in England.

It is estimated that at 31 March 1988, about 39,300 children and young people were on child protection registers in England. This is a rate of 3.6 children per thousand in the population aged under 18. These figures are slightly lower than the NSPCC estimates at the end of 1987. They estimated a total figure of 43,985, equivalent to a rate of 3.8 per thousand of the under-18 population.

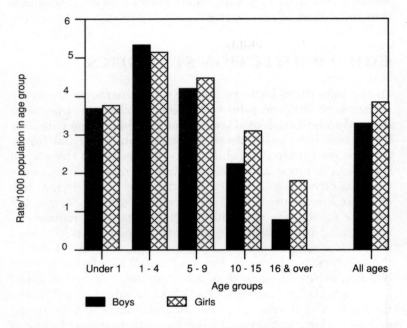

Fig 1 Survey of children and young persons on child protection registers, year ending 31 March 1988, England. (Department of Health, Personal Social Services, Local Authority Statistics, May 1989.)

It can be seen at a glance that the under-10s represent a particularly vulnerable group. Also of significance is the fact that as girls become older they seem to appear much more frequently on the register. This could relate to them being more likely targets for sexual abuse than boys. For those children aged 16 and over, girls were three times more likely to be on the register than boys.

As regards the kinds of abuse for which children were

50

registered, the figures are less reliable, because there are significant variations in the categories used by different registers. About 28 per cent were on the register under the category 'physical abuse'. This represents a total of 11,000 children having been physically abused, and placed on the register. A seventh, 5,800, were on the register under the category 'sexual abuse' and 10 per cent were on the register under 'neglect'. One-third of all the children on the register were deemed to be children about whom there was grave concern, but who may not have actually been abused at all. Only 4 per cent were registered under the category 'emotional abuse', which amplifies the hidden nature of the problem.

The registers are not static. A child's name can be removed, just as it can be added. During the year ending 31 March 1988, 21,300 children were registered, at a rate of 1.9 children per thousand under 18.

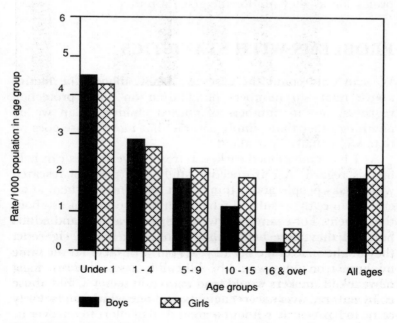

Fig 2 Children registered during the year ending 31 March 1988

Included in these national statistics are breakdowns of register figures for each local authority area. These figures show a remarkable variation, which may be the result of a variety of factors. Two possible explanations for this might be that some areas are more likely to produce abuse than others, and that there is a significant variety in the criteria used by different local authorities for registering cases and in management practice in this area generally. There may be some truth in the first suggestion (*see* Chapter 4) and, from my own experience, I can assure you that the second suggestion is the truth. Some people may well wish to argue that there ought to be a degree of similarity between authorities on the circumstances which would lead to registration. However, we have already seen some of the reasons why this agreement about definitions is very difficult to achieve, and these difficulties would appear to be just as insoluble for the social work profession as they are for the general public.

PROBLEMS WITH STATISTICS

We can only count the cases we know about. The figures above relate to numbers of children on child protection registers, not to numbers of abused children. Can we do anything other than simply assume that more abuse goes on than we actually hear about?

As I have mentioned earlier, retrospective studies can help in this regard. A retrospective study is a piece of research which asks people about things that happened to them at an earlier time, the results of which can help to inform us about the present. For example, if we were to ask a thousand adults how old they were before they smoked their first cigarette, they might on average say 12 years old. The fact that the same might be true today would be difficult to assess, because most 12-year-old smokers would tend to do it in secret. Child abuse is, by nature, a very secret activity and one which tends not to come to light easily without a great deal of effort to uncover it.

With regard to retrospective studies in child abuse, let us

take as an example the survey conducted in 1985 by Anthony Baker and Sylvia Duncan, called 'Child Sexual Abuse: A Study of Prevalence in Great Britain', in *Child Abuse and Neglect Vol. 9* (*see* Bibliography). Baker and Duncan discuss the results of a MORI survey of a nationally representative sample of the UK. A total of 2,019 men and women, all aged 15 and over, were interviewed. Ten per cent on average claimed to have been sexually abused before they reached 16 years of age, 12 per cent of women and 8 per cent of men. The average age of victims when first abused was substantially lower for females. Of those who said they had been sexually abused 51 per cent said that it had harmed them. Baker and Duncan say:

'We estimate that there are over 4.5 million adults in Great Britain who were sexually abused as children, and that a potential 1,117,000 children will be sexually abused before they are 15 years of age. At least 143,000 of these will be abused within the family. The social and mental health implications are enormous, and the authors suggest that an effective intervention and prevention policy is urgently required.'

The definition of sexual abuse which was used in this widely quoted survey is as follows:

'A child (anyone under 16 years) is sexually abused when another person, who is sexually mature, involves the child in any activity which the other person expects to lead to their sexual arousal. This might involve intercourse, touching, exposure of the sexual organs, showing pornographic material or talking about sexual things in an erotic way.'

As you can see, this definition is rather wide, (*see* Chapter 1) and accurately reflects the huge range of activity to which the term 'sexual abuse' refers. If we compare the frightening statistics to come out of this retrospective survey with our earlier material from the DHSS, we can easily see that we appear to be registering a very small proportion of actual cases of sexual abuse. Even given the undoubted fact that statistics can be manipulated to prove almost any point, the difference between numbers of registered cases and the expected number based on the Baker and Duncan material is simply staggering. If it is true that about 10 per cent of people are sexually abused before the age of 15, we are failing to detect all but a very few cases. Other retrospective samples tend to support the general findings of the Baker and Duncan survey although the figures each of them arrived at about incidence of abuse vary a little. All point to the fact that abuse on a wide scale escapes the notice of the authorities.

The same is true, to varying degrees, of physical abuse and of neglect. It is highly misleading to use register numbers as accurate guides to the amount of abuse which goes on. Child protection registers are also extremely misleading in another significant way. By far the greater proportion of children on the registers come from the lower socio-economic strata of society. Many families who have children on the register are poor, live in unsuitable accommodation, have low wages or no work at all. It is therefore very easy to claim a simple link between poverty and abuse. This is wrong. Whilst there may well be evidence to suggest a link of sorts between physical abuse, neglect and poverty, there is no such link in the research with sexual abuse nor, as far as I am aware, with emotional abuse. Yet, the register statistics would have us believe otherwise. Why is this?

Many people with financial worries, with housing problems, living in depressed areas of our cities, are inspected (whether they like it or not), by more outsiders than the rest of the population. The rent man, the health visitor, the debt collector and a range of others may well visit regularly. Some of these families may seek help of varying kinds from social workers and therefore come into contact with people who are on the look-out for abuse more frequently than others. If the spotlight is on one section of society more than another, it is reasonable to suppose that this section will provide more candidates for the register of abused children.

I have conducted numerous investigations into child abuse in the past, and I am well aware of another, rather less wholesome, reason for the imbalance of registration. The articulate middle-class family is often more able to fend off disturbing enquiries from suspicious social workers than is a one-parent family living on income support in the middle of a run-down council estate. I know this is a sweeping generalisation, but I do believe it to be true. What is more, the family which falls nicely into the idealistic picture of house and mortgage, double glazing and 2.2 children is more likely to be believed than is the working-class family whose outward appearance is one of a struggle with authority, pressure and stress. It is more difficult to believe that the village headmaster is assaulting his children than it is to suspect this of a man who is unemployed and recently out of prison, having served time for burglary. None of us ought to have preconceptions and a biased view of others, but all of us have, including social workers.

I'm sure there are some social work professionals who might hotly dispute that statement and who would claim to be totally objective and perfectly non-judgemental about these things. If there are such people about, I have yet to meet them. Social workers are human beings too! I was told by a colleague of a case involving a child who was taken to hospital suffering from significant, but not dramatic physical injuries. The doctor who examined the child in accident and emergency was unsatisfied as to the explanations given to him by the parents and referred the case to his superior. This happened to be a friend of the family concerned who dismissed the idea that the injuries could have been deliberately inflicted on the boy. He was discharged from hospital. The following day he was returned, having sustained injuries of such severity as to warrant a lengthy stay in hospital. The parents admitted causing the injuries. It is not only social workers who sometimes struggle to remain objective.

A look at the figures on the register might lead us to suppose that abuse is not a significant problem. Not true. We may suppose it only happens in working-class communities. Not true. We may feel satisfied that we have the situation well under control. Not true.

SUMMARY

I have tried to give a brief outline of the development of our acknowledgement of child abuse as a major social problem, beginning with our knowledge of history, and particularly of Victorian England. As a result of the growing development of social awareness and medical science, the concept of child protection began to take shape, coloured along the way by numerous reported child abuse tragedies on both sides of the Atlantic.

I have discussed this development in such a way as to point out the struggle which society has had, and is still having, to come to terms with what we are capable of doing to our children. I have given as up-to-date a picture as I can of the current knowledge which we have of the incidence of notified child abuse. I have advised caution in interpreting these first national figures, and would suggest that readers who wish to know more about the incidence of abuse refer to retrospective studies which have been conducted, principally in the USA, over the past few decades.

3 Case Examples

INTRODUCTION

We now need to consolidate some of the material looked at so far by placing it in a practical context. In order to do this, I shall discuss a variety of case examples, offering some commentary and comment after each one. I have selected cases which point out the difficulties of working in the child protection field for all concerned. The cases I shall examine are not necessarily the most extreme or clear cut examples, but those which realistically reflect the diverse nature of the phenomenon of child abuse. They may be seen as being typical of the kinds of situations with which local authority social workers have to deal on a regular basis.

I have grouped the examples under various headings, beginning with 'multi-problem families'. This section will hopefully point out the dangers of trying to explain child abuse by way of labelling it and putting it into mutually exclusive compartments. The reality is that it is rare to find a child whose experience of abuse, within the home at least, can be labelled solely under one of the categories discussed (*see* Chapter 1). Social workers often deal with families who present a whole range of problems, whose children are subject to the risks of various types of abuse, and which are so chaotic and confused in nature as to be impossible to label in any meaningful way at all. As we have said before, labels can be misleading, and this will be especially the case with the types of situations that are described in the first section of this chapter.

Examples of physical abuse will follow, which will again aim to portray the variety of different presentations involved in this type of abuse. I shall illustrate a case of emotional ill-treatment and neglect, highlighting the particular difficulties which these forms of abuse create for those professionals attempting to identify children at risk. I will conclude with examples of sexual abuse.

Some of the issues and themes which are highlighted in the commentaries on the cases which follow will be dealt with in more detail in subsequent chapters. Whilst these cases are based upon real situations, they have been heavily edited to disguise the identities of those involved. The aim here is to illustrate themes and general issues, rather than to focus upon clinical detail. For this reason, some of the material is a composite of more than one case.

MULTI-PROBLEM FAMILIES

Case 1

This involves a young woman, Andrea Smith, whose own experiences of childhood no doubt did a great deal to limit her subsequent ability to parent her own children adequately. Andrea was the middle child of seven, born to parents whose marriage was bedevilled by unemployment, drink problems and marital violence. In later years, Andrea was to say that she had been 'dragged up'. Her mother died when she was nine years old. She was systematically indecently assaulted by a number of men when she was about eleven years old, and on the re-marriage of her father, was basically abandoned by the family and came into care.

She returned home shortly before she left school but could never forge a happy relationship with her father and his wife. She left to live in lodgings in the area, and met and married a man much older than herself who lived in the same lodging house. Andrea's husband was a very quiet, rather timid man, who found his wife to be volatile and unsettling. Violence between them was a feature of their relatively short time together, and Andrea would often assault him. Shortly after giving birth to a son, the marriage foundered. John's was a difficult birth, but during his first few months of life he was adequately cared for. When Andrea left her husband to live with another man, whose home was very close to the one she left, John was just over two years old. Andrea's new relationship followed a similar pattern of violence to the one she had left, except that now she was on the receiving end.

A daughter was born some months after Andrea left her husband. Andrea maintained that her husband was the father, but he disputed the fact. Both children were living in an atmosphere of violence and confusion. Andrea's husband would see the children quite frequently, and would spend time with John in particular, who would go to stay at his home from time to time. Soon after the birth of her daughter, Alison, the social services department had its first contact with the family. An anonymous telephone call was received, complaining that Andrea was leaving her children alone in the house at night whilst she and her boyfriend went out. This was hotly denied by a verbally aggressive Andrea when the social worker called round. It was made perfectly clear to the social services that they were not welcome or needed in the house. The children were boisterous and extremely noisy, but seemed to be physically well cared for.

Andrea lived with her boyfriend for two years until she decided to leave with her children to make a home for herself. She allowed access to the children by their father whenever she felt like it. This was an extremely *ad hoc* arrangement, which must have brought a great deal of confusion into the lives of the children. Andrea became more and more susceptible to violent mood swings, varying from almost childlike optimism and enthusiasm to the depths of depression. Although she maintained that she had made the correct decision in deciding to leave her boyfriend, it was a time of great sadness and anxiety for her. She was being supported on a frequent basis by a health visitor, who called to see her quite regularly, and persuaded Andrea to take her children to a local playgroup. This was perhaps the first time that the children were able to be observed in a meaningful way over any length of time.

John presented himself as being a completely anti-social, almost uncontrollable little boy. He was extremely aggressive both with other children and with toys and furniture. His concentration span was very short indeed. Unlike most of the other children, he was unable to sit still at story-time and failed to respond to reprimands from playgroup staff. At the age of almost four, he couldn't dress himself or use cutlery. His vocabulary was limited, except where abusive language was concerned. Alison, who was about two years younger than John, was much quieter in large groups. She seemed timid of men, and tended to cling to her mother. Outwardly, she displayed none of the rather disturbing characteristics of her elder brother.

The social services began to visit Andrea on a frequent basis after John was found to have a hand-mark on his cheek. Andrea said she had lost her temper and lashed out at him. Andrea seemed to sink into more and more prolonged periods of desperation at this time. She would contact a variety of helplines, such as the Samaritans, and speak for lengthy periods about her feelings of desperation and her inability to cope with the pressures of single parenthood.

John and Alison were placed in the care of the local authority when Andrea assaulted John a second time. Again, the incident was the result of her losing her temper at some aspect of John's behaviour. Both children were fostered. Their behaviour in foster care supported Andrea's descriptions of their behaviour at home. The children were upset and confused at leaving home, and initially their behaviour was extremely difficult for the foster parents to contain. Contact between Andrea and the children was regularly maintained, and over a period of months the behavioural excesses of the children began to subside. Andrea was overwhelmed with feelings of rage and guilt at having her children removed. Over a period of time, and with the help of a variety of different professionals, this reaction gave way to sadness and relief. An acknowledgement was made on Andrea's part that the children ought to have been removed when they were. Although the children remained in care, Andrea was able to maintain fruitful links with them, and thereby play a significant role in their future care.

Commentary

For me, Andrea encapsulates the essence of a great many of the parents with whom social workers regularly work. The most starkly obvious aspect of this case is the way in which problems in one generation seem to be replayed in later ones.

Andrea shares so much in common with her children. Like them, she suffered, through no fault of her own, from a confused and highly unsatisfactory childhood, marked by loss, in Andrea's case the death of her mother, and in the case of her children, the break-up of their parents' marriage, and the subsequent break-up of the relationship with her boyfriend (whom John, at least, had come to regard as his father). Both Andrea, and subsequently her children, were brought up in a confused environment and were unable to benefit from the stabilising influence which appears to be a feature of settled families.

Andrea seems to have married hastily. One could speculate that she was seeking support and a fatherly influence. Perhaps she was looking for something which she missed out on earlier in life. It is possible that, because she missed out on so much of the normal experiences of childhood, she was quite an immature adult at the time when she was trying to cope with her own children. Her childhood hadn't adequately prepared her for the task of parenthood. For this young woman, how much did she still need to come to terms with events from her own past, not least having been sexually abused and being placed in care, before she could be ready to invest her energies in the upbringing of her own children? Did her experiences of motherhood bring back sad and angry memories of the way in which she was dealt with as a child? She had lived all her life in violent surroundings and was starved of affection. When under pressure, did she tend to replicate these experiences with her own children?

Imagine then, that you are the social worker attempting to help Andrea to be a 'good enough parent'. There is a sense in which, for some people, the damage has been done too long ago and left to fester, disabling the client to a significant degree by the time the social worker turns up to look at the way in which current children, in the current family, are being dealt with. Andrea loved her children, and they loved her. There was never any malicious intent in her behaviour towards them. John was physically abused. Both were emotionally abused and neglected, to varying degrees. What, then, does a social worker do? Children must be protected, and often, as in this case, this means removing them from home. But social workers often know that the parent, from whom the children are being taken, is often at least as much of a victim as the children themselves. We often deal with symptoms, not causes. An assessment must be made about the risks involved in allowing the 'Andreas' of this world (of which there are many), to keep their children, whilst the unresolved issues alluded to above are examined and explained.

In this case, as Andrea herself was later able to acknowledge, the risks to her own children were too great not to take action. There is a sense in which Andrea used her children to draw attention to her own plight.

Social workers have been criticised, quite rightly in my view, for allowing situations like the one described above to drift until too late, failing to protect children and over-identifying with parents. We must protect children, we must endeavour to keep families together and help parents. The unit of measurement used to balance these often contradictory elements is risk to the children. Limited resources often mean removal of children from home and little or no subsequent work with the parents from whom the children are taken.

Case 2

Janice was born at a time when her two elder brothers were already in care. Her mother was in her late 30s, of low intelligence, with a history of petty theft and living with her husband in a council house whose level of decoration was appalling. There was no wallpaper on the walls, several windows were broken, and soiled bedding and clothing were strewn around the place. Janice's brothers were in care because their father had asked social workers to take them away whilst his wife was in hospital during the last few weeks of pregnancy. Mr Jones played very little part in the care of his family. He had problems with drink, and gambled to excess. His wife was often unable to provide the basics for the children with the small amount of social security money which her husband didn't take to indulge his expensive habits. When Mrs Jones came home with Janice, her two boys were returned home from care, where they had both been looked after in the same foster family.

When Janice was about two years old, social workers began to receive a steady stream of referrals from the nursery school attended by her two brothers. The boys' development seemed to be way behind that of the other children. They often had headlice, smelt strongly of urine, and wore the same kind of clothing winter and summer. Mr and Mrs Jones regularly approached the social service department for food, clothing and money. This was sometimes given, the alternative being the removal of the children into care. Mr Jones was regularly sent to prison for not paying debts, or for failing to pay court fines imposed for offences of petty theft. Mrs Jones became more and more worn out. She looked much older then her years, and received no support whatever from any of her extended family, all of whom lived in the area, most of whom shared similar domestic problems.

Suddenly, Mrs Jones left the family home and went to live with another man whom she had been seeing for some time. She claimed much later that she had intended to come back for the children, but that she found a sense of freedom and release when she first left which softened her resolve. The custody of the children was granted to their father in divorce proceedings. Although Mrs Jones was granted reasonable access, she never saw the children on a regular basis until about six years later.

For the next two years, Janice and her brothers suffered a sustained period of persistent and severe physical neglect. The children were often absent from school. Janice developed a very chesty cough, often had time off school due to ill health, and was a rather thin, pale, tired-looking girl. The education department continued to draw these matters to the attention of the social services who were visiting the home from time to time, in an attempt to prop up a disintegrating family, whose membership had now been increased by Mr Jones' re-marriage. A steady trickle of material help, such as clothing and items of furniture, was provided, but nothing had any significant effect upon the material standard of the home, which became steadily worse and worse.

Eventually, the social services department instituted care proceedings and all three children were removed from the home due to their neglected condition. At the time they were brought into care there were no foster homes available locally which could take them all in together. Janice was placed in a children's home, separated from her brothers. Early records of her time in care indicated an introverted, emotionless girl who seemed unable to cope with any but the most basic of social skills. She was not particularly intelligent, but was performing at a level far below that of which she ought to have been capable. She was six, and her life up to then had been one long, relentless struggle.

For the next three years, several attempts were made to place Janice with foster parents. She had two placements of over six months in length. Both broke down as a result of the foster parents' inability to cope with her almost complete lack of responsiveness to them. She began to run away from placements, and struck up a new relationship with her mother, often running back to her from either foster homes or the children's home. She would never talk about her early life, she seemed to have forgotten about her brothers, with whom contact was never adequately maintained, and invested all her energies into attempts to integrate herself into her mother's home. Mrs Jones had, by this time, produced a son. Although the condition of her home was not ideal by any means, it was a marked improvement on the conditions in the home she had left several years earlier. She was now married to a man who seemed committed to building up a viable home environment for himself, his wife and their child.

Janice was allowed to live with her mother, still on her care order (which could last until she was eighteen). Over the next twelve months, her two brothers also came to live with their mother, with whom they had had little contact for the previous eight years. During the next two years, the reunited family suffered innumerable problems. Janice persistently truanted from school, got into trouble for fighting with staff and pupils, and became gradually more difficult for her mother and stepfather to deal with. She had a poor relationship with her brothers, and became increasingly resentful of her half-brother, who she claimed received all the attention, both emotionally and materially. Her elder brothers became involved in petty crime, and made numerous court appearances. The condition of the home, along with that of its occupants, deteriorated markedly. Mrs Jones began to look increasingly haggard and unkempt. Her husband, who had helped Mrs Jones to begin to rebuild her life with their baby son, became a distant figure who played little part in his wife's attempts to deal with the children. The family became ostracised within the neighbourhood, and had no support system outside the home.

When Janice was eleven, the situation collapsed. Firstly, she was noticed at school with bruises on her face. Although neither Janice nor any of her family disclosed how it had happened, her stepfather was strongly suspected. She was soon expelled from school, as staff found her behaviour to be intolerable. She would not respond in any way to efforts to discipline her. She disrupted all lessons, and had no friends.

Mrs Jones eventually requested that Janice be removed from the home and taken back into care. This request was eventually acceded to, and she never returned home. Mrs Jones subsequently revealed that there had been suspicions of sexual activity between Janice and one of her brothers. It was this suspicion which made her take the traumatic decision to relinquish the care of her daughter for the second time. Janice never made it back into a family, spending the rest of her time in care living in residential establishments, where she presented extremely serious management problems.

Mrs Jones was able to disclose the extent to which her early life had also been a very disjointed one. She had spent large periods of her childhood in care, due to the behavioural problems she caused to her own parents, and her mother's disability.

Commentary

The situation has a variety of components which are similar to those discussed in Case 1. Again, we see the effects of inconsistent caring upon the development of children. Janice never was able to benefit from a family life which was settled, either socially, economically or emotionally. Mrs Jones was another parent who herself was a victim. The affection which she never had in her own childhood was also missing to a significant degree in her first marriage.

One might wish to ask why it was that the children were allowed to suffer so dramatically when they were being cared for by Mr Jones after his wife left him. He had been given custody of the children by the court, but demonstrated his inability to provide for their physical well-being. They were being physically neglected. They were badly clothed. They looked ill, had a lot of time off school, and were shunned by their classmates due to their poor hygiene and lack of social etiquette. This is an example of the special problems which the diagnosis of neglect, or emotional ill-treatment presents. How much neglect is permitted before action is taken? How many times do we allow children to turn up to school in February without a winter coat before we decide they are being abused? Mr Jones was not in work. He spent more money than he should have on alcohol and gambling. But, as far as we know, he never physically abused his children. He stuck by them when his wife left. They didn't starve, and they were a family. With the benefit of hindsight, were the children, and Janice in particular, damaged more by being cared for by their inadequate father, or by being placed into care and moved around from placement to placement at an alarming rate?

Social workers must try to balance these risks in such situations, and where neglect is involved, the task of quantifying these risks becomes very difficult indeed. I have purposely selected a case here which demonstrates the problems which a lack of resources creates. Any ties which Janice may have had with her brothers were damaged, probably irrevocably, when they were separated from each other. This is often a problem with large families. Is it better to keep family groups together in residential care, or to split them up so as to give the children an experience of family life in foster care?

No real attempts were made in this case to retain adequate links between the children and either parent. They were allowed to drift apart. When Janice began to vote with her feet, as it were, and ran away to be with her mother, she was running to a stranger. She may well have had an idealistic image of what her mother was like based on the popular culture of the 'nuclear family'. Advertisements on the television, story books she will have read at school, snippets gleaned from school children who will have consistently taunted her about being in care, may well have contributed to a burning desire to possess something which perhaps doesn't actually exist – the ideal mother-figure.

Janice descended on her mother and her hapless second husband. She was confused and angered by her experiences to date. She had no consistent history on which to build a settled personality. When things began to go wrong, all her resentments about the past flooded out, and were aimed at authority figures (school and social workers), which represented for her the extent to which she had been victimised, through no fault of her own. Her mother failed to live up to her ideal expectations. Her half-brother she especially resented for having a place in a family which, for her, was an unattainable goal. The tension and stress in the household was unbearable. Most of its constituent parts were ill equipped to deal with it. They tried desperately to keep together, but closing ranks and withdrawing from society only served to increase the stress at home. Although it was never established whether any sexual behaviour had taken place with her brother, this may not have been surprising in view of the complete lack of family feeling between them.

Janice was used in the reconstituted family as chief housekeeper. She undoubtedly suffered significant emotional abuse as a result of the disparity of status between herself and her half-brother. Mrs Jones subsequently admitted that she was aware at the time Janice came back to her that things would deteriorate. She felt that she had to take her back in order to offset some of the guilt she had always felt for having left the original family home all those years ago.

This case has within it varying degrees of emotional neglect, physical abuse, the possibility of sexual abuse, and significant levels of physical neglect. I feel frustrated at times about the way in which tragic cases are dealt with by the media. They often seem to be very clear-cut and portray social workers and other professionals in a simplistically bad light, which often masks the extent of the problems with which they have to work. In my view, the two cases which I have just outlined demonstrate another side of child abuse. They raise issues about balance of risk, problems of resource and the influence of the past on the present, which often combine to present major obstacles to constructive work. Neither case contains elements within it which would make the headlines, although in both examples children suffered significant harm from a variety of sources.

In both cases there were many different potential clients. Whether we invest in work with parents or with children is often an issue. Resources often limit the extent to which both are done adequately. Both sets of parental figures were crippled by major financial burdens, to some degree of their own making. However, the fact is that many families are poor, and always will be poor. If we accept that there is a link between poverty and some forms of abuse, where does that leave the social work role? How can a family concentrate on therapeutic relationships with a caring professional when the gas board are coming to disconnect the supply at any moment? I pose these questions, but unfortunately I do not possess the answers. I wish the reader to understand the complexity of the social problems which some families can present, and the limited influence which social workers can often have. Sometimes, all we can really do is pluck children out of environments like those described in the two examples, as a damage limitation exercise, and hope that we can provide alternative arrangements for their care which can help to repair the damage. This is done whilst realising that many of the factors contributing to the child's experiences of abuse are beyond the scope of individual social workers. The underlying message from the two cases could be that social work can sometimes deal with effects (although in the case of Janice even this is questionable), but that some causes, and in particular the stress created by poverty, are very much wider issues.

One may be forgiven for believing that social work has little relevance to situations of the kind just mentioned. However, although the overall impression left by such cases is one of desperation, the descriptions I have given have focused on events and circumstances, rather than on the social work role. In both cases, a great deal of effort went into helping the adults and children cope better with their lives and unlock the confusion and negative feelings which were the inevitable result of the impact of their situation on all the clients. Andrea is settled with another man, and sees her children regularly, both of whom are being cared for in a very settled foster home. Janice has her own family now, and has been able to negotiate a reasonable relationship with her mother, whose marriage is stable and caring.

I shall now go on to describe some situations of physical abuse, attempting to illustrate the wide variety of situations to which this particular label relates.

Case 3

A 13 week-old baby was admitted to the casualty department accompanied by her grandmother. She had some small bruises to her forehead, which her grandmother claimed were caused deliberately by both parents, her son and daughter-in-law. She had red marks on her cheeks which closely resembled the impressions which would be left by pressure from finger nails. Her left eye was partially closed as a result of swelling caused by quite a hard blow to the face. The left side of her face had reddened and dark areas, suggestive of having been hit by a fist at different times. The medical opinion was that the injuries were consistent with having been deliberately inflicted by more than one adult.

The little girl, and her elder sister, were removed to a place of safety by social workers and the police began an investigation. It transpired that the parents failed to admit to having caused the injuries, or adequately to explain them in any other way. There were no signs of ill-treatment on the elder girl.

The parents lived in private rented accommodation. The father worked in a local engineering firm, and material standards were good. His wife was of low intelligence. She was uncommunicative, very self-conscious, and relied on her husband to a great extent. Their children were made subject to care orders, so that parental rights were transferred to the local authority. After a period of foster care, during which time both parents maintained close contact with them, the children were prepared for a return home. This took place over a two-month period, during which time the children stayed with their parents for increasing lengths of time until, after one or two weekends home, they returned full time.

Twelve months after the return home, the same little girl was back in the same casualty department, this time brought by her father. The mother had lost her temper because the girl wouldn't eat her midday meal. Her right arm was broken in four separate places. Her left arm was also broken in one place. Mum admitted to the police that she had bent her child's arms deliberately and at one point had thrown her on the sofa, no doubt inflicting more injuries to the damaged and immobilised arms in the process. It subsequently transpired that the mother had assaulted the girl the first time. This time her husband had colluded with a cover-up. Both children, who were still legally under the care of the local authority, were placed with foster parents. Their parents split up. Their father is now living with his parents, their mother is living with another man. They plan to have children. There is no contact between the children and either parent, and there is every chance that both girls will be adopted in the near future by their foster parents.

Commentary

This case is different from the previous two. The marriage appeared to be a secure one. There were no dramatic financial pressures and there was a significant amount of contact between the family and the outside world. Only one child in the family was ever abused.

Imagine the dilemma faced by the social worker subsequent to the discovery of the first series of injuries. It was established that the baby was injured more than once. The adults wouldn't admit to what had happened, and even the grandmother said she was unable to substantiate her claims that the injuries had been deliberately caused by one or both parents. In fact, as time went on, she retracted her allegations, claiming that she had been so shocked at seeing her granddaughter, she accused the parents hastily.

Social workers took immediate action to protect the children, who were removed to a safe place. Police enquiries were unable to shed any new light on the affair, and neither parent was prosecuted. The parents seemed to have a caring relationship with each other. They had a nicely furnished home, and demonstrated their desire to resume the care of their children by complying, to the letter, with any advice concerning arrangements for access which the local authority gave to them. There was no history of abuse in either of the parent's families. The mother wasn't particularly intelligent, but that constitutes no grounds for taking the significant step of permanently splitting up the family.

If the social workers had kept the children in care, away from their parents, is there any justification for believing that they may have been criticised for being too harsh on the parents, who, after all, had been convicted of no crime? Might

71

not a court have instructed the local authority to return the children (or at least the elder child, who had not been injured) if their parents had applied for the care order to be revoked?

The decision was taken, after having assessed the interaction between parents and children in a planned increased amount of contact, to return them home under the protection afforded by the fact that the care order was still in force. Mum's temper snapped, which it very rarely did, and one child was badly injured. In hindsight, the wrong decision was made. Had the child been killed, as she could quite easily have been, no doubt the local authority would have been hauled over the coals for not possessing hindsight in advance!

In some ways, these situations are the most dangerous in that it is difficult to quanitify risk to children from parents who have a capacity to lose their temper to such an extent as to assault their children severely. Their mother was, and no doubt still is, a placid and easy-going person whom it would be difficult to imagine capable of violence in any way.

Case 4

A twelve-month-old girl was taken by her mother to the GP. Apparently she had been crying all night and would not settle. Upon examination, the GP was horrified to find that the area around the little girl's anus was blackened and cracked. The mother could give no adequate explanation. The GP took the child, with her mother, to the local hospital. The diagnosis was that the girl's skin had been burned on several occasions, and that although it was impossible to determine how these injuries had been caused, they were certainly not self inflicted, nor were they accidental. The police questioned the child's mother and her relatively new cohabitee. It transpired that the boyfriend had been stubbing his cigarettes out, using the child's bottom as an ashtray. This man was imprisoned for a substantial length of time. The child was placed in care. Her mother maintained that she was unaware of what was happening. Whilst her boyfriend didn't implicate her in the statement which he readily gave to the police, the social workers couldn't believe she didn't know something was wrong, or that she had failed to notice the pain which her daughter was suffering. The courts shared this view. She was placed on a probation order. The child, who suffered no permanent damage, was subsequently adopted.

Commentary

This case represents another category of physical abuse, which in my experience is relatively rare. A man or woman who takes sadistic pleasure in inflicting severe pain on children in the way described above presents a danger to society which I feel doesn't diminish with the passage of time, nor with punishment. I also doubt the extent to which such people could be deemed to be safe enough to care for children in the future after any amount of therapeutic intervention from social workers, psychologists or psychiatrists.

Cases 3 and 4 have represented the severe end of the spectrum of physical abuse. In some senses, when a child receives ill-treatment to such a degree, the task for those responsible for child protection is relatively straightforward. Let us now look at examples which demonstrate more difficult areas of the work.

Case 5

A young couple, both of whom had children from previous relationships, began to live together when their marriages broke up. Mrs Anderson had two children under five, and Mr Allen had one child aged four. When they began to live together, all three children joined the new family. Mrs Anderson soon became pregnant and produced a son. As the other children were all girls, this child was particularly welcomed into the home. Mr Allen had a job, and was able to provide enough income to allow the family to live comfortably. The children were all well cared for, always immaculately dressed and well fed. When the baby was about six months old he was taken to the GP with a badly bruised and cut lip.

This had been caused, said his mother, when he had rolled off the sofa and hit his face on the edge of a toy car which was lying on the carpet. This was accepted as being a reasonable explanation. Some weeks later, he bruised his arm and back when he fell down the stairs during an unsupervised moment playing on the landing. During the course of the next few months, the little boy was dutifully taken by his mother to the local health centre with another four separate injuries, all of which were accounted for to the satisfaction of the doctor or health visitor, both of whom were impressed by the conscientiousness of Mrs Anderson.

One evening, the emergency social work team received an anonymous phone call about the family. The child, the caller claimed, was being badly beaten by his father and was crying all the time. When the household was visited, a very angry and abusive Mrs Anderson refused to allow the social worker in the house at first, only agreeing after being told that the police would be involved if she wouldn't co-operate. The boy in question looked perfectly well. Mrs Anderson denied that her husband had hit him, and said he had been out all evening. The girls were upstairs in bed. Although no action was taken at that time, social services contacted the health centre in the morning. It transpired that Mrs Anderson was due to bring her son for a routine check up later in the week. Alerted to the events of the previous evening, the health visitor made a note for the examining doctor.

When the boy was examined, he had several recent and distinct hand-marks across his back, and what looked like a faded linear bruise across his chest. Mrs Anderson broke down and told the doctor her husband had done it. He often hit his son, who he suspected of being fathered by Mrs Anderson's estranged ex-husband. During the course of the subsequent case conference, the pattern of probable assaults could be traced over the previous five months. Each incident, taken individually, was adequately explained, but pieced together they gave a much more sinister picture.

Commentary

This is an example of the grave difficulties faced by workers who have to decide the seriousness of a series of superficial injuries. Perhaps the health visitor could be criticised for not detecting the pattern, or the GP? However, faced with each separate incident, it was impossible to detect the problem.

Children do get bruised, frequently. They fall, have fights, bang their arms and legs on bikes, climbing swings and playing sports. How many injuries is a five-year-old allowed before we look suspiciously at it?

Case 6

A ten-year-old boy was the youngest of four brothers. Their parents were caring people who loved their children, but who had great difficulty in controlling their family who fought amongst themselves frequently. The youngest boy was often the recipient of beatings from his bigger and stronger brothers, and turned up at school one day with a swollen cheek and a partially closed eye. The teacher took him to hospital, after having collected his father on the way. On examination, the boy had innumerable bruises on his body, the source of some of which he could remember. He told the doctor he came off worst in fights with his brothers. His father readily admitted that this was true. There was no question that either parent was involved directly in inflicting injuries on the boy.

Commentary

Is this child being abused? Again, what is the point at which boisterous behaviour between brothers and sisters becomes intolerable? It could be argued that his parents were guilty of failing to protect him, and were being neglectful, but the boy himself accepted his treatment as a way of life, loved his parents and his home, and was a healthy young man.

Case 7

What attitude would you adopt towards a father who brought his daughter to see you, showed you several angry red marks across the back of her thighs, and said that he had administered them with his belt because she had repeatedly sworn at her mother? This man was ashamed and embarrased, but defended his right to chastise his nine-year-old daughter if she behaved in the way described. The daughter, when threatened with the belt had said, 'You daren't touch me or I'll tell the welfare!' For this reason she was brought by her dad to the welfare!

The little girl's knowledge of social services came from earlier, unrelated contact with the department. Her father was known to be a very caring, if quite strict parent. Had the child been abused, and was she at risk of future abuse? Yet again, answers to these questions depend on personal opinions about the way in which children should be disciplined, and the limits beyond which physical discipline becomes assault.

We will now look at an example of emotional abuse, bearing in mind the proviso that emotional abuse is bound to be a feature of all other aspects of ill-treatment to some degree.

Case 8

John lived with his mother and stepfather. Mr and Mrs Andrews had two young children of their own, John's half-brother and half-sister. When John was seven, and the other children were one and two years old, Mrs Andrews, ably supported by her husband, requested that John be taken into care. They couldn't cope with his detachment. He never spoke, didn't have anything to do with the two younger children, and stole money from the house. Efforts to persuade Mr and Mrs Andrews that a removal from home would be likely to add to the difficulties rather than deal with them failed, and John came into care.

He was placed in a small residential unit, and observed closely. He was a very popular boy, presented no problems for either staff or other children, and became more and more relaxed and confident the longer he was there. He saw his mother and stepfather every week when they came to visit him on Sunday. Staff noticed that they rarely asked them about how he was doing, and spent most of the time talking about the exploits of their two remaining children. After about eight weeks in care, Mr and Mrs Andrews decided John was cured, and took him home, which they were perfectly entitled to do as the arrangement for his care was a purely voluntary one.

John's behaviour, according to the Andrews, lapsed quickly to what it had been prior to his earlier reception into care. Mrs Andrews came to ask the social workers to remove John a second time. He was deliberately soiling himself, would not speak, refused to participate in normal family life, and was stealing vast quantities of money. Mrs Andrews was particularly concerned that John may harm his half-brother and half-sister, although she was not able adequately to substantiate this fear.

John was visited at home. He sat on the sofa staring down at his shoes. The television was on, but he ignored it. He looked sad and depressed, much older than his eight years. He said that his time spent in care had been good, and that he had no friends at home. The other children in the house were too young to play with. He said that he did steal money from time to time and could offer no explanation for it. He hadn't spoken to his stepfather for about a week, because his stepfather had sent him to Coventry. At meal times, John would sit in the same room but separated from his family. They said he had poor table manners and preferred not to have to eat with him. There seemed to be no communication with John at all in the house. John found it very difficult indeed to express any kind of opinion about himself, possibly because he was unused to being asked.

The social services decided to ask the court to grant a care order in this case, so as to transfer the parental rights over John's care to the local authority, to prevent the Andrews moving John back home as had happened in the past.

On the day when John came into care, his belongings were

stuffed into two plastic carrier bags. His stepfather accompanied him to the health centre, where a routine medical examination was to take place prior to John's reception into care. Mr Andrews didn't speak to John much, and John showed no emotion whatever at leaving the house. There was an unreal, almost trance-like quality to John at this time. He spoke barely at all, and would only give short clipped answers to direct questions. He never seemed to cry. If he fell and hurt himself he wouldn't cry. If he was told off for behaving badly he wouldn't cry.

After a few weeks back in care, he began to become more communicative. He started to smile occasionally, something he rarely ever did. He would offer information about himself without waiting to be asked. He became more boisterous. His school teachers suddenly noticed a change. He had been a quiet, well-behaved boy in the past. Now he was much more animated and occasionally got into trouble.

Commentary

The key point to note here is the comments made by the school. This indicates the tremendous difficulty of detecting this form of abuse. John was, in some ways, an ideal pupil to have in a class full of noisy children. He never stepped out of line, was always polite and well mannered. He was unusually quiet, but steadily got on with his work. He never seemed to mix very well with other children, but he never got involved in any trouble either. This boy was displaying a great many symptoms at school indicative of serious problems. Emotional abuse is easily missed – it isn't traumatic, nor does it occur quickly. It develops over time, so much so that the adults who are guilty of it are often only minimally aware that it is going on. A pattern developed over many years in that household which, for the participants, became the norm. There was nothing unusual in separating one child at meal times, nor in punishing a child by sending him to Coventry. Thankfully, these parents were able to acknowledge that something was wrong, even if the blame was placed squarely with John himself. Had they not come forward, it would have been difficult to imagine circumstances in which John's predicament would have come to light. John became the scapegoat for the family. Obviously, many issues around his relationship with his stepfather, and who John actually represented to these two adults are at play in this situation. Whatever the causes, I would contend that this form of abuse can be at least as horrific in its own way as the more lurid and dramatic cases of physical abuse, and is capable of inflicting more lasting damage to a child than one or two episodes of over-chastisement.

Case 9

This case will hopefully illustrate what is meant by physical neglect. Again, this form of abuse has an infinite number of manifestations and can be present to many degrees of severity. This case example has elements within it which I would describe as typical of severe neglect.

Pat and Nicholas Jones' marriage broke up. They were both nineteen years old, and had a seven-month-old baby boy. Pat gave the child, Darren, to Nicholas, and he was apprehended wandering the streets late at night with the child, with nowhere to go. Pat went to live with relatives, and Darren went to live with her. The social services department was concerned due to Pat's obvious immaturity and the fact that she was living in a house where a physical assault on a child had occurred some time previously. Pat had been in care as a child, and there were three generations of physical abuse in her family background.

Soon after the marriage break up, Pat Walsh (she reverted back to her maiden name when she left Nicholas) began to live with Paul Hoskins. He was a year younger than Pat, and had also been in care. For the following twelve months Pat and Paul, with the unfortunate Darren, moved address no less than nine times, staying in lodgings, or with friends or family, until they were thrown out. Naomi was born when Darren was eighteen months old. The council house provided for the family had no central heating, was unfurnished, and was without wallpaper. Naomi came to the house from hospital when only a few days old. It was unheated, and other than a few chairs and a bed, there was no furniture at all. No preparations had been made for the baby, other than a pram and a few items of clothing. Naomi was slow to gain weight, and suffered from severe nappy rash.

Paul left the house when Naomi was a few weeks old. Pat placed Naomi in care as she said she couldn't cope alone. When Paul returned a few days later, Naomi was allowed back home. Both children were placed under the statutory supervision of the local authority by the courts with a condition that they be medically examined at the discretion of the supervising social worker. This meant that a social worker would now be seeing the family and the children on a regular basis.

The next twelve months saw several breakdowns in the relationship between Pat and Paul. They also moved house, again. Soon after the move, Darren was taken to the GP suffering from a badly burned hand. He had apparently fallen against the electric fire the day before. It had taken twenty-four hours before his mother had sought attention for a nasty burn. Money was provided for a fireguard. It was never bought. Home conditions in the new home were appalling, with no carpets, no toys and very little heat. Naomi had a cot upstairs, where she seemed to be quite often when social workers visited. There were no bedclothes on the bed which Pat and Paul shared with Darren. Bedding consisted of old overcoats and jumpers. A half-empty bucket of urine in the room served to negate the trip downstairs at night with Darren if he wanted to go to the toilet.

A social worker asked to see Naomi on one occasion when she was in her cot, allegedly asleep. She wasn't asleep, but was staring listlessly around. The bedding in the cot was wet with stale urine. Naomi lost over two pounds in weight in a few weeks, between trips to the GP for medicals. The situation was reaching crisis point. Naomi was sitting up by the fire (still unguarded) during one visit. She had just been bathed, in almost cold water, very close to the fire. Her left leg was noticeably swollen and red. Her foot was rather swollen also, with mottled discoloration of red and bluish markings. Mum said she had been sitting too close to the fire, but the social worker asked the health visitor, who also called regularly, to check the situation in the morning. Naomi was subsequently admitted to hospital suffering from frostbite. She was spending so much time lying in a damp cot with inadequate bedding and no heating that she suffered a cold injury.

The children were removed.

Commentary

Just as in Cases 1 and 2, this presentation is compounded by a multiplicity of problems. Looking at the whole picture, you might be horrified at the level of neglect to which the children were exposed, and at the amount of time which they were exposed to it. However, the family did have some strengths which persuaded the authorities to go on working for some time with what increasingly became a hopeless situation. Pat remained with her children throughout most of their traumas. There were sporadic episodes during which her volatile and unpredictable relationship with Paul was settled. The children were not being physically abused in the traditional sense.

These parents were obviously not equipped, for a variety of reasons, to cope with children. They were both young and emotionally immature. Both had a background of rejection and confusion in their own childhoods. Basic child care skills were never taught to them, and by the time this was considered, much of the damage had been done. Neither parent would undertake the responsibilities which go with the physical care of small children, nor did they have any insight into concepts of emotional care. This case illustrates the physical risks to which children can be exposed from parents who would never deliberately set out to injure them. The damage in this case was due to acts of omission, not commission.

Another feature of the case was the importance, in terms of

assessing the children's welfare, of collaboration between agencies. By involving the health authority in administering regular medical checks, it was possible to discover Naomi's failure to thrive. Her weight loss was cumulative, over a period of time. It was not obviously detectable. She looked well nourished and was quite a plump little girl. When she came into care her weight increased almost immediately. No one will ever know how many hours Naomi spent upstairs in her urine-soaked cot, being largely ignored by a couple whose own needs for care and affection had never been met either, and who consequently were unable to provide it for others. Again, in this case, who is the victim?

Lastly, then, let us examine two cases of sexual abuse which contain aspects common to many situations which fall into this category.

Case 10

Tracy was sixteen years old. She lived with her parents John and Margaret Clark, her ten-year-old brother, James, and Linda, her sister aged seven. Mr Clark was a long-distance lorry driver, although he spent most nights at home with his family. They lived in a small village which was quite a close community. Mr Clark originated from another part of the country, but his wife had spent all her life in the area, and most of her extended family lived close by. Mr Clark earned a good wage, and material standards within the house were high. To the outside world, the picture was of a contented family. However, there had been an occasion twelve months earlier when James had run away from home with a friend. He stayed out overnight, but was returned to his parents the following day. When Tracy was fourteen, she had been admitted to hospital after having taken an undisclosed quantity of her mother's sleeping pills. Around this time, she had also told a school teacher that her dad was touching her breasts. The police followed this case up, but were never able to get a clear story from Tracy, and the rest of the family denied all knowledge of the incident.

One night, after having watched a television programme about sexual abuse, Tracy, during the course of an argument, told her mother that her earlier allegation (two years ago) had been true and that her father had been sexually abusing her for as long as she could remember. For the past six years, he had been having sexual intercourse with her on a very regular basis, once or twice a month.

Mrs Clark was horrified. When her husband came in from work, she confronted him with the disclosures. He admitted it all and broke down. Mrs Clark called the police, who arrested John. Tracy was taken to the police station with her mother, both of them in a state of complete shock. She was medically examined by a male police doctor and subjected to intensive questioning by the police. Both she and her mother made statements that night and were taken home confused, anxious, angry and very upset.

Mr Clark was retained in custody and eventually received a three-year term of imprisonment. He had corroborated much of what his daughter said, except that he refused to admit to having had intercourse with her before she was thirteen (which, for some reason, is deemed to be a graver offence).

Apparently, Tracy would usually arrive home first from school. Her mother worked in a local shop and usually got home at about 5 p.m. Between 4 p.m. and 5 p.m. Mr Clark would regularly abuse his daughter. She would go upstairs to get changed out of her school clothing, and Mr Clark would have intercourse with her. It later transpired that Mr Clark was a man about whom some people in the village always had doubts. On one occasion he took Tracy and a group of her friends for a picnic in a local wood, and there he made improper suggestions to several of the girls. On at least one occasion he exposed himself to a little girl who had called for Tracy years ago.

On occasion he would physically assault his son, which is why he ran away from home. Tracy said she had been tempted to disclose what was happening earlier, but had been very much put off by the fact that she had not been believed in the past. Out of desperation she had taken the overdose of her mother's tablets, but had never hinted at the reason for her despair whilst in the hospital.

Linda had not been abused, as far as anyone could ascertain. Mrs Clark obviously felt guilty at not being able to protect her daughter and at not being aware of what was going on.

Mr and Mrs Clark are now divorced. There is no contact between Mr Clark and the children.

Commentary

In some senses, this is a rare example of a relatively straightforward case. Tracy discloses abuse, and her mother thankfully supports her. Mr Clark admits his involvement, up to a point, and is removed from the home. Tracy is not required to give evidence in the criminal case against her father who is sent to prison. It is decided that there will be no contact between the children and their father. Neither Tracy nor James want to see him, although for a time Linda, who is made aware of the reasons for her father's departure from the scene, is understandably upset.

A common question in cases like this is, 'Why didn't Mum know what was happening'? Mothers often don't know, and those who do are usually under all kinds of pressure not to say anything at all. Why didn't Tracy tell anyone? Both of these common questions nicely deflect responsibility for what has happened on to the victims, rather than allowing it to rest with the offenders, who are usually men. It is wrong to invest children with this level of responsibility; not only do they have to cope with the undoubted confusion created by being abused by their father, to whom they may well feel significantly close, but they often also have to cope with threats of violence and of being made to feel responsible for breaking up the happy home.

These issues are demonstrated further in the next case to be examined, which presents a less lurid and more confused picture altogether.

Case 11

Joanne is fourteen. She lives with her mother and stepfather (her own father left home when she was a baby) in a comfortable council house on the edge of a large estate. Joanne is a normal, happy girl, who has discovered boys. She has a variety of boyfriends with whom she visits the local youth club, along with groups of other young teenagers. On one occasion, when she was thirteen, she had reported a man to the police for having allegedly put his hand up her skirt whilst she was shopping in town with a friend. The police made some enquiries, but eventually the friend told the police that she had been with Joanne the whole time and no such incident had occurred. Joanne admitted she had made the whole story up.

One morning in school, Joanne broke down and began to cry. She eventually told her teacher that her stepfather had raped her last night when she was upstairs in her bedroom. Joanne was interviewed by the police and a social worker. She was medically examined. The results of the interview and the examination were inconclusive. The medical examination showed that Joanne was not *virgo intacta*, but this in itself is not evidence that the hymen has been pierced by a particular object. There was no medical evidence either to support or deny Joanne's version of events which, by the time she came to make a statement to the police, was beginning to look rather less clear-cut than her earlier graphic description at school. She was now saying that she was unsure as to whether her stepfather actually penetrated her with his penis, but that it had felt like it. She had not at this stage had intercourse with anyone else, although her mother certainly thought that she might be involved in some degree of sexual activity with pals from the youth club.

Joanne's stepfather categorically denied having touched her at all. He was supported by his wife. He had no previous convictions, and became increasingly angry at being detained by the police for questioning. He felt that Joanne may have made up the story to try to get him into trouble for making her stay indoors for the past few nights as she had been coming home later than she should.

With the information collated in the way described, the police had to decide what to do with the stepfather, and the social services had to protect Joanne. The one decision influenced the other. The police decided that they had no reason to detain him due to the confused picture given by Joanne, and the vehement denial by her stepfather. This decison may well have been coloured by the knowledge of the incident twelve months previously when Joanne had made a false statement about another incident. The social workers were then placed in a dilemma. What if intercourse had taken place and she was sent home? What if it hadn't and she was put into care?

Joanne was made the subject of a Place of Safety Order, giving the local authority the right to detain her for up to twenty eight days. She was placed in a small residential children's home. From the moment she arrived, she denied all she had previously said, and retracted the whole of her statement. She said she wanted to go home and that she had made up the story to get back at her family for making her stay in. Meanwhile, a great deal of work was being done with her mother and stepfather. He felt she was a difficult girl to deal with and he felt threatened by her rapidly developing sexual knowledge, as well as her physical development. He said that when they were play-fighting, he may from time to time have touched her breasts, over her clothing, by accident, but that he had never deliberately acted in a sexual way with her.

Joanne remained in care for three weeks, during which time she was seen by her stepfather and mother under the supervision of a social worker. Gradually, a different picture emerged. Joanne had been touched by her stepfather, who had on one or more occasions put his hands underneath her clothing and touched her naked breasts. He mentioned that he had never done anything else. Joanne agreed with this interpretation. She was returned home under the supervision of the local authority. Her stepfather received a non-custodial sentence in the criminal court. She was seen in the family and on her own on a regular basis. No further incidents were noted or reported.

Commentary

Here is a very clear example of the impact on children of disclosing abuse in general, and sexual abuse in particular. Joanne's world fell apart. She was whisked away into care. She was responsible for the destruction of the home (or so she felt). Here we have double abuse in practice. Joanne is allegedly abused by her stepfather, but then she is the one treated as the guilty party and removed from home, rather than the alleged offender. Whatever the truth of the allegations, and this will no doubt always remain clouded in mystery, the system we have for dealing with such circumstances can be detrimental to children.

Do children lie? Joanne says she did, in the past and again at the time when she accused her stepfather of rape. Undoubtedly, children do not always tell the truth, but in the circumstances outlined above, it is usually the case that children, younger ones in particular, are likely to underplay, rather than to overstate the situation. Even if it is the case that a child has lied about a sexual assault, the very fact that they chose that particular topic to tell lies about may be indicative of problems – the proverbial cry for help. It may be that, in Case 10, Tracy's overdose of sleeping tablets served a similar purpose to Joanne's story about being assaulted in town. 'Please take notice of me. I can't tell you the truth because it's too painful, but I can draw attention to an area of my life which needs to change!' This is what, in their own ways, both girls may well have been saying.

There are innumerable examples of sexual abuse which are much more dramatic and sensational than the ones I have described. However, these cases have, I hope, given an indication of the kinds of issues which are around for professionals who have to deal with such situations. In many ways, sexual abuse is singled out from other forms of abuse because it appears to be that much more difficult to contemplate. The problems it presents can be exceptionally complex and stressful for all concerned.

SUMMARY

Hopefully, this chapter has helped readers to conceptualise some issues which have been discussed earlier, particularly in relation to definitional difficulties. The cases were chosen simply·to illustrate general themes and common scenarios, hopefully highlighting the problems with which those who work in this field have to deal. I discarded some more sensational and harrowing cases, as I did not wish the reader to be deflected too much from the study of the case material by feelings of despair and hopelessness. I am very well aware of the potential impact such material can have on the reader when it is grouped together in this way, with no respite. If it helps to bring home the reality of the subject, and the way in which some children have to live on a daily basis within our society, then the chapter will have achieved its main objective.

4 The Effects of Abuse

INTRODUCTION

This chapter is concerned with the impact, both initially and in the longer term, of abuse on children. An examination of these issues will inevitably involve some discussion of indicators which can be used to alert us to the possibility of abuse. For example, bruising is one obvious effect of physical abuse, so it is something which can alert us to the fact that a child is being physically maltreated. However, I feel compelled to stress at the outset that there are no foolproof indicators of abuse, and that almost any physical sign or behavioural indicator could have a perfectly innocent explanation, or, just as importantly, no available explanation at all.

The chapter is split into two sections. The first part deals with physical effects/indicators, whilst the second part concentrates upon social, emotional and behavioural effects which are sometimes much more contentious and speculative. Having said that, the events in Cleveland during 1987 created a tremendous amount of debate in the media and within the medical and social work professions, highlighting the problems of interpreting physical signs of sexual abuse. These issues, and others, are looked at in the first part of the chapter.

PHYSICAL EFFECTS

Physical Abuse

Bruises

Young and active children usually have bruises. In fact, it would probably be exceptional to find an active youngster who didn't have bruises on his or her body. However, bruises located in unlikely places on a child, or with incompatible or absent explanations, begin to give cause for concern. For example, bruising to the face, back, ears, hands, buttocks, upper thighs and soft parts of the body are more suspicious than are bruises to the shins, knees and elbows. If a child falls, it is usually forwards. For this reason, bruises to the back can give cause for concern. Also, as a result of a fall, the bony areas of the body are usually the places where bruising occurs. Children seldom injure their faces, and are careful to protect the head, almost as an unconscious reflex action, when they fall, or as an accident is about to occur.

I once took a child to a local hospital after he had complained of being beaten on his bare buttocks by his father. Sure enough, there was ample evidence of this, with clearly defined weals. However, the examining doctor, in the presence of the child's father, was able to count a further seventeen individual bruises on the boy's legs and arms, which the boy assured us were caused by playing football with his friends. It is important to be extremely careful not to over-react to signs of bruising in children for which there seems to be a reasonable explanation.

Pressure marks on the face are a common feature of some physical assaults. The classic presentation of this is one circular bruise in the centre of one cheek, and a row of two or three other small marks on the opposite cheek. These injuries are the result of the child's face being held, very hard by fingers and thumb.

There are medical conditions which make some people susceptible to bruising. These conditions, in particular blood disorders, need to be borne in mind before conclusions are reached in uncertain cases. Other errors of judgement can easily be made. I was once involved, with a colleague, in removing a baby from its home, due to reports that a man who had a history of violence to children was staying in the same house. When we went to the house to collect the baby, I noticed several bruises on the baby's head and on both cheeks. I pointed these out to the hospital doctor who examined him. The bruises were washed away with soap and water!

Head Injuries

Skulls can be fractured if sufficient force is used. Children can be dropped on the floor, thrown in anger on the bed or against a wall. The resultant fracture is not life threatening in itself, but the potential brain damage to the child is. The child could be killed instantly, or could recover well only to deteriorate due to continued bleeding in the head. Unlike some injuries which result in bruising, it is very difficult to infer the cause of a fractured skull from the actual presentation of the injury. Often, a bruise will outline the object with which the skin came into contact. For example, teeth marks can often be quite clearly seen on the skin of a child, in the form of bruises which match exactly the teeth of the offender. Fractured skulls present more potential problems in terms of investigation.

Bleeding inside the skull around the brain can be caused without a fracture being present. This type of injury can be extremely damaging because it is not easily detectable. Subdural bleeding can follow a sharp bang on the head, and it can also be caused by shaking the child rapidly – especially in very young children, since the head is not adequately supported by muscles in the neck. Rapid shaking of the child may result in its head being tossed violently back and forth, and this can damage veins on the surface of the brain. The resultant bleeding may lead to vomiting or fits. The child may become drowsy. However, it may be that this bleeding only comes to light when it has continued over a period in which the build-up of blood under the skull begins to impair the function of the brain. Outward physical indicators such as a developing bulge on the head, signs of bleeding in the retina at the rear of the eye, and behavioural indications in the child may not be immediately present, so that the detection of the subdural injury occurs some time after it was inflicted.

Tyra Henry was twenty-two months old when she died in September 1984. Her death resulted in a public inquiry which was subsequently published in 1987 entitled *Whose Child? The report of the public inquiry into the death of Tyra Henry* (*see* Bibliography). On 24 August 1984, Tyra was hit and dropped

91

on the floor by her father for wetting the floor or bed. He also, around the same time, bit Tyra in the area of the left nipple. On 28 August, whilst her mother was out, Tyra was attacked by her father, who inflicted a large bruise on the left side of her forehead and temple. The following day, a fight occurred between the parents. Tyra was in her mother's arms, and was dropped to the floor. Her father picked her up, threw her on the bed and she struck her head on the headboard. She was put to bed. Later in the day, whilst her mother was out, Tyra was again attacked by her father. Tyra was taken to hospital in a semi-conscious state, but died in the early hours of 1 September. She had about fifty bite marks on her body, and a skull fracture which may have been caused by the blow when she hit the headboard. She had severe bruising all over her body.

Bone Injuries

Young and relatively immobile babies rarely break their bones. Fractures in the very young are to be viewed with suspicion. Clean breaks in children are less common than splits and hairline cracks. 'Greenstick fractures' can often be the result of the violent mistreatment of limbs in youngsters. They can outwardly be difficult to detect due to minimal bone displacement. An immobile limb in a child, or particular pain and tenderness may well be the only indication. Major breaks usually are accompanied by a visible deformity, as the bones are displaced to a significant degree. There are other kinds of bone injury which do not involve an actual break of any kind. If the growing long bones in a young child's arms and legs are violently pulled, the end of the bone may partially separate, as this represents a weak area. Similarly, if the thin envelope of tissue surrounding bones is squeezed too hard, this may cause bleeding to occur between the outer membrane and the hard bone. This can lead to swelling and the eventual production of a callus, which X-rays will be able to detect. These presentations markedly heighten the possibility of deliberate injury, as they are unlikely to be the product of an accident.

However, there must always be an awareness of the possibility that most presentations could be accidentally caused, or be the result of a medical condition. For example, some medical commentators have pointed out that brittle bones (*osteogenesis imperfecta*) is a condition which could in some cases lead to wrongful accusations of abuse. Young babies can sometimes receive injury at the time of birth which may go undetected. However unlikely the possibility, a person must always be aware of alternative explanations, especially where babies are concerned, since you are not going to receive an accurate verbal account from the client.

Burns and Scalds

Some children are physically abused by being forced to be in contact with very hot objects. Children have been seen in hospitals with perfect imprints of the fireguard branded on their bottoms and other parts of their anatomy. Cigarette burns are commonly seen (although I have sometimes seen infected insect bites look remarkably like cigarette burns). Forced contact burns are often detected as a result of the clear mark which the burn leaves. If you accidentally touch something hot, you tend to move away quickly and the resulting burn mark is therefore often difficult to distinguish. Clearly outlined marks, from toasting forks to electric irons, indicate suspicion.

Immersion scalds are also often seen on younger children. In order to scald a child badly, the water has to be quite hot. In order to present a child in hospital with badly scalded feet and a clear line above which the skin is normal, a person has to forcibly immobilise the child's feet in water which is hot. If a child gets into a hot bath by accident, it scrambles to get back out quickly. Water will splash everywhere and will not be localised to the extent that one can see straight lines between scalded and healthy skin. A colleague of mine once dealt with a baby whose bottom was very badly scalded. The mother insisted she had held him in the bath for a split second before realising the water was too hot. The scald was severe.

93

At best, this mother was negligent, at worst it was an example of a deliberately inflicted injury.

Other Physical Presentations

There are many other physical indicators of abuse. For example, there are examples of children being poisoned by their carers. Some commentators, expert and otherwise, have argued that a number of cot deaths may be attributable to deliberate murderous acts on the part of their parents. Whilst I sympathise with those parents who have suffered tragic losses due to legitimate cot deaths, I am also able to accept that there may be occasions when youngsters are murdered which go undetected, or which are wrongly attributed to this syndrome.

Internal injuries to children, whilst not being common, are seen from time to time. As a result of a violent blow or blows, the liver, spleen and kidneys can be susceptible to rupture. Various instruments can be pushed into children's mouths, ears, rectums and other orifices which can cause serious injury.

The variety of abrasions, weals, scars and other types of injury which are routinely seen on the bodies of children and young people is vast. Often, it is dangerous to diagnose deliberate injury in all but the most obvious cases without being able to assess the wider picture of the whole presentation.

Sexual Abuse

Genital Injuries

The physical effects indicative of sexual abuse have become extremely contentious since events in Cleveland, which were reported on by Lord Justice Butler-Sloss, in the *Report of the Inquiry into Child Abuse in Cleveland 1987* (*see* Bibliography). As a result of the occasionally hysterical media coverage which these events attracted, the debate surrounding the validity or otherwise of a variety of physical effects of abuse has, if

94

anything, become more confused. The Cleveland crisis demonstrated quite clearly the fact that, in terms of physical effects at least, there is anything but consensus as to the meaning of certain physical presentations. The problem with sexual abuse is that there are often no physical effects. And, in order to assess the presence of physical effects, one requires some degree of consensus as to what constitutes an abnormal as opposed to a normal presentation. They hymenal opening (which is the hole in the membrane that stretches over the entrance to the vagina in girls), demonstrates this problem of presentation, because the absence of this membrane has often been equated, probably inaccurately, with loss of virginity. There is no consensus of medical opinion as to the normal size of the opening in females of various ages. If a man penetrates the young, immature vagina with his penis, the hymen will be stretched and broken. Medical evidence will be able to say that something caused the break, but in the absence of semen, blood or hair which can be traced to the alleged abuser, it will not be able to prove that a sexual assault took place.

In my experience, vaginal penetration of young girls is not as common as are other forms of abuse. Forcing an adult penis into a child's vagina is likely to be painful for both parties, and could result in skin tears, bruising, swelling and reddening skin around the genital area of the girl. Repeated penile penetration of the vagina may cause smoothness of the skin around the entrance to the vagina. Penetration could cause tears of the vaginal walls, as the child's body is compelled to accept an object for which it hasn't yet developed a capacity. Whilst these findings are not conclusive proof of sexual abuse, they would be strongly suggestive of it and would become rather compelling in the absence of other explanations. It may perhaps be because potential abusers are aware of the physical damage they could cause that vaginal penetration with young children appears to be not as prevalent as other forms of sexual abuse. Young boys involved in forced oral sex, or in acts of masturbation with adults, may present, like girls, bruised and swollen genitals. There may well be bite marks and evidence of soreness.

95

Sexually transmitted diseases can cause serious harm to children who are being abused. Venereal diseases and other sexually transmitted conditions can lead to a variety of medical complications, as well as providing very strong evidence of sexual abuse.

Anal Injuries

As with genital injuries, there seems to be little which proves conclusively that abuse has taken place simply by observing the physical presentation of the anus, other than the presence of foreign bodies (semen, for example) in the rectum or anal canal. Most medical practitioners are agreed, though, that anal intercourse with children can produce a variety of physical effects. The most well known of these, following Cleveland, is 'reflex anal dilatation'. The passage of faeces through the anal canal and out of the body, is controlled by two rings of muscles called sphincters. The internal sphincter operates automatically whereas the external sphincter (located at the opening of the anus), can be relaxed or tensed voluntarily. Reflex anal dilatation is sometimes used to describe the opening of both sphincters when the buttocks are parted, allowing a clear unobstructed passage through the anal canal to the rectum. The inference is that the sphincters perform in this way because they have become conditioned to relax to allow penetration by the abuser. There is some measure of agreement that the sign is one which merits suspicion, but it is for the medical profession to attempt to clarify its position further on this issue, if it can.

Buggery (in my experience more commonly practised by child molesters than vaginal penetration, especially in relation to young ▪children), can lead to a variety of physical conditions. It can cause bleeding and tears around the opening of the anus, in the anal passage and rectum. Fissures and lacerations of the anal opening, bruising, distended veins and abnormally textured skin suggestive of persistent rubbing can all be indicators of abuse. The sphincters can lose their normal muscle tone and become lax as a result of persistent abuse. This makes it impossible for the child to retain faeces, and the child will soil itself.

Other Physical Indicators

Pregnancy is sometimes an immediate physical consequence of abuse. Many children have expressed concern that they may be carrying their abuser's baby. The medical examination, much maligned in some quarters, has an invaluable role to play in alleviating these fears. I have talked to a child as young as six years old who was anxious that she may be having a baby because she was playing with her brother's penis! Of course, some children do become pregnant as a result of abuse and, as can be imagined, the implications in terms of counselling in these situations is immense.

Many children who have been sexually abused are also subject to physical abuse, and vice versa. The use of force, actual and implied, is a means by which some abusers protect themselves from being found out. I would argue strongly that all presentations of physical abuse require careful assessment on the basis that sexual abuse may also be present.

Although serious physical damage is not common in relation to sexual abuse, there are examples of horrific sexual practices being responsible for internal and external injury of a very serious nature. Although difficult to imagine, if a six-ft tall, fourteen-stone man indulges in intercourse with a two-year-old girl, the capacity to cause significant physical damage is quite apparent. Girls and boys can have a variety of objects pushed inside them which can sometimes result in serious internal injury, and the link between physical assault and sexual gratification is often ignored or understated.

Neglect

Physical neglect of a child often involves acts of omission on the part of its carers. That is to say, they fail to provide the basic physical requisites for healthy and normal development. These basic necessities would include things like food and

97

shelter, clothing, warmth and supervision. Adequate medical and dental care, along with assistance in personal hygiene can also be added to the list. If a particular child is deprived to a significantly severe extent of any or all of these basic practical requirements, a whole host of physical effects will be the result. Children can be killed because neglectful carers fail to protect them from obvious harm such as fire, busy roads and poisonous household substances. Severely neglected children often appear to be more susceptible to a variety of childhood illnesses. The persistently coughing child, or the child who appears perpetually exhausted and listless ought to give rise to concern, given that there are no valid explanations for the conditions from which the child suffers.

Children whose dietary needs are severely neglected may often appear to be thin and pale, lacking in energy and are usually more likely to pick up infections and bugs. Neglected children will often have voracious appetites which are difficult to satisfy. They may be wearing clothing which is completely unsuitable for the weather conditions. They could be persistently dirty and smelly. Carers of children may not sometimes make provision for basic health care. Immunisations can be missed, appointments to see the GP not met and home visits by health personnel fail to result in the child being seen. Bad teeth and poor eyesight may fail to elicit a response from those charged with the care of the child, whose personal appearance will often markedly distinguish him from other children of the same age.

Physical neglect of children is every bit as harmful to children as physical abuse. In fact, some would say that the cumulative effects of persistent neglect are likely to be physically more detrimental to a youngster than an assault. Neglect is a form of ill-treatment which seems to be consistently applied to a child over a period of time, whereas physical abuse can be more erratically inflicted. A neglected child is, without intervention, likely to remain neglected, whereas a physically abused child may experience lengthy spells during which he is treated well. Because the effects of neglect are often cumulative, a great deal of harm, over a long period of time, can be caused before the child's predicament comes to the attention of the authorities.

Non-Organic Failure to Thrive and Centile Charts

Although this phenomenon is usually discussed in terms of neglect of children, I feel that it is connected in many instances with all types of abuse. At its simplest level, children will fail to develop at an acceptable physical rate if they are not being fed adequately, if their nutritional needs are not being met. Some children will be small due to a variety of illnesses, and perhaps because their parents are small. However, there are those children who fail to grow properly due to the poor standards of physical care which they receive.

In recent years, there has been a growing acceptance of the need to monitor the height and weight of children about whom concerns are expressed. These developmental checks are often done by way of plotting the child's physical development on special graphs, called centile charts. Basically, these charts comprise details of the normal range of weight, height and head circumference displayed in the form of a graph. The normal range is usually depicted by lines displaying the upper 3 per cent and the lower 3 per cent. So, if a five-year-old child's weight is plotted on the graph, and falls below the lowest line, this means that his weight is below 97 out of every 100 weights within the normal range. These lines are called centiles. A child on the fiftieth centile is in the middle of the normal range. Plotted over time, height, weight and head circumference can be judged according to where, in relation to the upper and lower normal limits, the development of this particular child is located. More importantly, the rate of gains and losses can also be assessed in a comparative way.

Centile charts can be confusing, and misleading. For example, it is quite wrong to suppose that because a child's weight is below the third centile, there is something amiss. By definition, 3 per cent of the population will be on or below the third centile, just as 50 per cent will be on or above the fiftieth centile, and so on. The important factor here is rate of change over time. If a child is on the third centile when she comes into care, and is just below the fiftieth centile after twelve months in foster care, this would presumably give cause to question the physical care which the child received from its previous carers. As a general rule, once a child reaches about six months of age, its growth ought to mirror the rate depicted on the centile charts, whether the child is physically large or small.

The clues which centile charts can give was illustrated by Kimberley Carlile's medical history. Kimberley's death resulted in a public inquiry during the course of which her medical history was closely examined. When she was four and a half months of age, her weight was recorded just above the tenth centile. When she was two years old it had dropped below the third centile. In May 1984 she weighed 11.5kg. At the time of her death just two years later, aged just over four and a half years old, she weighed 10.26kg. If she had remained on the growth rate depicted by the third centile, she ought to have been about 14kg at four and a half years old. The importance of checking rates of development over time by using centile charts ought never to be underestimated.

Emotional Abuse

'Failure to thrive' (FTT) is, according to some writers on the subject, a potential physical effect of emotional abuse. This is as yet a contested and controversial assertion. How is it that a child, deprived of love and affection, can suffer in terms of physical development, especially if its physical needs are being met? Perhaps the term 'starved of affection' has some deeper meaning? Again, emotionally abused children sometimes appear to be more prone to illness, and are often sickly, appearing sallow, worn out and unhealthy. They may be unable always to control their bowels and bladders, and can suffer from a whole variety of eating disorders. Emotional abuse is a largely unexplored subject (*see* Chapter 1), about which a great deal more research needs to be done. It is usually associated with all other forms of abuse, and therefore can be present in conjunction with a very wide range of physical presentations originating from physical abuse, sexual abuse and neglect. At this point, I can only say that my experience of emotionally abused children leads me to be extremely sympathetic to the notion that (whilst it obviously is associated profoundly with social, emotional and behavioural effects), there is a connection with the physical well-being of children.

Summary of Physical Effects

There is a whole host of literature which describes in graphic detail a seemingly inexhaustible catalogue of physical effects associated with the abuse of children. I have tried to select a few of the most common. I hope that I have balanced these descriptions by pointing out the uncertainties involved in making diagnoses on the basis of any individual physical sign. The following section will explore other effects of abuse, which, taken in conjunction with physical findings, will often lend weight to assumptions based on physical presentations alone.

OTHER EFFECTS OF ABUSE

For all forms of child abuse, it can be said that the child has been dealt with in a way which would be likely to limit the child's ability to trust. This will be particularly the case if the abuser is a member of the same household as the child, as is often the case.

Lack of trust This key issue of trust is one which is often damaged by abuse. The child can develop an obviously abnormal and guarded approach to the outside world, displaying fearfulness and becoming particularly wary. The child may create barriers which hinder the development of normal social relationships. In later life, an inability to trust others can severely hamper a person's capacity to enter fully into adult relationships. Adult partners of some people who were abused as children can sometimes detect an aloofness, an intangible atmosphere which limits the closeness which the couple are able to achieve. A lack of basic trust underscores many of the effects of abuse, both initial and long term, which I shall go on to mention.

Poor self-image   Children who are treated badly, particularly over a lengthy period of time, may begin to justify the ill-treatment they receive by blaming themselves for it, believing that they deserve no better. Young children have a view of the world which revolves around them. They can only see events in terms of the way they influence them. For example, if a parent dies, children will often make sense of this tragedy by feeling that they were to blame, that their behaviour had caused the event to happen. When a child is abused, the sense of worthlessness which this can create often has lasting implications. Some victims can become lifelong under-achievers, never reaching their full potential because they almost expect to fail. They may never have been encouraged and praised as children, but subjected to verbal and physical abuse, or ignored.

Some abused children display a high degree of anxiety and are very eager to please, possibly because any attention or love they receive at home is conditional, and has a price. They may be extremely fearful of the consequences of their actions. For example, a boy aged nine was removed from home where he was being physically abused by his father, and placed in foster care. After two nights, he soiled himself whilst getting ready for bed. He hid his dirty underpants behind a wardrobe. This went on for a few days until his foster mother discovered the source of the smell. The boy cowered in a corner, thinking that he was going to be hit. Apparently, whenever he had an accident of this type at home, he used to be badly beaten by his father. He was expecting a dose of the same treatment.

Poor self-image, fear of abuse and a lack of self-worth can create a whole range of possible effects, as follows.

Self-abuse This seems to happen particularly with adolescents. They may mutilate themselves, take overdoses of tablets and lose interest in their appearance. In adulthood, a reliance on alcohol and/or drugs of various kinds may be noted.

Depression This can often be manifested in the behaviour of abused children as withdrawal, unassertiveness and an inability to be happy. This form of depression is worrying from a diagnostic point of view. An abused child who is quiet, unassertive and slightly withdrawn can often, by definition, go unnoticed. In a classroom situation such a child may display behavioural signs of abuse related to depression but appear to be a model pupil. 'She never seems to complain, always does as she is told and never causes us a moment's trouble.' If the anger and resentment associated with the abuse is turned outward instead of locked away inside, the subsequent behaviour may be very different. The child, young person and adult, may be very demonstrative and aggressive, violent and destructive. It might be argued that this outward display of anger is more healthy than the inward-looking depressive behaviour, in that the victim is releasing his or her feelings, but it may also be interpreted that the demonstrative person is more disturbed than the withdrawn individual.

Over-alertness v passivity If children are brought up in an environment where they expect to be abused either at regular intervals, or all the time, they may well develop a highly-tuned self-preservation trait. They become overly watchful and guarded. Various writers have alluded to the term 'frozen watchfulness', to describe the mesmeric fixed gaze of young physically abused children. This concept holds true in some cases for all forms of abuse, because some children are forever alert, overly so, to the potential dangers they perceive in adults.

Conversely, some victims become resigned to a life of abuse. They are anything but guarded, and almost see themselves purely in terms of their role as victim. They become passive observers of the abuse done to them. This may well be one of the factors which contribute to the marked extent to which victims are prone to re-victimisation. Abused children who develop a passive coping mechanism obviously make compliant targets for future abuse. Self-assertive, confident children are less likely to be repeatedly victimised in this way, either as children or in adulthood.

Inappropriate maturity By this is meant behaviour which seems too grown-up for the child's age. Some children seem to be extremely well aware of the mood swings of the adults around them, and can appear perceptive beyond their years. Often their carers have been unable or unwilling to treat them as children, and have dealt with them as equals in terms of age and experience. I have often been struck by the impression that some children have a relationship with their carers more akin to husband/wife or brother/sister. Perhaps the eldest child in the family is allocated duties in relation to the other children which is completely inappropriate in terms of the child's age. One child I can recall, who would often turn up for school very late and who also seemed tired and pale, would have to get her brothers out of bed, give them breakfast, make sure they were washed and dressed and off to school before her parents got up. She was also responsible for them in the evenings, when her parents would go out. Her brothers were aged five and seven, and she was ten years old.

Importantly, if children miss out on childhood experiences to the extent that they cannot recall a time of freedom from responsibility, they may develop into adults who have a need to 'catch up' with missed sections of their lives. Some adults, as a result of being given too much responsibility too soon in life, can revert back to childlike behaviour in an often vain attempt to recapture something that may well be lost for ever. The adolescent adult can be a long-term effect of having been dealt with inappropriately at a much younger age.

Running away This particular effect of abuse is often cited as being particularly relevant to sexual abuse, more often than not relating to adolescent girls. It has certainly been my experience that both sexes, admittedly very often in their teens, will run away from all manner of abusing situations, sexual or otherwise. One reads about the numbers of children who run away to large cities, where they often fall foul of exploitation of various kinds, ranging from prostitution to drug abuse. In many cases, these young people have been brought up in households where they have been physically and/or sexually molested, neglected and emotionally deprived.

Relating this to the earlier point that some abused people are prone to re-victimisation due to their passivity, the runaway presents an easy target for an extended period of re-abuse and possibly a lifetime of ill-treatment.

Manipulative personality Adults will often threaten children with violence and a variety of other sanctions if they tell anyone that they are being mistreated. The child may well learn to keep secrets, and to misrepresent the truth to the outside world as a means of ensuring that the abuse is not uncovered, for fear of reprisals. These children can develop into manipulative and devious people who appear to be very untrustworthy individuals. The coping mechanisms they acquire in childhood can, for some, be impossible to shake off. This can make them extremely difficult people to get to know. They are fearful of human relationships and afraid of making meaningful commitments in case they are hurt. It is easy to see a vicious cycle developing here, underpinned by a lack of basic trust. The child is abused – the child doesn't trust – the child develops a self-protective coping mechanism of lies and deceit – the child grows into adulthood but these feelings remain – the adult is difficult to get to know and is isolated – the adult expects rejection – the adult is rejected – reinforces poor self-image – heightens isolation and depression – increased feelings of self-protection – lack of trust.

I have come across adults who were abused as children and have subsequently had their children removed because they became abusers themselves. On numerous occasions I have been struck by the extent to which these adults have resigned themselves to failure, and have almost relished the process by which they have been labelled 'abuser'. Some people expect to fail and to be rejected. They are unable to comprehend and cope with anything other than criticism because achievement and praise threatens their own view of themselves. This view was formed years previously as they tried to make sense, as children, of the abuse which they received.

Desensitisation to abuse in others   Another possible long-term effect of any form of abuse is an inability to accept and respond to pain and suffering in others. If you are brought up in a very violent household, where physical assault between adults and children is the norm, you may become so used to this as a way of life, and may try and live with it, perhaps even ignore it, for so long that you become unable to appreciate its effects upon others, in later life. The same would be true of other forms of abuse. Many theorists claim that this is one reason why adults who were abused as children may develop into abusers themselves or be less likely to protect their children from other abusers. 'It happened to me and never did me any harm', is a comment one hears from time to time from parents whose children become victims.

Delinquency   Steele and Hopkins studied 100 adolescent offenders who were brought to a juvenile detention centre for the first time. The results were seen in their article 'Violence Within the Family', in *Child Abuse and Neglect. The Family and the Community* (*see* Further Reading). Of these youngsters, 84 had been abused or neglected in some way before they were six years old, and a staggering 92 had been ill-treated or sexually abused within the previous 18 months.

Learning difficulties   Some abused children do seem to be under-achievers in terms of academic performance. When removed from the abuse, their school work can sometimes show significant improvements. This may well relate to the general level of stress under which abused children are living on a regular basis. Their mental energy is being diverted into seeking means of hiding the abuse, avoiding its recurrence and making sense out of what must often be an exceptionally confused world of mixed messages to a child. For example, if a child is being sexually assaulted at home on a frequent basis, or physically threatened and assaulted, it must be extremely difficult for the child to apply its concentration to academic work. Unavoidable preoccupation with the threat of abuse, real or imagined, is almost bound to limit the degree to which the child is able to reach its academic potential. It is a measure of the phenomenal resilience of children that some are able to cope in anything like a normal fashion.

I was once aware of a case of a six-year-old girl whose father was extremely verbally threatening to her. He used to set great store by her progress at school, and became obsessed with the development of her literacy and numeracy skills. He would threaten her with all kinds of horrific physical sanctions if she didn't make the required rate of progress. She had to be able to handle more difficult basic arithmetic than the other children in the class. She had to have a more advanced reading book than her friends. She happened to be a very bright girl who, for a while at least, was able to cope well under the increasing pressure. However, her father's demands grew, until he was expecting levels of achievement beyond the capacity of an intelligent six-year-old. He began to hit her, and her work suffered. She became sullen and quiet in class. She would occasionally soil herself, and began to display clinging behaviour towards the teacher when it was time to go home. Eventually, these problems were successfully sorted out, but for a period of months, that girl and her father were locked into a spiral of emotional and physical abuse which could easily have got out of hand. The more she achieved, the more pressure she was under. The greater the pressure, the less she was able to achieve.

To summarise so far, it would appear that children who fail to receive an acceptable level of physical and emotional care can become incapacitated at many different levels. For some, the lack of 'good enough parenting' means that, as adults, they too become inadequate parents. If children are unhappy because of experiences of abuse, they may be unable to express their feelings for several reasons. They may not feel able to trust anyone, they may be unable to put into words the confusion they feel, or they may be threatened if they were to tell. Many may be too young to say anything at all. In these circumstances, some victims will begin to communicate in other ways, as we have seen. These behavioural, social and emotional effects, only a few of which I have highlighted, become very important to social workers (and others whose job it is to diagnose and deal with child abuse) because they are often the only indicators available that things are not as they should be.

One four-year-old girl was referred to the GP due to a persistent soiling problem. She would soil herself in bed, on a frequent basis, occasionally smearing some of the excrement on the bedroom wall. Her mother became extremely worried. The GP could find no physical problem which could explain it and the child was referred to the hospital, where she underwent a variety of tests. No physical abnormality was detected. The child's problem subsided. Some years later, she told her mother that a cousin who used to babysit would sexually abuse her by putting his finger in her anus. For this girl, the soiling was an outward expression of the fear, confusion and anger she felt about the abuse, which she couldn't bring herself to divulge to her mother with whom she enjoyed a normal and caring relationship.

POSSIBLE EFFECTS OF SEXUAL ABUSE

I now wish to concentrate, albeit briefly, on some of the possible consequences of sexual abuse which have not been highlighted so far. I have done this for two main reasons. Firstly, child sexual abuse is currently a matter of extensive debate and concern for both professionals and parents alike. Secondly, there appear to be a range of implications for some victims of sexual abuse, which seem not to be present to the same degree in those who are victims of other forms of ill-treatment.

Childhood sexualised behaviour Sometimes, young children who are the victims of sexual abuse, particularly if it has been going on for some time, will begin to behave in a sexual way which is beyond the bounds of what would normally be expected. Referrals are often made to social workers about children in schools who appear to be acting in a sexually provocative manner in class. These children may, for example, be displaying a degree of sexual knowledge and experimentation beyond the level which would be deemed normal for that age group. They may relate to any form of contact with either adults or children in a sexual manner. They may simulate intercourse and other sexual acts with playmates and with toys. They may masturbate to an excessive degree, in too open a fashion.

There are some rather important points to note here. Firstly, children, including very young children, can find sexual behaviour enjoyable. Children (and adults) of all ages do get enjoyment from the act of masturbation. This fact is often unpalatable to adults. It is as if children are not to be seen as sexual beings until they wake up one day with the capacity to enjoy what we like to think are adult activities. People of all ages can get pleasure from sexual activities. This is normal. What may be abnormal is the extent to which this natural pleasure in the discovery of sexual activity indicates a degree of knowledge and sophistication which is inappropriate for a young child. The sexually abused child may well display a sexual repertoire which singles him or her out as having special knowledge from that of his or her age group. A child who rubs a teddy bear on its genitals may be viewed in a different light from a child who simulates oral sex with the toy. In the first instance, the child may well simply have discovered that a particular activity makes them feel good. In the second case, one would question the depth of knowledge which the child has gleaned.

Young children who are sexually abused may have learned

that the only interaction they have with adults is sexual. They can therefore adopt a sexually provocative demeanour with all adults with whom they are in contact, because they know of no other means by which they can receive any attention.

Adult sexual disfunction There have been numerous research studies conducted in the past few years which have linked sexual abuse in childhood ·with subsequent sexual problems in adulthood. The guilt and anxiety which some victims carry around with them for a long time following abuse can hamper their ability to enjoy a normal adult sexual relationship. General problems, to do with intimacy, frigidity and promiscuity, have all been cited as the potential long-term effects of sexual abuse. The reader might justifiably claim that there is a big difference between frigidity/impotence and promiscuity. However, both extremes along this particular sexual continuum have been ascribed to child sexual abuse. In terms of frigidity, early abusive experiences may have left the victim feeling tainted and damaged, so much so that subsequent legitimate sexual activity becomes impossible to cope with. Alternatively, a child may, as a result of early exposure to extensive sexual activity, grow up to be unable to have other than sexual relationships or feel so worthless, and have such a lack of self-respect, that they feel unable to comprehend themselves other than as objects for sexual gratification.

For some, sexuality has such powerful associations related to negative early experiences, that it become a preoccupation, almost an obsession. For such people, the basic enjoyment of a sexual relationship is forever clouded by feelings of anger, guilt and confusion. Some become unable to experience any sense of sexual fulfilment, which only serves to add to the anxiety and confusion with which they are already struggling.

Homosexuality There is some research material to suggest a possible link between the sexual abuse of both boys and girls and subsequent homosexuality. These findings are tenuous and controversial. Different research projects appear to produce different findings in relation to this issue. I have no personal case experience which would either support or refute this alleged link, and so feel unable to comment. However, I would observe that the (in the main) intolerant heterosexual community would probably like to be able to establish such a link (so as to argue that some homosexuals derive their particular sexual preferences from unnatural activities between adults and children), in a predictable attempt to discredit the homosexual community. This is not a view to which I would personally subscribe, nor do I feel it is one which is supported by the available research. Our general knowledge about the potential long-term effects of sexual abuse is limited at present, so that we should always be wary about theories which claim to show definite links between cause and effect.

Prostitution   Again, a number of researchers have claimed a link between sexual abuse as a child and subsequent prostitution. I have certainly come across adult females who have had a history of sexual abuse, and who have been prostitutes. Perhaps this link relates to some issues already discussed on early sexualisation, an early introduction to the connection between reward (sweets, not being physically harmed, positive attention, and so on) and sexual behaviour, lack of self-respect and worthlessness, and desensitisation to the situation. We have also seen how runaways can easily become targets for ruthless people, some of whom may introduce young people to a life of crime, drugs and vice.

Poor body image   In a desperate attempt to avoid further abuse, some children will try to change the way they look to a radical extent. They will lose weight, or put weight on, as if deliberately to make themselves unattractive to their abuser(s). In adulthood, these behaviours can often continue and develop into serious clinical problems. I am aware of at least one study which found that a majority of women being treated in a clinic for anorexia nervosa had been victims of sexual abuse as children. Often a simple lack of interest in personal hygiene and general health can be an outcome of abuse.

111

Victims of abuse, as has been pointed out earlier, often develop a very poor self-image, lack any self-confidence and view themselves as the guilty party. This can lead people to be over-zealous or completely neglectful in respect of their own appearance.

Unattributable stomach complaints Some victims of sexual abuse, in particular women, can suffer for years with stomach pains and a variety of abdominal and genital complaints for which no medical cause can be found. A client of mine had been sexually abused by a variety of male members of her family when she was a girl. Into her thirties, she would regularly seek medical assistance via her GP and consultant gynaecologist, complaining of severe period pains and regular stomach aches. No physical problem was ever diagnosed. It was only after she was able to begin to talk about events which had occurred twenty years previously that the frequency and severity of her symptoms began to subside.

CONCLUSION

I have tried to outline some of the most significant initial and long-term effects of child abuse. The effects discussed are by no means an exhaustive list, and nor are they mutually exclusive. I hope that I have shown that abuse is bad for children, and that in some circumstances the effects of abuse, particularly in the long term, can be devastating.

Underpinning the effects is the basic issue of trust, which has been broken by the abuser. The sense of powerlessness with which the victim is left has major implications for intervention by the social services and other agencies, which will be discussed in more detail later (*see* Chapter 9).

It is important to stress that there is no easy formula to gauge the impact of a particular form of abuse on a particular child. Much will depend on variables, such as how old the child was at the onset of the abuse, what the relationship was between the abused and the abuser, what form the abuse took, and how long the abuse went on. Each child is different. Some cope better with the aftermath of abuse than others. Some are devastated by what would seem to be fairly minor episodes of abuse. Some seem to be unaffected by serious and protracted periods of abuse. In general, it would appear that healthy children make the healthiest victims, that is to say, if a child seems to cope well with life in general, it is more likely to cope with abuse than a child for whom the everyday stresses and strains of life are a struggle.

Many people are not unduly affected by experiences of abuse. Social services and other agencies get to hear about only the small minority of cases. There must be vast numbers of adults and children who are experiencing, or have experienced in the past, a variety of abusive episodes in their lives, but who are able to lead normal, happy and productive lives.

Finally, I would repeat what I said earlier; most of the signs, symptoms and effects discussed could easily have a perfectly innocent explanation. It is highly dangerous, and potentially a form of abuse in itself, to attempt to label children (or adults for that matter) as having been abused simply on the basis that they seem to display symptoms which have been identified as being indicators of abuse. Of course such signs and symptoms are important in alerting us to potentially dangerous situations, but a positive diagnosis rests on the collation and assessment of a whole range of factors, unique to every particular case.

5 Why are Children Abused?

INTRODUCTION

I now want to examine some of the more popular explanations which have been formulated in answer to the question, Why do people do it? Abuse takes a variety of different forms, and can occur in isolation or in combination with other types of abuse, therefore, the potential explanations vary, and rarely appear to operate as single exclusive causes of abuse. It is very unusual to come across a readily identifiable and distinct episode of abuse for which there is one discernible and unique explanation. Life is never quite that simple. People must always be wary of the dangers of believing that abuse of any kind can be understood in a simple 'cause and effect' way. The issues are unclear and complicated and it is difficult to be clear and concise about them.

I shall begin by discussing two issues which are of primary importance as explanatory factors across the whole range of abuse – 'socio-economic stress' and the 'cycle of abuse'. I shall then look at specific categories of abuse with reference to some of the more significant theories which have been suggested to explain them.

SOCIO-ECONOMIC STRESS

It is now relatively well established that abuse of all types can and does occur in all sections of society, that it cuts across divisions based upon class, wealth, status and culture. However, it is a fact that a great deal of abuse of children occurs in the more deprived areas of society. There are at least two reasons why this should be the case. Firstly, as I have already mentioned, there is a significant bias towards the detection and reporting of abuse within the lower strata of society. This is due to a variety of factors, one of which being that the middle classes are often better equipped to deflect suspicion of abuse away from themselves. In this they are ably assisted (it has to be said) by agencies whose staff are often comprised of people from similar backgrounds, eager to minimise signs of abuse which emanate from sections of society to which they themselves belong. Secondly, some sections of society are subject to greater degrees of stress than others.

It would probably not be unreasonable to argue that adults under stress are more likely to behave badly towards children. When we feel under intense pressure, or are under any form of stress for a significant period of time, we often say and do things which would, under normal circumstances, not be said or done. The case studies on pages 57–88 graphically demonstrated the extent to which some people live their lives under tremendous stress. Poor housing, unemployment and financial constraints are problems which bear down heavily on large numbers of people in the UK today. These factors, taken together and experienced over long periods of time, can wear down a person's ability to cope. Life becomes a struggle from day to day. Being forced to contend with these external socio-economic stresses can gradually inhibit the capacity to respond to other pressures. As those of us who have had children will readily agree, a young child in the home, as well as being a source of pleasure and fulfilment, is also a source of great stress. Sometimes, people will behave badly towards a child because their tolerance to stress has been gradually eroded by the social and economic situation in which they live.

Of course, this is not true of every person. Nor is it to be seen as an excuse for abuse in any individual case. However, there does seem to be a definite link between lower social class (for want of a more adequate expression) and some forms of abuse, particularly physical abuse and neglect. For society as a whole to ignore this link, and to expect individual social workers to deal with individual cases without acknowledging the wider socio-economic scene, is problematic. Many would argue that without a fundamental shift in perception of the problem of child abuse away from individual responsibility towards an acknowledgement of wider social, economic and political factors, our capacity to develop effective preventative strategies to ameliorate the problem will at best be limited and at worst be pointless. It is beyond the scope of this book to expand into these wider issues. Suffice it to say that I have often worked with clients whose lives are shaped and manipulated so starkly by factors beyond their control, that I have felt totally helpless to prevent their children from being abused. The parents are themselves being abused all the time, by being located at a particularly disadvantageous position in the general scheme of things.

I am very well aware that vast numbers of the population live in circumstances of disadvantage and would never abuse their children. I said earlier that in my opinion such factors never excuse the actions of individuals. I feel that it would be wrong of me to bypass this controversial aspect of child abuse simply because it brings into play factors over which social workers and their clients have little control. If we lived in a community which enjoyed full employment, which housed its citizens in adequate accommodation and in which minority groups were not disadvantaged, I feel sure, from my experience, that we would see less child abuse. It is important to be aware that I use the word 'less' here, to denote the fact that there do exist adults who, whatever their situation, will abuse children.

In my opinion, the stress factors which emanate from the relationship between many individuals and the state are perhaps the most significant indicators of potential abuse, particularly in relation to physical assault. This relationship is also responsible for a large proportion of the stress felt by social workers who work in this field, and this issue is addressed in a little more depth later (*see* Chapter 10). When thinking about other factors which may explain why adults abuse children, it is often important to bear in mind these wider considerations which can underpin much of what is wrong in the relationship between the adult and the child.

To what extent are issues of socio-economic deprivation prevalent in society today? Well over one million children under sixteen are living in families where at least one parent is unemployed. At least one-third of the unemployed males in the UK have dependent children. There is evidence to suggest that the divorce rate for the unemployed is twice the national average. About 10,000 families sleep in emergency bed and breakfast accommodation every night. Homelessness is a major problem. Many people live in inadequate accommodation from the point of view of amenities and safety, and more than one million people are on housing waiting lists. Whether we like it or not, and whatever the causes, there are huge numbers of children living in the UK today whose principal carers are suffering from the effects of the stress caused by socio-economic forces which are complex and difficult to understand. The link between stress and some forms of child abuse are, in my opinion, not difficult to understand. The potential consequences of this for thousands of children in the UK are enormous.

THE CYCLE OF ABUSE

R. S. Kempe and C. H. Kempe sum up the cycle of abuse in their book *Child Abuse* (*see* Bibliography) thus:

'The most consistent feature of the histories of abusing families is the repetition from one generation to the next, of a pattern of abuse, neglect and parental loss or deprivation.'

This often quoted cycle of abuse appears to have been elevated in recent years, to a point where one could be forgiven for supposing that all abused children are destined to become abusing parents. This is not the case. However, a significant proportion of adult abusers (figures vary according to which research data is consulted) have been abused as

117

children. Social and economic stress plays a significant role in child abuse, and economically and socially disadvantaged children often grow up to be disadvantaged adults. This produces a situation in which socio-economic stress is transported from one generation to another.

If an adult's own experience of being parented is inadequate and abusive, they may have little or nothing from their past on which to base their conduct with their own children. Both consciously and subconsciously we tend to pick up so much, both good and bad, from our early experiences. Some abused children lose out on much that is necessary for the adequate development of a rounded personality, and as a result, their subsequent ability to give to their children that which they never had (and therefore are unable to see as necessary), in terms of emotional support in particular, is severely impaired. To illustrate this, I know of a whole range of cases, where parents have failed to see the significance of their children being accessible to adults who are known abusers. A colleague was working with a young woman who found it very difficult to understand the importance of strictly supervising the contact which her four-year-old daughter had with her grandfather, who was a known sex offender. This man had sexually assaulted his daughter frequently when she was a young girl. Whilst there was no deliberate intent to harm her daughter, this woman had a worryingly cavalier attitude to contact between her own child and this man. In this case, there was possibly a lack of insight on the part of a mother whose own history had left her sadly devoid of any concept of the protective duties of parenthood, and whose own experience of abuse had impaired her capacity to judge potentially dangerous situations in a realistic way.

There is much which we have yet to understand about the transfer of patterns of behaviour from parent to child. Some adults appear to replay negative events from their childhood with their own children. When some background information is available, it often seems to be the case that the child has been abused in similar ways, at around the same age, as the parent was abused in childhood. It is as if some adults need to make sense of the past through their children. By replicating episodes from their own childhood, they are trying to get in touch with unresolved psychological issues, of which they may not even be aware. Certainly, in terms of an assessment of risk in any particular case, knowledge that one or both parents were abused when they were children is something which needs to be taken into account. This is especially important if no help of a therapeutic nature was ever given to the adult, to help them deal with any long-term psychological effects which may have resulted from their abuse.

Theories have been offered by way of attempting to explain the occurrence of abuse in its different forms. Because the categories of abuse are not mutually exclusive, many of the explanatory factors which follow are not unique to one form of abuse. I categorise them here only in so far as it might be possible to enhance clarity, by ascribing explanations to those forms of abuse to which they appear particularly associated.

PHYSICAL ABUSE

Many early research studies argued that physical abusers were grossly disturbed people with a variety of psychopathic tendencies. Perhaps early researchers were keen to distance the offender from the population at large and to ascribe mental illness as the reason for their actions toward children. However, in 1972, Kempe and Helfer argued that less than 10 per cent of abused children were injured by adults who would be described as being seriously disturbed (*see* Bibliography).

There have been a wide variety of psychiatric models of abuse put forward which may help an understanding of why certain individuals are more prone than others to injure children.

Low Frustration Tolerance

Adults who find it difficult to relax, and whose capacity to deal with the stresses of everyday life (children, mortgage, marriage, job, unemployment, and so on) may tend to be more prone to violent episodes than others.

Rigidity and Inflexibility

Some parents appear to impose excessive and unrealistic rules of behaviour on to their children, and appear to conduct their lives generally in a very regimented and clinical way. For people such as these, children can pose inordinate problems as they go through the normal developmental process, whereby they learn, often by mistakes, about how to behave and how to interact with other people. Too rigid an approach can set up unnecessary tensions and create a situation where the relationship between parent and child becomes little more than an unresolvable war of attrition.

Aggression

Impulsive and overly aggressive adults may also display a propensity to abuse their children physically. Where does this aggressiveness originate? As we have already seen, some children brought up in a violent household will display a developing immunity to physical violence and may become aggressive and violent themselves. Protracted exposure to significant stress factors is also thought to increase the impulsivity and level of aggression which adults display. (Sources of stress other than those which have already been discussed are examined a little later in this chapter.)

Punitive Control

Some adults use physical force more than others in an attempt to control their children. It may be safe to assume that those parents who resort to physical force are more likely to abuse their children than others. However, it could be argued that the opposite is in fact the case. Those parents who physically check their children may be less likely to be presented with behaviour from the child which warrants punishment, whereas those with a more liberal approach to child-rearing who allow their children too free a rein, may be storing up trouble for the future.

Low Intelligence

It has been argued in a variety of studies that parents of low intellect are more likely to physically abuse their children. I doubt this view. If the reasons why such parents are of allegedly low intelligence are examined closely, they are likely to show that these parents have perhaps not been allowed to achieve their potential due to socio-economic factors beyond their control, rather than because of a basic lack of intellect. There is also the fact that this group is likely to be over-represented in the official statistics, because they are less able to fend off enquiries from public agencies.

Unrealistic Expectations of the Child

It has certainly been my experience that some parents who physically abuse their children have very unrealistic expectations of the child. I can recall cases where young babies have been hit because they cried, where school-age children were abused for not coming top of the class in exams, and a variety of other examples where children have been assaulted simply because they were unable to reach the unreachable goals which parents set.

We tend to assume that if adults produce a child, she will be a good mother and he will be a good father, as if the process of conception and birth allows the adults access to knowledge they didn't have before. We do not teach people enough about children. Very few adults are given any degree of training in basic child care craft or human growth and development. It is not too surprising, therefore, that some adults develop strange views about the kinds of behaviour and levels of achievement to be expected from children, at various stages in their development.

Sociological Sources of Stress

Single-parent families   Without any chance of sharing the burden at all, normal child-rearing can become overwhelming to a degree where physical assault takes place.

Lack of network of support   Isolated families, families without grandparents and other relatives to assist, can be placed under more stress than other, more adequately supported family groups, and abuse may be more likely to occur.

Marital discord   This is another obvious, and all too common, source of family stress which in some cases can lead to the physical or other kinds of abuse of the child.

The characteristics of the child   This aspect of the nature of abuse is being examined much more closely than in the past. There are a number of obvious features which would make the prospects of abuse more likely, especially if coupled with the other factors already mentioned.

Illness can be a problem, and children with severe handicaps or other illnesses appear to be more likely to be abused than children who do not have any physical difficulties.

Prematurity also seems to be a relatively common feature in the abuse of children. It may relate to the possibility of the parents being denied the chance to bond adequately with the child in its first few days, particularly if it is receiving special medical attention. It may be that a premature child creates added stress to parents, to whom its arrival is something of a surprise. Recent studies have suggested that there is something about the look of a premature baby which makes it more prone to abuse. Babies look appealing, soft and round. They are designed, so the theory goes, to elicit a protective response from adults. Premature babies often do not look appealing and therefore are denied the chance to have the appropriate placatory effect on the adults who care for them. It seems that ugly babies may be more at risk of abuse!

Demanding children are less easy to care for than others. Many children sleep and eat at the right times, say and do the right things, and generally are a pleasure to be with, but others place a great many more demands on their carers. They are irritable, are poor sleepers and feeders, and, as they grow, seem to be constantly in trouble. Whilst it is difficult to know the means by which each individual develops in such different ways, it is easy to see how the more demanding child is likely to be more at risk of abuse.

So far I have mentioned a series of possible factors which may help to explain the occurrence of abuse in a variety of situations. I think that those of us with children of our own would perhaps be sympathetic to some of the explanations. I can recall occasions when, after feeding a baby in the middle of the night and spending a long time winding him, I have changed his nappy only in time for him to urinate over the carpet. Having cleaned this up, and put a new nappy on him, I have finally put him back in his cot. It is now 5.15 a.m., I am due to get up in two and a half hours. The feeling of relief as I finally get back to bed, and my sense of achievement is immediately shattered by a muffled cry which grows steadily stronger and stronger. I feel tense and agitated. I argue with my wife about who should 'see to him'. At difficult moments like that, it is almost possible to understand why some people resort to abuse.

Before moving on to look at possible causes of neglect and emotional abuse, I shall conclude with a brief description of a situation of physical abuse, concentrating upon the case from the abuser's point of view.

Case Study

Joan Robinson is thirty-two years old. She lives in her own home with her fourteen-year-old son Mark. Joan has never married, and Mark's father lives in another part of the country, rarely making visits to see Mark and never helping his mother with any financial contributions. Joan is a nurse, and works in a busy Accident and Emergency Department in a local hospital. The work is demanding and tiring. Because she works rather long hours and changes the pattern of her shifts quite frequently, her social outlets are minimal, although she sees her mother when she can.

Mark is of average ability at school. He has numerous days off, being unable to motivate himself to get ready to go on those occasions when his mother isn't at home. He has few friends, spending his time at home watching video films. He does quite a lot of housework, cooking and cleaning for his mother. Occasionally his mother has bouts of heavy drinking which often result in her beating her son with items of furniture, or her fists. He is eventually admitted into the care of the local authority. His mother admits she can no longer cope.

This case is based upon a real situation with which a colleague has been working for some time. If we list those factors which, from the brief summary of the case, might seem to have contributed to Joan Robinson's situation the following picture might emerge. She is a single parent suffering from social isolation and a variety of stress factors, including her job and its unsocial hours. She has anxiety about her ability to care adequately for her son, concerns about his schooling, and unrealistic expectations of the boy (he was being used by his mother as principal housekeeper which may not be an appropriate role for an adolescent to play). There is also the possible drink problem. Joan undoubtedly presented a significant risk to her son on occasions when things just got too much for her. However, in order to begin to do something to help, you have got to move beyond the simple label 'abuser' and try to analyse those factors which may have contributed to the outcome.

NEGLECT AND EMOTIONAL ABUSE

I have combined all forms of neglect and emotional abuse because I feel that there seem to be innumerable strong similarities between theories which attempt to explain why it is that some adults abuse children in these particular ways. However, as I have said before, I would not wish to create the impression that any of the following factors belong exclusively to any particular form of abuse. One of the great challenges within the field of child protection is the fact that there is very little of any substance which can be said about the subject which is not itself open to dispute and controversy.

Bonding

This term is used to describe the process by which an infant and its parents (in particular its mother) develop an early relationship of warmth and affection. There appears to be a widespread, but by no means universal agreement that the process of bonding is the most critical part of infancy. If that initial relationship between parent and child fails to materialise, or is in some way irreparably impaired, then the prospects that the child will be abused are increased. This is particularly the case in respect of emotional abuse. Indeed, some would argue that the lack of adequate bonding in the first days of an infant's life constitutes a form of emotional ill-treatment of itself. Certainly, if its parents have no deep-seated bond of love and affection for the child, you can readily imagine that youngster being ignored, unprotected and generally receiving less than adequate care as it grows through childhood. We have already seen that prematurity is one way in which the process of bonding can be hindered. Other possible difficulties can relate to various factors.

Unresponsiveness can be a problem. For a variety of reasons, either the child or the parent may be unable to demonstrate the normal range of audio-visual responses. This could be due to physiological problems, post-natal depression, or a number of other factors. The child may be a particularly demanding baby, whose temperament does not naturally endear it to its parents.

The baby may be the 'wrong' sort of child, unwanted, and the result of an 'accident'. It may be the wrong sex, or it may not fit the idealised expectations of young parents whose images of babies have been gleaned from nappy commercials on television.

There is a significant amount of controversy surrounding both the concept of bonding, and its potential effects. My own experience leads me to believe that the concept of bonding is an important feature of the early development of a child. However, the long-term effects allegedly associated with its impairment, in particular, the extent to which these children are more prone to neglect and emotional abuse, are much more debatable. This is especially when you consider the number of successful adoptive placements which are made, where a child has been removed from a parent with whom it may or may not have successfully bonded. Put at its most basic level, if a relationship between a mother and child starts out badly for any of the reasons outlined above, it may continue on a downward, neglectful and abusive path, if no effort is made to intervene. However, bad beginnings can be recouped, either by giving help to the adults or, in the more serious cases, removing the child.

Communication

This factor appears to have particular significance in relation to neglect and emotional abuse. At one level, it is obviously related to the concept of bonding, which is about the ability of adults and infants to develop means of communicating feelings and needs to each other without the benefit of speech. However, parents/carers who have a poorly developed pattern of communication, and who seldom, if ever, describe to each other their wishes and feelings, particularly in relation to emotional needs, can often be neglectful of the needs of their children. If the family doesn't encourage this level of communication, unmet needs can remain unmet, and the child may be deprived of basic social, emotional and physical requirements and also of a means by which to articulate those requirements.

This leads on to the question of feelings, and the problems which some people seem to have in articulating them. There is a sense in which some adults, and in particular men, find it unmanly even to acknowledge that they have a yearning for emotional closeness. Many people are brought up in a pseudo-stoical environment where we avoid physical displays of affection and deny closeness to others. For these people, of whom there are many, the notion that children have emotional needs may be beyond their comprehension, or may be minimised to an extent that the child suffers as a result.

Immaturity

Adults who find themselves in the role of principal carer to a child, yet who have failed to achieve a level of personal maturity themselves and who possess a multitude of unmet 'childlike' needs may be neglectful and/or emotionally ill-treat their child. Dependent personalities, demanding, and emotionally frail people may well see the child as competing for the attention from the other parent which they themselves crave. They may block the child's attempts to have its needs met and may resent the responsibility which the task of raising a child imposes to a degree where the child is punished, consciously or subconsciously. Please remember that immaturity doesn't simply relate to the age of the parent. I have met innumerable mature teenaged parents, and many immature and incapable older adults.

Obviously, this phenomenon relates in part to the cycle of abuse which was discussed earlier, in that an immature adult may well by symptomatic of an inadequate childhood. Whatever the cause, immaturity can certainly be a big problem in terms of an impaired capacity to deal with children.

I have had many clients who, for a variety of reasons, have missed out on large sections of the normal development process when they were younger. One woman in particular had married her boyfriend, by whom she was pregnant, when she was sixteen. She had a baby daughter. All was apparently well for the first four years of the child's life, but the marriage then hit problems. The child's mother often went out with a group of other young women to nightclubs in the town at weekends, leaving an increasingly resentful husband at home babysitting. The marriage broke up, and she was left at home to care for her daughter. She began to drink heavily, became involved with a number of young men in the town, and on two occasions was arrested for drunk and disorderly conduct. She presented as a rather moody person, who would be high one time and depressed the next. Her daughter received little or no attention, and was left at home with various babysitters whilst her mother went out.

This woman was obviously caught up in a situation where she became increasingly resentful at having lost out on her late adolescent years. Her behaviour was that of a recalcitrant sixteen-year-old, and the responsibility she had towards the care of her daughter began to diminish to an extent where she became actively neglectful, as if she wanted to punish her daughter for the trap in which she felt she had been caught.

Large Families

Some theorists have argued that big families, of necessity, create certain difficulties which can promote abusive situations and can, in particular, lead to neglect and emotional abuse. Large families are more susceptible to economic stress. They may make communication difficult. Parents will feel more stressed as a result of having to care for more children. Attention may be at a premium, and family members may be in competition with each other for affection. I have no evidence from my own experience either to support or reject this view. I have known happy large families who seem to have benefited from being large, and I have seen other situations which have not been quite so happy. It seems to me that, if there is enough financial provision, if the family is adequately housed and the relationship between the carers is sound, children do not appear to suffer by being in a large group. I doubt whether the quantity of parental attention/affection is anywhere near as important as the quality of that contact when it occurs.

Psychological Problems

Adults for whom everyday life is a constant struggle are more likely to abuse their children. Depressed people may lack the motivation to provide for their families. This can be a cumulative, spiralling scenario. Maybe the depression is reactive to a major traumatic event, such as unemployment, bereavement, the birth of a child, and so on. Perhaps the depressed adult gives less physical and/or emotional attention to the children. As a consequence, the behaviour of the children deteriorates. They become more demanding and difficult to deal with. This accentuates the pressure on the depressed adult, whose capacity to be a parent is further impaired, and so it goes on.

Psychotic people are those with severe mental impairment which makes them lose their grip on reality from time to time. The problems which they can create for children in their care are obvious. Mental retardation may also be a contributory factor, particularly in relation to neglect and emotional abuse. This is linked to knowledge of parental tasks, both practical and emotional. If a parent is unable to carry out the basic functions and duties in relation to the child, then it is self-evident that the child will suffer as a consequence.

Similarly, if one or both parents suffers from a serious physical disability, this could sometimes lead to problems. My experience, however, of families in which one or both parents have been physically disabled leads me to conclude that the potential benefits to children often outweigh the obvious drawbacks. The strength of the relationship between a child and its disabled parent can be quite dramatic, and of immense benefit to both parties, who can often share an openness and an intimacy which may be beyond the scope of other people.

EXPLAINING SEXUAL ABUSE

In a variety of ways the phenomenon of sexual abuse differs from other forms of ill-treatment. In acts of physical abuse,

129

neglect and emotional ill-treatment it is more often than not the parents who are primarily responsible. Children are sexually abused predominantly by people who know them, often their parents. However, grandparents, aunts and uncles, brothers and sisters can also be involved in the sexual abuse of children. It can be an activity which pervades whole family groups, and is not necessarily confined to one or two family members. I have been aware of cases of sexual abuse involving a number of different households, some of which may be linked by marriage, in which children have been an interchangeable commodity, passed from one family to another for the purpose of sexual assault.

The association with socio-economic stress is much weaker with regard to sexual abuse than seems to be the case with other forms of mistreatment. Although some research studies do point to the assertion that it occurs more frequently in families of lower social and economic status, these findings are more tenuous than with other types of abuse, and may, again, bear more significant relation to the extent to which certain types of families are easier to label and supervise than others.

Sexual abuse is often much more difficult to detect than other abuse. It is heavily cloaked in secrecy, and is surrounded by denial and disbelief, both on the part of the public and the professions alike. It is often not possible to detect routinely by simple observation or medical examination. For these reasons, our knowledge about its origin is limited and much of the research upon which the following material is based is quite new, and open to question. More than any other form of child mistreatment, sexual abuse is controversial, and it is difficult to be able to say anything too definite about it. I shall endeavour to discuss a few of the more popular theories which have been advanced in recent years, in order to explain why sexual abuse of children might happen, but the scope of this book is too broad to be able to give this particular topic the space it deserves. The reader will have to look elsewhere in the specialist literature for more detailed discussions of the subject. It is sufficient here briefly to describe some of the more prevalent theories, in the knowledge that none of the following information is without its controversial aspects.

Mental Illness

As with other forms of maltreatment, it is interesting to note that some of the early theories strive towards being able to say that the sexual offender is 'crazy'. This is, in part at least, a function of our continual desire to put a distance between offenders who engage in abhorrent acts and ourselves, as if to demonstrate our normality in contrast to the 'very sick' people who molest children. This is one of the reasons why sex offenders are sometimes singled out for violent treatment by fellow inmates in prison. The 'normal' prison population sees itself as being threatened by an involuntary association with these 'sick' individuals. Although a certain number of offenders are undoubtedly ill, are extremely predatory and have hundreds of victims, the great majority are not like that at all. They function perfectly well in most areas of their life and in the main do not conform to the stereotypical image which we may have of them as being 'dirty old men', offering sweets to children.

Masculinity

Sexual abuse is predominantly a male activity. There are cases where women have been convicted of sexual abuse, but these are relatively rare. Why should this be a male problem? The growing feminist literature in the mid to late 1970s firmly places the responsibility for sexual abuse in the wider context of the dominance of men over women, and the way in which they are conditioned to be powerful and to exercise control. Successful men are supposed to search out sexual conquests and their ability to attract females is one important criterion upon which their very 'maleness' is judged by their friends and associates. There are all kinds of pressures in the modern world which try to reinforce this view. Advertisements on television sell all manner of objects, from cars to jeans, on

131

the basis that the purchaser will be awash with sexual opportunities.

The timid, reticent man who is devoid of any degree of confidence may find it impossible to see himself fitting into this scheme of things. He may project his unfulfilled sexual needs on to less threatening people, such as children. His desire for dominance and control, ingrained perhaps at a very early age (John gets a toy gun and is expected to shoot 'baddies', whilst Joan gets a doll and is told to be gentle and subservient), finds expression in relationships of a deviant nature with children. The children may be persuaded to accede to the man's demands by being threatened, bribed and tricked.

Addictive Cycle

There are numerous commentators who assert that the sexual victimisation of children is often addictive. Adults may have deep-seated fantasies about becoming involved in a sexual relationship with a child for a variety of reasons. They may have been abused themselves and feel the need to replay the experience, they may be threatened by adult sexuality and may be sexually immature, or they could lack knowledge about sexuality and be simply reacting to an external stimulus, maybe a pornographic video film. Perhaps they begin to masturbate whilst thinking about abusing a youngster. Masturbation is enjoyable and reinforces the nature of the fantasy. In time, the fantasy may take on obsessional proportions to the extent where the prospective offender begins to search the community for potential victims, in order to bring the fantasy to life. The more the potential offender thinks about abusing a child, the more revolted he is by his thoughts. Maybe he doesn't like himself too much anyway. He has problems in other areas of his life. He thinks he is unattractive. He is going bald. The mortgage is hard to pay. He retreats more and more from the real world into compensatory fantasy. This increases in importance the more often he fantasises. It may then be only a matter of time until

132

he offends. This may revolt him at first. He may hide away from the reality of what he has done and return to his fantasy world, and so the process continues.

This raises another crucial difference between sexual and other types of abuse. In time, the act of assault becomes enjoyable. I realise that there are some damaged individuals who get a thrill out of physically harming children, but sexual fulfilment, in general, is more commonplace and the abuse occurs more frequently simply because it develops into a very pleasurable experience for some people. Whether the satisfaction derives from sexual orgasm or from strong feelings of power, dominance and control depends upon the nature of the offender. There are those, of course, who combine physical and sexual abuse (some would argue that they are inextricably linked anyway), and who are extremely dangerous individuals.

Unresolved Past *Blockage*

Early victimisation, whether by acts of commission or omission on the part of the child's carers, can lead to a host of unresolved issues, as we have already seen. The adult can grow up to fear adults, to mistrust the extent to which adults will protect, and to crave love and affection which was denied them by their own parents. Some experts argue that there is a particularly strong link between having a history of abuse, and becoming a sexual abuser.

If the offender's development is arrested at an early stage, by virtue of abuse, then this may mean that they feel a particular affinity with youngsters who are around the same age at which they are developmentally blocked. They may seek out love and affection from children as a way of compensating for the past. They may identify with their abuser(s), and play the role of offender, in order to conquer their own feelings of being victimised. Some practitioners have described the homes of middle-aged sexual offenders as being completely incongruous to their chronological age, with records and pop posters on the walls. It is as if they are locked

133

into an emotional time trap and seek escape by identifying with children, with damaging results.

Selfishness

Many sexual offenders are completely oblivious to the needs of those around them, and in an infantile way recognise only their own needs. They are unaware of the pain they cause others and are completely fixated by their deviant behaviour pattern. Again, this tendency to regress to an early level of social and emotional functioning is likely to relate to arrested development caused by trauma in their own childhood. Of course, this selfishness has massive implications in terms of the management of sexual abuse. Rational argument about the hurt which their behaviour can cause is often ignored, or accepted on only a very superficial level. They have often grown up in an environment where self-reliance was the only sure way of avoiding pain. Confiding in others was not productive. These inward-looking and self-centred needy adults become extremely hard to reason with and are very adept at warding off responsibility and shifting blame on to others. Their patterns of denial, no doubt reinforced by a retreat into fantasy are often impossible to break down.

Stress Relief

Sexual experiences are enjoyable for most people, and this can also include children. Youngsters brought up in an uncaring environment where they are either ignored or treated badly in some other way, may often seek solace in sexual behaviours, and in particular masturbation as a way of self-medication. It may be the case that some adults, when under particular stressful conditions, will revert to this early self-medication behaviour as a retreat from reality. If this becomes linked to deviant fantasies, then one may see the development of a regressed offender. The regressed offender is someone who is not permanently fixated by sexual feelings towards children, but who can resort to this behaviour in certain circumstances.

134

Disinhibitors

If we accept the unpalatable supposition that some adults have a tendency towards the sexual abuse of children, then we must try to explain how it is that the inhibitions surrounding this abnormal and unacceptable behaviour are overcome. Such inhibitions would include the following:

- Fear of being caught
- Fear of being punished
- Societal taboos against sexual activity with children
- Guilt and shame
- Adult sexual outlets

However, a variety of experts have suggested a number of factors which weigh against these inhibitions, some of which I have already mentioned, such as history of abuse, pornography, masculine stereotypes, deviant fantasy. There are a number of others:

Lack of supervision   If, for any reason, young children are made available as potential targets of abuse, any fear of being caught may diminish. So-called 'latchkey children', youngsters who are cared for by a succession of babysitters about whom the parents know very little, and children whose parents are often unavailable due to work commitments, divorce and separation, and illness, may all be at increased risk of abuse.

Step-parents   The lack of a blood relationship between an adult and a child may militate against the alleged incest taboo, and make children more acceptable as sexual objects.

Substance abuse   As many of us may be aware, we can do things we regret if under the influence of alcohol and/or drugs. Adult males who abuse their bodies in this manner may often be disinhibited with regard to the abuse of children. Indeed, in my experience, being under the influence of drink is the most

135

common excuse which sex offenders use when their behaviour is discovered.

Inadequate sentencing   This is an extremely controversial topic. There is a body of opinion which strongly believes that the punishments inflicted on convicted sex offenders are too lenient, and that this can lead to the commission of more offences. However, I feel that there is a problem in terms of being able to prove that this link is a real one, and is not simply a reflection of the natural disgust which most people feel toward those convicted. Certainly, from the point of view of the victim there is some justification in supporting the notion that sentencing policy is lenient and erratic. I have met several victims of sexual abuse who have felt extremely angry that the person who assaulted them received what they perceived as being a light sentence. If we are to put the needs of the victim first, then we ought to take these views into account. The extent to which prison modifies the behaviour of sexual offenders is a topic worth discussing (*see* pages 260–1).

The Role of the Non-Abusing Adult in Intra-Familial Sexual Abuse

This is another controversial subject. Some feel that the inability of the child's mother to act in a protective capacity, or to fulfil her partner's sexual needs, is a factor which can create a situation of sexual abuse. Whilst I can understand these arguments, I have great personal difficulty in accepting them. On the first count, were the adult male member of the household a reasonable mature person, in control of his impulses and desires, there would be no need for his partner to act in a supervisory capacity towards his relationships with children in the home. As regards the possible paucity of the adult sexual relationship, this may well be a problem which creates tension and frustration for both partners. In no way ought it to be projected on to deviant activity with children. There is a subtle danger in relation to theories of child sexual abuse which lay great store on the role of the female adult.

136

They talk about dependency, immaturity, passivity and collusion. They seldom talk about control, domination, physical violence and threat. I am anxious about theories attempting an explanation of the causes of sexual abuse, which do anything to deflect responsibility away from where it really lies – firmly with the adult male offender. Such arguments are basically flawed by the way in which blame and responsibility can become dissipated.

In a similar way, the children themselves can also be blamed, and their behaviour is cited from time to time as a cause of the abuse. Adolescents who wear alluring clothing, who use a lot of make-up and who flirt with men are often felt to be responsible for their sexual abuse. Of course, such factors may well contribute to the occurrence of abuse, but it is in my view worryingly easy for these issues to take the focus away from the real roots of the problem.

Case Study

John Clark was thirty-eight years old, a physically small man who worked as a driver for a large warehouse. He was married with two daughters. He was convicted of sexually assaulting his eldest child when she was fourteen years of age. He later admitted that he had abused her for a number of years. It was very difficult indeed to engage John in conversation. He seemed to be an anxious, nervous man who very seldom seemed able to relax.

His wife tended to answer questions on his behalf, and often spoke about him as if he was not present in the room. There was rarely any interplay of speech between the two. John would often go out alone at night and was guarded about divulging where he would go. He seemed to have very few friends, and his parents, brothers and sisters all lived some distance away. When he was not out in the car, he would sit at home watching television or work in the garage making things for the house (he was a qualified carpenter).

He was extremely strict with his daughters. They were not allowed out to friends' houses and were discouraged from

137

bringing friends home. Similarly, they were rarely involved in school activities, spending most of their time at home. When they did go out, it was invariably in the company of one or both parents. When the abuse came to light, John admitted his actions to the police, but the subsequent content of his letters home from prison gave the impression that he minimised the enormity of his behaviour, tending to blame his actions on alcohol and on his wife, with whom he had had a rather poor physical relationship. On his release from prison, he lived for a time in a probation service hostel. He began to deny his behaviour, saying that he had been coerced into making a false statement by the police. His wife divorced him, and his daughters refused to see him.

This pathetic story highlights some of the problems encountered in relation to the origin of sexual abuse. The guardedness of so many offenders, their inability to conduct adequate relationships with other adults, and their highly developed sense of self-preservation combine to make it very difficult to get to know them and to form anything other than assumptions as to the cause of the abuse. Perhaps John had himself been abused. He may have been able to find a relaxed social relationship possible only with children. He was never able to allow anyone to breach his defensive shield in order to really know him. Like innumerable other sexual offenders, John remained a largely shadowy figure, about whom little was known.

SUMMARY – HIGH RISK CHILDREN

To summarise, certain conditions which may constitute high risk for children should be highlighted, taking into account the knowledge which is available with regard to the origins of child abuse.

Parents were abused The cycle of abuse is a prevailing issue in much of the available literature and has certainly been demonstrated on innumerable occasions in my working experience. Some of the case histories described earlier in the book highlight this phenomenon strongly.

Poor socio-economic conditions Families who exist in poor housing, with inadequate finances, whose children may receive poor education and little material aid, certainly seem to contain a disproportionate amount of most types of abuse. There is a reasonably well-established link between abuse and stress. There is little which is more productive of stress than socially and economically disadvantaged lives. There is some truth behind the stereotypical welfare benefit 'scrounger', the person to whom work is anathema, and who would never make any realistic attempt to improve his conditions. However, this stereotypical image is grasped eagerly by a great many self-satisfied, maybe even slightly guilty people for whom the system is working well, in order to dispel any feeling of unease which, in their more altruistic moments, they may have towards the large groups of people within society who, through no fault of their own, find everyday life a constant struggle. If people were to grasp this link vigorously, the whole nature of the way in which we view the problem of child abuse would shift. It would then no longer be about perverts, sadists and incompetent social workers. All of the scapegoats would disappear. The problem would belong to everyone. Perhaps that is too unpalatable a proposition for us to accept in a meaningful and collective way.

Marital turmoil Divorce, disharmony and dispute, involving the principal caregivers in any family, may, in certain situations, place children at risk of all types of abuse. I would not for one moment wish to suggest that this is self-evident. Parents who try to sustain an unworkable relationship may well provide a much more harmful environment for children.

Isolation Families who are socially isolated from their extended family relationships and from the community in which they live may be more prone to abusing their children. The isolation may be a product of the abuse (adults may not

139

wish to be found out), but may also be responsible for producing conditions in which it can thrive.

Illness in the family An ill child or adult is a significant cause of stress in all families. Some writers have suggested that this heightens the risk of abuse.

Prematurity There do seem to be links between prematurity and some forms of ill-treatment. This, as has been discussed, may well relate to the contentious issue of bonding.

Unwanted child The unwanted child may well be resented, rejected and neglected. This will depend on a variety of other factors to do with the extent of stress which the child imposes upon the family and the strengths and weaknesses of the relationships within the existing family group.

Step-parents The lack of a blood relationship with a child can, some argue, make the risks of abuse by step-parents greater than would be the case with a natural parent. Again, for some people this may well be true, but much depends on the constellation of other factors already discussed in this chapter and much more besides.

Finally, I would wish to reiterate a comment I made at the beginning of this chapter. I have placed the issues which have been discussed under headings related to specific areas of abuse. Whilst this implies that they are often most closely linked with particular types of ill-treatment, these categorisations are not in any way rigid. Just as all forms of child abuse are often interlinked, so are the reasons why abuse might originate.

6 Legal Aspects of Child Protection

INTRODUCTION

The reader needs a general overview of some of the more important legal issues relating to child protection. My purpose here is to provide enough information to permit an understanding of general concepts, rather than to present complex legal explanations. For a more detailed analysis of the law, I would advise that more specialist texts are consulted.

The law, as it relates to children, is extensive and complicated. The development of procedures to deal with child protection was, to some extent, a process of evolution, informed by an analysis of cases which were subject to public inquiry, and by representations from a variety of organisations and pressure groups. In a similar way, the law relating to child protection is an evolving phenomenon. Over the past twenty-five years, our knowledge of child abuse has expanded dramatically. This has led to the need for the legal process to take into account new issues, and a steadily increasing volume of cases. The controversies surrounding child sexual abuse in Cleveland in 1987 have significantly heightened debate around the subject. The recommendations of the ensuing report which received evidence from a variety of professional organisations have had considerable impact upon subsequent proposals for changes in the law.

At the time of writing, a major piece of legislation, the Children Bill, is in its final stages of development in Parliament. The aim of this Bill is to rationalise the law as it relates to children, and to pay particular attention to, amongst other things, the authority necessary for social workers to carry out their tasks in child protection. It will be my aim in

141

this chapter to contrast some themes in current legislation with proposals in the Children Bill, pointing out issues of practice which the new legislation is attempting to address, concentrating upon the nature of emergency powers in particular.

THE CIVIL AND CRIMINAL LAW

The main distinction between civil and criminal proceedings relates more to the outcome of the case than to the circumstances which led to the case being brought to court. Criminal cases end with a sentence being passed by the judge or magistrates. A case is brought against someone (the defendant), they may then be found guilty of an offence (convicted), and a sentence passed. The sentence can range from an absolute discharge to imprisonment.

Civil cases end with a judgement being made by the court, often compelling someone to stop doing something, or to do something which they have been failing to do. In civil proceedings, a prosecution is not brought, but an individual or an agency (the plaintiff) sues someone (the defendant), and after hearing all the evidence, a judgement is reached. No one is convicted and punished, but a ruling is made which attempts to establish and enforce the rights of individuals who may be suffering an injustice. Obviously, the civil and criminal law cannot be separated so easily, and there are cases where both civil and criminal actions could be brought. For example, in the case of a road traffic accident where a drunken driver knocks down a pedestrian, the driver may be prosecuted under the criminal law for breaking various rules related to driving. The driver may also face a civil action, having committed the civil wrong of negligently injuring someone.

In terms of child protection, an adult who abuses a child may be charged in the criminal courts with a variety of offences. A case may also be made in civil law to remove the child from the adult's care, if it seems likely that the child may suffer further abuse in the future. A major problem for child protection agencies is the difference in the way in which evidence is weighed in civil and criminal cases. Under the criminal law, a conviction will only be made if a jury is satisfied *beyond reasonable doubt* that a crime has been committed. In relation to civil proceedings with which social workers are involved, a court need only be satisfied that a case is made on a balance of probability. This distinction may seem small, but in practice it is often the case that, although an alleged abuser cannot be brought to trial due to lack of evidence, a local authority may be able to bring a case in the civil courts. Unhappily, a frequent consequence of this is an element of system abuse for the victim, who sees the abuser left alone whilst they are ordered into the care of the local authority by the courts.

A wide variety of groups, both inside and outside the legal profession, are well aware of these problems and a debate is currently taking place about ways of improving the system. However, a person must bear in mind the need to achieve a balance between increasing the chances of making abusers account for their actions in a court of law, and protecting the innocent from being wrongly convicted.

It is beyond the scope of this book to provide a detailed account of the different powers in criminal and civil law which are vested in different courts. Some courts deal with one branch of law or the other, some with both. However, with regard to civil law relating to child protection, the proposals in the Children Bill attempt to simplify complexities surrounding these relationships. Cases are most often heard in the Magistrates' Court (which is split between juvenile court and domestic court) or the County Court. Although at present the High Court is sometimes used by local authorities as a route into care for children about whom they are concerned, it seems likely that the new legislation will limit the use of the High Court to a consideration of only the most complex cases.

CRIMINAL OFFENCES IN CHILD ABUSE

The Children and Young Persons Act 1933 remains the major source of legislation covering offences of abuse. Over the years, parts of the Act have been amended and expanded to take into account lessons learned through experience of its operation in practice and the developing knowledge of child abuse issues. Schedule I of this Act lists a number of separate offences against the person which relate to child abuse. Currently, one of the grounds upon which a child can be placed in the care of the local authority is that they are living in the same household as someone who has been convicted of an offence listed in this Schedule. These offenders are commonly termed Schedule I offenders. I do not propose to list all of the offences contained in this Schedule, but will select a few upon which to comment, in order to give the reader an impression of the range of offences which are contained in the Act.

Cruelty to Persons under Sixteen

Part I Section I of the Act states:

'If any person who has attained the age of sixteen years and has the custody, charge, or care of any child or young person under that age, wilfully assaults, ill-treats, neglects, abandons, or exposes him, or causes or procures him to be assaulted, ill-treated, neglected, abandoned, or exposed, in a manner likely to cause him unnecessary suffering or injury to health (including injury to or loss of sight, or hearing, or limb, or organ of the body, and any mental derangement), that person shall be guilty of a misdemeanour. . . .'

I have quoted this passage from the Act for two reasons. Firstly, it is the broadest definition of abuse in the Act, and covers many aspects of abuse, and secondly, it demonstrates just how open to interpretation the law can be. Words like ill-treat, assault, neglect and abandon are, as has been suggested

144

earlier, very difficult to apply in a consistent way. Over time, pieces of legislation like the one quoted above are tested and interpreted in courts, and decisions are appealed against, until an interpretation of the words is generally accepted. The problem with child abuse is that it will always mean different things to different people depending upon a whole range of circumstances which the law is not always able to take into account.

Allowing Persons under Sixteen to be in Brothels

This offence relates to the moral danger in which children might be placed within brothels. There seems not to be an exact correlation between this offence and child abuse as it has been defined in Chapter 1. Are such children being neglected and emotionally abused? Might this be an example of a situation in which an adult might be convicted of an offence on the basis of potential harm to a child, but where it might be difficult to describe the nature of that potential harm?

Intercourse with Girl under Thirteen

The interesting point to note about this particular offence is the way in which the law differentiates victims under the age of thirteen from victims over thirteen. Often, such an offence carries a harsher penalty than a similar conviction with an older young person would attract. I have been involved in a variety of cases of sexual abuse where the offender has admitted intercourse with the victim after she became thirteen, but would not admit to offences prior to that time, even though the victim was able to recount earlier incidents. Obviously, this must be a consequence of the way in which the law draws the line with regard to the age of victims.

Incest by a Man or a Woman

The crime of incest, which involves sexual intercourse between adults and children who are closely related, has

145

always been separated in law from similar offences between people who do not have close family ties. In my opinion, there have been some unfortunate consequences as a result of a separation which has probably accurately reflected public opinion. As we have already seen, the sexual abuse of children often occurs within families. When this happens, it is often viewed as being qualitatively different from abuse involving children who are not related to the abuser. In the past, there has probably been a greater reluctance on the part of the authorities to interfere in family matters, because the family is seen as a private organisation. When incest offenders are brought to trial, it has often been the case that more mitigating circumstances are highlighted, in comparison with trials involving defendants who abuse non-relatives. As we begin to learn more about abuse, we find that the distinction between incest (intra-familial abuse) and unlawful sexual intercourse (extra-familial abuse) is less pronounced than was previously felt to be the case. Many incest offenders also offend outside the home. Some victims suffer just as much whether the abuser is a family member or not. This distinction, based upon the relationship between participants, is less defensible than it appears, and can tend to impose gradations of sentencing by the courts which may be unjustifiable in terms of the effects that abuse can have on offenders. It may be the case that incest offenders are dealt with more or less harshly by the courts, and this can create confusion.

Any offence which involves bodily injury to a child or young person (murder, manslaughter, infanticide, grievous bodily harm, and so on) falls under the category of Schedule I offences. Other offences, such as assault, which may or may not involve the commission of an act of violence also are included in this list.

146

LOCAL AUTHORITIES – THEIR GENERAL LEGAL DUTIES

Much of the work which social workers do relates to their own professional judgement. For example, they can choose to work in a voluntary relationship with a family until such time as they feel it to be no longer necessary. They can choose to offer some people help rather than others. However, some aspects of the social work task are proscribed by law, and are not open to the same degree of interpretation as are other parts of the work. The general duties which the law sets out in relation to child protection are as follows.

Promoting the Welfare of Children

Under current legislation, the local authority has a duty to promote the welfare of children and to take action to prevent children being brought into care. Section I of the Child Care Act 1980 lays a duty on local authorities to:

'make available such advice, guidance and assistance as may promote the welfare of children by diminishing the need to receive children into or keep them in care. . . .'

The proposed new legislation contained in the Children Bill has a similar passage, although it redefines the role of the local authority somewhat by stressing the need to safeguard, as well as promote, the welfare of children 'in need'. Neediness relates to a lack of reasonable health or development, or disability. The interpretation of 'reasonable' in this context is likely to prove difficult.

This legislation creates a very wide-ranging role for social workers, who are obliged to act in those situations where they feel there is a need to safeguard and promote the welfare of children. The Children Bill is likely to set out specific duties under this general legislation, obliging local authorities to identify need, publicise their services, and take reasonable steps to prevent abuse and neglect. The Children Bill stresses

147

the duty to promote the upbringing of children in need by their families, emphasising family life as being the most appropriate environment in which to bring up children.

The Duty to Investigate

The law imposes a duty upon the local authority to cause enquiries to be made in respect of a child (under fourteen years old) or young person (aged fourteen to seventeen years) about whom information is received which suggests that there are grounds for bringing care proceedings. In effect, this means that if the social services department hears about a child who may be at risk of abuse, they are compelled to investigate, unless preliminary enquiries indicate that the information received is inaccurate. If someone were to ring the social services to complain that their neighbour was persistently leaving their very young children alone at night, or were seriously mistreating them, there is a clear obligation in law to make enquiries into the case. This may well mean that a social worker would have to call on the family in an attempt to check out the circumstances, armed only with the information provided by the anonymous caller.

The Children Bill is likely both to simplify and extend this duty. Under the new proposals, the local authority must investigate and take appropriate action if it is informed, or suspects that a child has suffered, or is likely to suffer significant harm. Under current legislation, the duty to investigate extends to situations where it is felt that there may be grounds for bringing care proceedings. These grounds generally relate to the present circumstances of the child. The Children Bill proposes changes to the wording of the law which would extend the general duty to investigate to cases where it is suspected that a child is *likely* to suffer harm. In practice, social workers currently will investigate such circumstances now, but the Bill's proposals, if enacted, would widen the duty of the local authority in the law.

148

EMERGENCY PROTECTION – PLACE OF SAFETY ORDERS

In many ways, the Children Bill's proposals about the emergency protection of children are its most radical aspects. They are also the most pertinent parts of the law concerning the protection of children. The new proposals have been made partly in response to events in Cleveland in 1987, but have to be seen in the context of a growing unrest about the powers which social workers appear to have at times of emergency. The current place of safety order appears to be a piece of legislation around which a more general debate about the extent of the authority of social workers seems to have been focused.

The Existing Law

Under Section 28 (1) of the Children and Young Persons Act 1969, any person can apply to a magistrate to detain a child in a place of safety. The applicant must show reasonable cause to believe that one of the primary conditions for care proceedings is satisfied in respect of the child. As we shall see later, these primary conditions include significant avoidable abuse, exposure to moral danger, and being a member of a household which contains a Schedule I offender. For the purpose of obtaining a place of safety order, the applicant doesn't have to prove that abuse is taking place, but must have reasonable cause to believe that this is so.

The order permits the applicant to place the child in a place of safety (for example, in the care of the local authority, or the home of a relative) for a maximum of twenty-eight days. There is no formal right of appeal by any party, and the order will lapse after the stated period unless further judicial authority is sought.

In practical terms, this order allows the applicant (who is usually a local authority or NSPCC social worker) to place a child in what they deem to be a safe environment, if they strongly suspect that the child is being abused, or is likely to

149

be abused by a known abuser. The parents of the child have no right of appeal for the duration of the order.

Problems with Place of Safety Orders

In some respects, the existing place of safety legislation is draconian, and in other respects it is of quite limited use. Firstly, a place of safety order does not confer the right to remove the child from home. Once produced, the child can be detained in a place of safety, but there is no power forcibly to remove a child from uncooperative parents in a situation of crisis. In such circumstances a magistrate must be approached for the issue of a warrant under Section 40 of the 1933 Children and Young Persons Act, which gives a police officer authorisation to search for the child and to take him or her to a place of safety.

A place of safety order does not transfer parental rights from the parents to the applicant. This has led to a great deal of confusion about what the local authority is able to do with a child who is the subject of an order. Curtailing access to the parents and allowing intimate medical examinations of the child in an attempt to gather evidence of abuse have all been practised in the past from time to time. Much of the debate in Cleveland in 1987 related to the use and, some would argue, misuse of place of safety orders. They were used to enable medicals designed to gather information (rather than to ascertain general health or to treat a medical condition) to take place, and to severely limit or prevent access to parents, neither of which is justifiable under a place of safety order (although the question of access by parents who may pose a threat to the welfare of the child is a more difficult issue).

Another difficulty with the present legislation is the maximum time for which the order can be enforced. The parents have no right to appeal against the making of the order, the order is often made by a single magistrate, based upon the hearsay evidence of an applicant, and neither the child nor its parents have to be present when the order is made. Because of these facts, orders can be open to misuse,

150

and may sometimes be relied upon in cases where the evidence of abuse, actual or potential, is limited. A worrying feature of these orders is the extent to which they often result in very lengthy periods in care for children. These orders should only be sought and enacted in times of crisis, so a significant proportion of the population of children in care will have begun their care career amid confusion and chaos. Also, if children have sometimes been brought into care under place of safety orders when the evidence available was minimal, it may be that this has led to protracted periods away from home for children who may have been better helped in other ways.

During the past few years the obtaining of an order for the maximum twenty-eight-day period has become more rare. Both social workers and magistrates have developed a healthy reticence about too dramatic a step being taken without evidence being presented before a court. Periods of seven or fourteen days are now much more common.

Proposals for Emergency Protection Orders

The Children Bill proposes the abolition of the place of safety order, and its replacement by an emergency protection order. With reference to some of the problems discussed above, the main changes are as follows.

Applications

Applications will normally be made to a court, rather than to a single magistrate. Some areas of the country already have an established procedure for obtaining place of safety orders from magistrates who are assisted by legal advisers (normally the Clerk of the Court), but the new proposals are an attempt to dissuade applicants from approaching single magistrates. (It is expected that Rules of Court will allow an order to be made by a single magistrate to cover for those occasions when a court is not available.) Under the new procedures, it is the court, rather than the applicant, which must be satisfied that the grounds for making the order exist. This will put the onus on the applicant to justify why the order is being sought more conclusively than used to be the case.

Grounds for Making an Order

The new emergency protection order will simplify the grounds under which emergency action can be taken. An order may be made only if the court is satisfied that there is reasonable cause to believe the child is likely to suffer significant harm if not removed from his current situation, or if not detained in it (for example, if the child is already in hospital when an order is made). The important point to note here is that the law will now allow action to be taken on the basis of what is likely to happen in the immediate future rather than on what has just happened. The court will need to be assured of the probability, rather than the possibility of significant harm. No doubt the definition of what constitutes significant harm will remain contentious.

Time Limits

The new order will be for a maximum of eight days, and can be extended by a further seven days (providing that the total time is less than fifteen days) on the application of the local authority or an authorised person (NSPCC). Should applicants wish to proceed through the courts to secure the legal future of an abused child, they will have to prepare a case to present to the court rather more quickly than in the past. The alteration in the time limits for orders is a clear response to the disquiet which has been expressed about the perceived powers which the place of safety order confers on the applicant.

Right of Appeal

Court rules are to allow children, parents and significant other interested parties the right to appeal to the court for the discharge of an order after seventy-two hours. Again, this is another means by which the powers of emergency orders are to be curtailed.

Rights and Responsibilities

The new emergency protection orders will transfer qualified parental responsibility to the applicant, who will be able to take such action as may be reasonably required to safeguard the child's welfare. This probably includes being able to agree to minor medical treatment, and an assessment of the child's short-term needs. At the time when an order is made, magistrates will be able to attach certain requirements, designed to clarify some of the contentious aspects of the existing legislation. For example, there may be a requirement that the child be medically examined, or be examined by a psychiatrist. There may be a direction that the applicant be accompanied to the house, when implementing the order, by a registered medical practitioner or a health visitor.

The granting of an emergency protection order will not allow the applicant to gain access to the child if the parents refuse to co-operate, but the court will be empowered to order disclosure of the child's whereabouts and entry and search warrants. This will replace Section 40 of the 1933 Act.

Access

Reasonable access to the child by parents is assumed under the new legislation, but the courts may wish to give directions about contact at the time when the order is made. A local authority will need to justify why it wishes to restrict or refuse access when an emergency protection order is in force.

This new piece of legislation is designed to clarify the existing procedures and to limit the extent to which current place of safety orders are misused. If enacted, the Children Bill's proposals will still give significant emergency powers to social workers, but within a more restrictive framework.

CHILD ASSESSMENT ORDER

There is the possibility that included in the new legislation will be an order whose effect will be to ensure that a child is assessed and/or medically examined, without the potentially damaging effects which are sometimes a consequence of removing the child from home. Such an order, if introduced, would occupy the existing gulf between voluntary co-operation between parents and child protective agencies, and the enforcement of a removal from home.

It would be an order, obtainable from a magistrate, that a parent take the child within a short period of time to a GP or a clinic so that an examination can take place. It would be designed to cater for those circumstances in which, for whatever reason, access to the child proves difficult, and the existing causes for concern may not warrant a place of safety order (or emergency protection order).

Such an order represents a development which I guardedly welcome. The main disadvantage relates to the stringency of the circumstances under which such an order will be applied for. If the grounds are too lax, it may mean that numbers of children are examined without good cause. If the grounds are too stringent, social workers may sometimes be inclined to opt for this less intrusive order in circumstances where a place of safety order (or its proposed equivalent) is more appropriate. However, an order which compels parents to take action to protect their own children, and which may limit to a minimum those occasions where children have to be removed from home before being medically examined, must be a welcome one.

OTHER EMERGENCY PROCEDURES

Currently, the police are empowered to detain a child or young person in a place of safety for up to eight days maximum (as opposed to twenty-eight). Under proposals contained in the Children Bill, police powers will be further curtailed so that they can detain children for a maximum seventy-two hours. As is the case with emergency procedures for other professionals, the police must inform parents of their actions as soon as is practicable, and must allow reasonable access.

The police have a further authority to intervene in cases of child abuse with a view to protecting life and limb. In the event of an emergency, a police constable is empowered to gain entry into premises and remove children without making prior application to the courts. This power is rarely used and must only be considered for use in particularly dangerous situations.

CARE ORDERS

As in the case of emergency procedures, the law in relation to care proceedings is about to be radically changed. At the moment, a child or young person can be committed to the care of the local authority by a court if one of the following grounds is satisfied:

a)   his proper development is being avoidably prevented or neglected or his health is being avoidably impaired or neglected or he is being ill-treated; or
b)   it is probable that the condition set out in the preceding paragraph would be satisfied in his case, having regard to the fact that the court or another court has found that that condition is or was satisfied in the case of another child or young person who is or was a member of the household to which he belongs; or
bb)   it is probable that the condition set out in paragraph (a) will be satisfied in his case, having regard to the fact that a person who has been convicted of an offence mentioned in Schedule I to the Act of 1933 is, or may become, a member of the same household as the child or young person.
c)   he is exposed to moral danger; or
d)   he is beyond the control of his parent or guardian.

155

There are other grounds related to problems of education and criminal activity, but the four I have mentioned relate most closely to child abuse. Not only does the social worker have to satisfy a court that one or other of these conditions applies, they must also show that the child is in need of care or control which he or she is unlikely to receive unless the court makes an order.

The court may make a care order, effectively transferring most of the parental rights to the local authority. They could make a supervision order. The supervisor then has a duty to advise, assist and befriend the client, although there is little help available through this order if parents/carers refuse to co-operate. They may decide, having heard evidence from the professionals involved, the parents, the child or his representatives and any others with relevant information to produce, not make any order. Most care orders are made using the first ground mentioned above, which contains a large number of words and phrases which are difficult to define.

The Children Bill proposes a simplification of the procedure. If the contents of the Bill become law, then in future care orders and supervision orders will be made if the court is satisfied that the child has suffered, or is likely to suffer significant harm, *and* the harm or its likelihood are due to the standard of care given to the child or likely to be given if the order isn't made. If this standard of care falls below that which it would be reasonable to expect the parent of a similar child to give, an order may be made. In judging the standard of care, the court must try to equate like with like; for example, a family on very low wages, or a single-parent family may not be expected to be able to provide the same material standards as a family whose financial status is higher. Although this may sound confusing, it simplifies the process to the point where each case can be judged on its merits without the need to fit each family situation into one or other of the existing categories.

Another aspect of current legal difficulties which the Children Bill has acknowledged is the time which it often

156

takes for cases to be processed through the courts. Usually, until all parties have been able to collate their evidence, and until reports are written, the case can be delayed for many weeks. In such cases, when it is felt that there is a need to protect the child, but the final court hearing isn't planned for some time, a series of interim care orders are made, usually at four-weekly intervals. These orders basically mean that a child is temporarily in care pending a final hearing.

The Children Bill will require the court to have regard to the detrimental effects on the welfare of the child which delayed proceedings can create. The court will be able to timetable events, giving directions to all those involved to ensure as speedy a conclusion as possible. Interim orders will be made for a maximum limit of twelve weeks, which ought to give ample time for the case to be prepared.

It is perfectly possible for care orders to be discharged, provided that a court is satisfied that grounds for retaining the child in care no longer exist.

VOLUNTARY CARE

Where it appears to a local authority that a person under seventeen years of age has no parent or guardian, or has been and remains abandoned, or its carers are prevented from caring for the child, it has a duty to receive the child into care. This is not a care order, and does not involve a court hearing. A similar provision is retained in the Children Bill. However, there is an important and controversial aspect to voluntary care which is to be deleted by proposed legislation in the new Bill. This concerns the 'assumption of parental rights'. Under the current legislation related to voluntary care, on specified grounds such as the death of both parents, or where it is judged by the local authority that parents have consistently failed to discharge their parental obligations, a local authority is empowered to take over parental rights to the child. In practice, it is usually the case that a group of the council's elected members take the decision to pass a parental rights resolution, weighing evidence provided by its professional staff. Whether the parents agree to the passing of such a resolution or not, there has been disquiet expressed by a number of pressure groups and organisations about a procedure which effectively places the child in care without there having been a court hearing. When the contents of the Children Bill are enacted, parental rights resolutions will no longer be allowed. Children placed in voluntary care will be looked after by local authorities until such time as the parents or guardians want them back. Should the local authority object, then it will have recourse to care proceedings and to emergency protection legislation.

WARDSHIP

There are some cases which present particular problems in relation to the law. They may be highly complex, or appear not to fit into specific categories as laid down in respect of grounds for care proceedings. Many of these cases will be dealt with by the High Court, where a child may be made a ward of the court. Once warded, the custody of the child is given to the court, who will allow day-to-day control to pass to another person, or the local authority. The High Court will make any order it feels is necessary to safeguard the child's welfare. In this sense, wardship is a more flexible procedure than others we have looked at so far. Anyone below the age of eighteen can be warded, and anyone with a legitimate interest in the child may make the child a ward of the court.

GUARDIANS *AD LITEM*

The scope of this book is such that it is inappropriate to dwell upon too much legal detail. Questions about representation, rules of evidence and court procedures must be followed up by consulting more specialist texts. However, one term is important – guardian *ad litem*. This describes a person who is appointed by the court to act as an independent voice for the child. At present a guardian will be appointed in a variety of circumstances, principally when there seems to be a conflict of interests between the child and parents. The Children Bill, when enacted, is likely to broaden the role of guardians *ad litem* in order to ensure that the court is able to avail itself of a report prepared by someone acting independently. This includes a brief to advise upon what action to take in the best interests of the child. The guardian will instruct a solicitor for the proceedings and will prepare a report for the court to consider which will help them to come to a decision. In order to carry out this task, the guardian *ad litem* must interview all relevant parties, such as children, parents, other significant family members, social workers, foster parents, and so on, and, on the basis of the information received, form a view as to the best way to promote the child's welfare. In this capacity, the guardian can serve the vital function of standing back from too direct an involvement in the case and can often provide a more objective and uncluttered view for the benefit of the court.

Guardians *ad litem* are qualified social workers who under-take this duty full time, or work on cases from authorities other than the one where they are employed as a social worker, so as to ensure fairness and independence.

PROBLEMS FOR CHILDREN

The difference which exists between the civil and criminal law poses tremendous problems for the victims of abuse. This remains the biggest difficulty as we try to fit the complex phenomenon of child abuse into the equally complex legal arena. The complexity of the legal process itself can be a source of confusion and stress to a child. In my professional capacity, I have attended court on numerous occasions, either as an observer or as a participant in the proceedings. I find the whole business extremely stressful. The language in which the law is couched is often idiosyncratic. The way in which a court case can transform a highly-charged and emotional issue into a rather clinical almost academic exercise must be very confusing for the child, and often for the parents.

We have already discussed the difficulties which can accrue as a result of the inordinate length of time it sometimes takes to bring a case to court. The anxiety which such delays can create need not be dwelt upon and I am pleased that there are parts of the Children Bill which allude to this problem.

In some respects, the court process encapsulates much that is wrong in our society in terms of the way in which children are treated. The law courts are an adult environment, and predominantly a male, white adult environment. They were certainly not designed to accommodate the particular needs of young children. Over the past few years, a vociferous debate has taken place about how to make the court process more 'user-friendly' to children, not so that they enjoy the occasion, but to make them more relaxed and to encourage them to contribute better-quality evidence. Of course, those professionals who are involved with the law relating to children are all very much aware of these problems, not least the legal profession itself. Experiments are taking place to introduce video technology into the court rooms, so that children may give their evidence either in a separate room, or screened off from the main body of the court. Rules of evidence are being reviewed in relation to the admissibility of uncorroborated statements by children in sexual abuse cases, in an attempt to increase the likelihood that sexual offenders will be brought to court more often than is currently the case.

My experience with children in court leads me to believe that they often make as good if not better witnesses than adults. If properly prepared and supported, I feel that the potential negative impact of a court appearance is grossly overstated. It is the delay between the commission of the act of abuse and the subsequent trial which has the more detrimental effect.

I wish to reiterate the fact that this represents an extremely brief and selective commentary on the law as it relates to child protection. At the time of writing, it is not possible to be sure of the final contents of the new child care legislation. I hope that I have simply given some of the main and most widely-used pieces of legislation with which child protection professionals have to work on a regular basis.

7 Local Authority Procedures

THE ROLE OF PROCEDURES

Since the mid 1970s, following the formation of the social services departments, procedures have been developed which provide a framework for those who care for children to carry out their responsibilities. It is worth discussing these procedures in some detail, and looking at their historical background, and the way in which they have evolved as a result of recommendations contained in some of the major child abuse inquiries of recent years, and in response to shifting opinions regarding the nature of child abuse itself. Terms such as 'case conference', 'review', 'registration' and 'key worker' also need to be analysed, as does the practical application of these procedures from the social worker's own point of view.

The central feature of procedures to deal with child abuse is their attempt to encourage all agencies to work together.

CO-OPERATION BETWEEN AGENCIES

There are large numbers of individuals and agencies who may have a contribution to make to child protection. In any one case, the following people could be involved: the child and its parents; the abuser/s, if not one or both parents; the police; the social services department; the family GP (doctor); one or more hospital doctors and consultants; school teachers and education social workers; health visitors, school nurses and midwives; psychiatrists and psychologists; probation officers; a variety of voluntary organisations, including the NSPCC; foster parents; and lawyers.

This list is not exhaustive, and for any abuse case there can be any combination of the above, plus other people, who may have a role to play. When the extent to which child abuse can involve co-operation between large numbers of people is realised, the need for clarity and procedural simplicity is apparent. There are a number of administrative and professional, as well as personal reasons why the process of working together can become difficult.

Administrative Problems

Many of the people named in the list outlined above work for large public organisations. There is a significant amount of research which describes how individual roles can become confused because of the size of the organisations involved. This is partly due to the wide range of functions which big organisations have to fulfil, partly due to the distance between customer and organisation which large bureaucracies some-times create. It may also be due to the variety of pressures which workers in organisations are under from clients and the organisation itself.

For example, it is a common complaint of social workers that the social services departments do not allow them the space to carry out the job they were trained to do. Often, a local authority social worker will spend less time in face-to-face contact with clients than you might expect. Some parts of the organisations demand that forms and reports are filled in thoroughly and regularly, as if this was the primary function of the department. We would all accept that administration is a vital part of any successful organisation, but sometimes you have the impression that the paperwork is of greater importance than contact with the customer.

Many social workers have often complained that senior management seems to be out of touch with the work which goes on. A rift between management and the basic grade workers is common within big organisations. Whether this rift is real or imagined, the result can often be that those workers who spend their time (or as much of it as the organisation will allow) seeing clients, can feel distanced from management and perhaps as a consequence feel unsupported. This can lead to a reluctance to take risks or to make decisions, and this can be detrimental to those who they are trying to help.

When considering these inbuilt tensions, which I would claim are shared by most large organisations, it is easy to see how problems of communication can arise when one organisation tries to talk to another equally large department. The processes of direct work with clients, and administration of that work, can cloud each other. Delays can be created, and information lost or misplaced. In *A Child in Mind*, the report of the commission of inquiry into the circumstances surrounding the death of Kimberley Carlile (*see* Bibliography), it was pointed out that a feature of the case, as with all the other inquiries ever held, was the problem of communication. Kimberley moved from the Wirral to Greenwich on 4 October 1985. In November, and twice in December, the health visitor in Greenwich requested the health records on Kimberley, unaware of the Wirral connection, which her authority knew about. Greenwich Health Authority received the health visiting records from the Wirral on 15 June 1986. Kimberley had died, as a result of extensive and prolonged child abuse, a week earlier. So, although the existence of the Wirral connection was known by Greenwich Health Authority, the person for whom this would have been valuable information was unaware of it at the time. The dissemination of information within and between organisations becomes more difficult the larger the organisation.

The nature of child abuse is a difficult and threatening subject. Social workers and other professionals, whilst developing a professional objectivity about the subject, also retain basic human instincts. It is at times tempting to encourage an administrative distance from the clients so as to be protected from the pain and emotional stress which the work involves. I would not wish to argue that the difficulties are created purely by the faceless organisations for which we work; they are also attributable in varying degrees to the individuals who make up the organisation. We all possess the capacity to hide behind the administrative functions of our

164

role, and to ascribe our own personal failings to the organisation, as if it were an individual over which we had no control or influence at all.

Professional Problems

Referring back to the list of people who may be involved in any particular case, although they may all share in common an overriding aim to help people, the professionally trained people on that list have widely differing training backgrounds and specific functions, as well as being employed by organisations with a variety of administrative structures. They all have different levels of responsibility within their organisations, and in the law, with regard to the protection of children. If we look at the primary functions of some of the individual professionals on the list, this point will become apparent.

The *police* have a central role in investigating crime, apprehending criminals and upholding the law. In relation to child abuse, this means that they will be particularly concerned with finding out the details of particular incidents from victims, and in determining whether there is a need to interview suspects if a crime has been committed. They do not have a central responsibility for the welfare of victims or families who have been affected by abuse. Of late, however, partly in response to a growing conviction amongst professionals that the key to productive intervention in child abuse is working together with others, the police have begun to adopt a more relaxed and wider role. They have been much more alive to the needs of victims and their families, and are trying to take a more rounded view of the whole picture of abuse, rather than simply concentrating upon the need to uphold the law. The latter, however, does remain their prime function and duty.

The family *GP* is obviously concerned with the health and welfare of the whole family. He may have an interest in, or knowledge of child abuse, but he may not. He is likely to have a limited amount of time available to devote to individual

165

patients, but is a key figure in child protection, because he may be a person to whom disclosures are made, or the first person approached with a suspicious physical presentation. He may be concerned not to damage his relationship with his patients, and be seen to be involved in assessing one member of a family on his panel of abusing another family member. He may have a long-standing relationship with some families which allows him either to make accurate assessments, or clouds his perceptions and makes him unwilling to accept that abuse is happening.

The *teacher* may also have a long-standing relationship with a family about whom suspicions are raised. The teacher knows that a professional relationship with the family is likely to be dented at the very least if a child is referred because of abuse. Teachers are in a vital position in that they, like GPs, are often likely to be the ones who are first alerted to suspicious situations. I do not suggest here that teachers as a group are likely to fail to report suspicions of abuse for fear of damaging their relationship with clients in the future, but I have been aware of several occasions when this has happened.

The *doctors* in Accident and Emergency suffer no such problems about ongoing long-term relationships. They will see a child who presents with physical symptoms. They can decide if they wish to treat the case as suspicious on the basis of what they see, and what they are told. They are less encumbered by problems of future contact, as their involvement in the case is likely to be very time-limited. Again, their knowledge of child abuse in its widest sense is likely to be extremely variable. Abuse will represent a fraction of the type of work with which they are involved.

Social workers occupy a central role in the protection of children; the perspective of this book is biased towards the social worker's role. They may or may not already be aware of the family at the time a referral about abuse is made. They, too, are sometimes affected by potential damage to ongoing case-work relationships which the investigation of abuse may cause. They have a duty to investigate cases of alleged abuse which are referred to them, and are required to work within a prescribed legal framework with which their professional colleagues in other agencies may or may not be familiar. They are more likely to be involved in all aspects of the referral, from investigation through to assessment and treatment, than most of the other agencies.

Social workers, like all other professional groups, are now becoming more aware of the need to work with other agencies in order to provide a service to clients involved in child abuse. Their own internal procedures usually emphasise the need for close co-operation with colleagues from other disciplines. Because the organisation of social work varies from area to area, and because of the differences which exist in social work training courses, it is not possible to say that all social workers are equally competent in dealing with child abuse. Some departments favour specialisation so that staff concentrate on one area of work, such as child care or the elderly. Other departments favour a more generalist approach, with their staff carrying a very mixed case load of all types of client. (For a more detailed examination of these issues, *see* Chapter 11.) It is important to note at this stage that social work is not a profession which is organised in exactly the same way throughout the UK. Significant differences do exist between departments.

Each agency, therefore, whilst encouraged to work together to deal with child abuse, is organised very differently and each has a different professional role and priorities. The need for some overall procedural clarity becomes more and more self-evident.

Personal Problems

Each professional has a view about their colleagues who work for other agencies. These views are formed partly out of an understanding of the role of other professions, but it seems to be the case that we also carry around some personal generalisations about each other. We often tend to feel that we know best, and that our job is to coerce other agencies into

167

adopting our view. The fact that others may take a different perspective is often put down to our prejudiced characterisations about other agencies, rather than the fact that they may simply be right and we are wrong.

An example of this aspect of interaction concerns a case I was working on some years ago. I was involved in visiting a particular family who had a whole host of problems, for about four years. During that time I developed a good working relationship with most of the family members. The eldest daughter became pregnant and set up house for herself. It became increasingly evident that she was failing to provide adequate care for the baby. After one incident, when it was found that the child had been left in the house unattended for a short while, a meeting was called to discuss the case. The police representative spoke at length about the risk to the child and felt that she should be removed. I and my social work colleagues disagreed. With the benefit of hindsight, the police were correct. I disputed their views partly on the basis of the facts, but partly because they were the views of the police! I used to have a caricature of the police as being heavy-handed, thoughtless and lacking in knowledge about child care matters. Perhaps this is true of some of them, but it is no less true of some social workers. I did not give that particular police officer's views the necessary credence because of my personal prejudices, not because his arguments were wrong. I also felt personally threatened by someone having the temerity to challenge my thoughts on a case I knew well, concerning an issue about which I felt I knew more than he did.

It may be the case that I am a particularly prejudicial person, but I think many people are just as susceptible to allowing unfounded prejudice to interfere with their thinking. How many readers think that social workers are wishy-washy do-gooders who drive around in little Citroën cars?

As a result of these factors, it is obviously the case that an agreed working protocol to deal with the issue of co-operation in child abuse cases was desperately needed. However, as with many self-evident truths involving child abuse, we have sometimes only responded as a reaction to situations which go horribly wrong, and which lead to the tragedy of a child death. Often when this happens, a public inquiry is organised in order to learn lessons for the future, and recommendations are made relating, amongst other things, to procedure.

PROCEDURAL DEVELOPMENTS

The most obvious example of change coming out of tragedy in recent years, was the frantic activity which followed the publication of the inquiry into the death of Maria Colwell. She died in 1973, having been killed by her stepfather. She was eight years old when she was killed. For the previous five years she had lived with foster parents, who were relatives of her natural father. Soon after being returned to the care of her mother, she was dead. Her death in Brighton became a topic of public concern. This was a result of the publicity which surrounded the case, because of the public inquiry which was set up to examine the circumstances surrounding her life and death. A pattern of press reportage was set which seems to have been followed persistently ever since. Her photograph was plastered all over the tabloids. The social workers were vilified, and actually attacked in the street.

This case, more than any other up till then, brought home to a sceptical public that 'battered babies' was a rather misleading term, and that older children were also being abused. The case had the classic 'tug of love' ingredients of foster parents losing out, after a lot of care, to natural parents, and the social workers were criticised for allowing blood ties to weigh more heavily than ties of affection and trust. Because these issues were already under parliamentary debate, due to the 1972 Houghton Committee report on adoption and the needs of children in long-term fostering, the scene was set at the time of the Colwell case for a great deal of government action. At the same time, the old children's departments, welfare departments and parts of the health authorities had been amalgamated into social services departments. The health services had been undergoing massive reorganisation in 1972–4. It was a period of chaos. There was a loss of specialisation as social service functions were amalgamated. Older inter-departmental relationships were dismantled and required renegotiation. The Colwell case was dissected and analysed against this rather confusing backcloth.

In the light of more recent inquiries, including Cleveland, it is worth pausing to look at the main causes for concern which were identified by the Colwell case. These were:

1.   Inexperience and lack of knowledge on the part of those concerned with the case.
2.   Lack of clarity about agency roles and poor communication between agencies.
3.   Poor recording and administration.
4.   Other agencies wary about giving information to social services.

Children keep dying as a result of inadequate care or physical attack. Inquiries keep being published which seem to say little more than was said in the aftermath of the death of poor Maria Colwell.

The Colwell Inquiry was published at around the time of a circular from the DHSS, which is the means by which advice from central government is passed to the local authority who are responsible for, amongst other things, social services departments. This particular circular entitled *Non-Accidental Injury to Children* (*see* Bibliography) lays the foundation for present procedures which are still being used and developed today.

The 1974 circular advised the establishment of 'Area Review Committees'. These committees, now-redesignated 'Area Child Protection Committees', are meetings of people drawn from all agencies concerned with issues of child abuse, and are meant to be the means by which local procedures for inter-agency co-operation can be established, maintained and reviewed. They should take the lead role in formulating policy, organising training, and informing the public about the means by which children are to be protected.

170

By 1976 all local authority areas had Area Review Committees, and an agreed set of working procedures aimed at enhancing inter-agency co-operation. Senior staff from each key agency now attend Area Child Protection Committees, which meet at least quarterly throughout the year.

The 1974 circular also called for the establishment of case conferences to meet to discuss cases of actual or suspected child abuse, so as to provide an inter-agency forum for planning action. The advice also went on to ask local authorities urgently to consider the setting up of a register of children who had been abused or about whom there was significant concern of abuse.

In 1975, advice was issued about the means by which persons who had been convicted of serious offences against children (violence or sexual assault) could be brought to the attention of local authority areas to which they were likely to go following release from prison. Other advice issued in 1976 attempted to consolidate earlier advice about procedures to follow in particular cases. Following the 1974 circular, various agencies in the same area had established their own individual registers of children about whom they were concerned. The 1976 circular suggested that this proliferation was confusing and asked that a central register be held by each local authority to which all agencies could refer.

Another important document was *Child Abuse: Central Register Systems* (*see* Bibliography). Note that the title of this circular has changed from 'non-accidental injury', with its bias toward physical abuse only, to 'child abuse', which signifies a broader definition, encompassing emotional ill-treatment and neglect. Sexual abuse was not a distinct category.

The latest, and the most comprehensive advice yet to come from central government is *Working Together, A guide to arrangements for inter-agency co-operation for the protection of children from abuse.* (*see* Bibliography). This guide, along with its accompanying circular, came at a time when child abuse was again hitting the headlines as never before. The Cleveland sexual abuse controversy was being reported regularly, and the document from the DHSS was published at the same time as the Cleveland Inquiry. Sexual abuse, not surprisingly, receives special treatment in *Working Together*, and advice is given about categorising sexual abuse as a distinct entity within registers. By this time, social services departments had already begun to respond to the growing referral rate of sexual abuse, and many local authorities, in collaboration with other agencies, had set up systems of co-operative working practices to deal with the issue. *Working Together* contained advice which had been gleaned from events in Cleveland, and some of the subsequent inquiry recommendations are echoed in the guidance from DHSS.

CHILD PROTECTION REGISTERS

The child protection register is a list of those children about whom there is some evidence of grave concern regarding potential abuse, about whom there is firm suspicion that they have been or are being abused, or who have actually been abused. Each local authority has a register of names, which is administered by a nominated custodian, who is often an employee of the social services department. However, in some parts of the country the NSPCC acts as custodian and administrator of the register.

The register ought not to be a static list of names, but should signify that there is some kind of inter-agency plan in operation which is designed to protect the child. In just the same way that the central government circulars have progressed from 'non-accidental injury', through 'child abuse', to 'child protection', so has the register changed in title. The idea of re-designating the register as the 'child protection register' signifies an emphasis upon prevention and upon the need to make plans for the future so that children are protected from harm.

One feature of many of the cases which have been subject to public inquiry is important. This is the fact that information which may have provided clues to abuse, had it been set alongside other information stored elsewhere, was often not brought to light. The register is an attempt to plug this particular gap.

The actual register itself is kept securely, and information contained in it is used only in so far as it helps to protect children. If someone wishes to check whether a child is registered, or whether other agencies are expressing concerns for the well-being of a particular child, they will usually call the custodian of the register. Most registers operate a call-back system and will not issue any information without being assured of the status of the person making the enquiry. The information which the custodian of the register releases at this stage will be very limited. They will normally only confirm that the child's name appears on the register, and will redirect the enquirer to someone who will be involved in the case. This person will then be able to discuss with them the nature of the enquiry, and will begin the process of consultation designed to ascertain the best way of co-ordinating any efforts to take action, if this is required.

Normally, a child's name will only appear on the register if it has been agreed at a formal case conference (an important aspect of procedure). A common and significant exception to this is when a child moves from one area to another, and is on the register in the area from which he has moved. This exception is important and worthy of note, because there is clear evidence that some parents who are involved in abusing their children will move around the country extensively, presumably in order to avoid detection. One aspect of the Kimberley Carlile case pointed out the administrative difficulties which such moves can create for large organisations, as they attempt to communicate with each other. Whether we feel these communication problems are justifiable or not, they certainly seem to exist. If a child who is on the child protection register in one area moves to another, there is clear guidance. The custodian in the old area should immediately contact their equivalent in the new area, and the child should immediately be included on the register of the area to which he or she has moved, pending a formal case conference at which discussion will take place about retention on, or removal from the register.

Criteria for Registration

The criteria for distinguishing one form of abuse from another are contained in recent guidelines. Bearing in mind all the problems associated with definition, those criteria are the basis for making decisions as to whether to register a child. Many areas are now also ensuring that registration indicates the formulation and implementation of an inter-agency plan to protect the child. Without the need for any such plan, there is no registration. If, for example, a child is so severely abused that it is removed from the care of its parents and placed in the care of the local authority, without any immediate plans for a return home, there is likely not to be any need for such a child to be registered. Social services are assuming the care of the child, and the child is being looked after by officers of the department. With the occasional horrific exception, the child's physical safety is thus protected without the necessity for elaborate inter-agency co-operation.

Removal from the Register

The decision to place a child on the child protection register is a significant one. It suggests that those agencies charged with the responsibility to protect children feel that the child is at significant risk of abuse, and that the situation demands formal co-operation in order to try and protect the child in the future. During the period of registration, the maintenance of the child on the register is kept under review. Each local area will have its own methods of review. Some will entail a periodic case conference at which those most actively involved in working with the child and its family will meet to assess the progress being made, and to make recommendations about removal from the register, amongst other things. Some areas have dispensed with the practice of holding formal meetings, and review cases by way of submitting reports to panels and standing committees. Whatever the arrangements, each registered child is monitored, and the decision to place a child on the register is periodically re-assessed.

There may be a variety of reasons why a particular child's name could be removed from the register. Family circumstances could have changed so that the adult deemed to pose a threat to the child's welfare is no longer in the area. It may subsequently be realised that the initial decision to register the child was wrong, and that the child's name can be removed. The work undertaken as part of an overall protection plan may be successful, significantly diminishing the need to retain the child on the register. The important factor to note here is that a child's name can be removed, and the register is not a static instrument from which there is no escape.

CASE CONFERENCES

For many years the case conference has been seen as the pivotal point of the procedures designed to protect children. Basically, a case conference is a professionals' meeting designed to exchange information about children who have been abused or who are at significant risk of abuse. When an agency receives a referral, and carries out initial enquiries which lead it to believe a child is at risk, an initial case conference is organised. The exact detail of how an initial case conference is organised varies widely throughout the UK. Initial conferences will take place soon after a case of abuse has come to light, usually within a week. Although some degree of liaison will have taken place between key agencies before the meeting, the initial case conference will often be the first opportunity for all concerned professionals to review events, perhaps hearing certain information for the first time, and to make a number of decisions and recommendations.

It is essential to be aware of the status of these meetings. There is no sense in which their decisions are legally binding on agencies who attend. They are means by which inter-agency co-operation can be facilitated under a procedural umbrella, to which all agencies subscribe, by virtue of their participation in the area child protection committees which produce the local procedures. Those invited to attend will usually include: representatives from the social services department; representatives from the police; a local authority lawyer; and health authority personnel (concerned with the case), including a consultant paediatrician, a hospital doctor, a midwife, a health visitor, nursing staff, a community physician, a GP, and a psychiatrist.

Where appropriate, representatives from the following might also be invited: the education department, the probation service, the NSPCC voluntary organisations, and foster parents.

Others can be added to this list, depending upon the type of case under discussion.

For the purpose of clarity, the functions of the conference can be split into two distinct sections: decisions and recommendations. The decisions the conference will make will include:

1. Whether abuse is substantiated, or if the degree of risk can be assessed.
2. Whether or not to place the name of the child on the register, dependent on 1 above.
3. Who to appoint as 'key worker' (this term is explained in detail later).
4. The identification of the core group. (Again explained later.)
5. Who will inform the parents or carers of the decisions and how this will be done.

Recommendations of case conferences (as distinct from decisions) will include:

1. What action is needed to protect the child/ren in the short term, such as legal action.
2. A plan is developed, designed to assist in protecting the child, including who shall visit the family, and what shall be

176

the general basis of the work they will undertake. The resources needed to carry out the plan are considered.

These recommendations, which are usually not deviated from except in unusual circumstances, will be made by the case conference to individual agencies for action. These must be recommendations as distinct from decisions, because each individual agency will have its own legal and professional duty to uphold. It would be unrealistic to expect any agency to relinquish its professional and legal obligations, by following a course of action determined at a case conference with which, after having given that recommendation due consideration, it vehemently disagrees.

Core Groups

At initial case conferences, it is now becoming accepted practice for a small group of workers to be identified as the ones who will be responsible for carrying out the bulk of the tasks agreed at the meeting. Whilst there may be ten or fifteen people at an initial conference, the 'core group' may comprise three or four. This group will need to maintain a very regular dialogue throughout the subsequent work with the child and family and remain mindful of the recommendations of the case conference.

Key Worker

The concept of 'key worker' has existed for a number of years. The idea is that the naming of one person, whose main function is to act as the point of contact between agencies, will help to ensure a co-ordinated and planned piece of work with the child and its family. The key worker will be a social worker or an officer of the NSPCC; these are the two main agencies who possess the requisite legal powers to protect children in urgent situations. Usually, the key worker will be the person who has the most contact with the family. For these reasons, his or her role is crucial.

177

SPECIALIST ASSESSMENT TEAMS

The idea for the creation of specialist groups of professionals to work with families and children at the point where there may be inconclusive suspicions of sexual abuse, was suggested in the Cleveland Inquiry. Lord Justice Butler-Sloss recommended that a social worker, a police officer and a doctor, all with specific training in dealing with child sexual abuse, could jointly undertake an initial assessment and, on the basis of any conclusions they arrive at, decide whether there is any need to take the case further. This idea recognises the fact that a large proportion of suspicious cases involve little, if any, conclusive proof, and require subtle and skilled early assessment, particularly in alleged sexual abuse cases. Some areas already have specialist units dealing with aspects of sexual abuse, which link in to groups of doctors and police officers to do assessments. Whether or not multi-agency teams of the type envisaged by the Cleveland report are commonly organised, to be called on to do this particularly skilful and demanding work in any systematic and standardised way throughout the UK, is difficult to say. Certainly, the suggestion can be seen as an attempt to consolidate the growing view that the only realistic way in which child abuse can be worked with effectively is by co-operation between agencies – these agencies possess different skills, and have different roles, but their contribution provides an indispensable part of the whole process.

PROCEDURES – A HELP OR A HINDRANCE?

There is no aspect of the job of social work which involves as much procedure and departmental policy as child protection. This may reflect the fact that child protection is a very complex and sensitive area, but so are most other areas of the general social work task. It is obviously also due in part to the need to work with other agencies on a regular basis. However, this 'cottage industry' which has sprung up in recent years, responsible for the development of ever-more complex and detailed procedures to deal with child protection, is in part the reflection of a crisis of confidence within the profession of social work itself, and on the part of other agencies and the general public at large. We are all now faced with the realisation of the extent of the problem of child abuse. There is a sense in which people take comfort from paper with rules and advice printed on it. If the agency has a procedure, then this in itself will help to protect children. If we write about the problems enough, they will go away!

Procedures can sometimes lead professionals into a false sense of false security. Child abuse work involves personal stress, and the careful assessment of risk, often basing judgements on the balance of probability rather than absolute fact; this is a major cause of that stress. Sometimes, it is easy to take comfort behind rules, procedures and guidelines emanating from your own agency, the Area Child Protection Committee, or central government. There can also be a temptation to turn into a mechanistic functionary, robotically following the procedures at the expense of being involved in the more threatening and ultimately more productive process of using professional judgement. I realise that this may well be seen as a contentious statement, and that in an ideal world, procedures and professional judgement go hand in hand. It is when procedures become a substitute for professionalism that problems can emerge.

Over the years, the case conference has been a focus for critics of procedure. Because there is a unique legal responsibility placed upon social services to protect children, I have been present at some case conferences where the collective anxiety of other agencies is handed over to the poor key worker by way of registering the child as being at risk. This is done without any real commitment on the part of some to be actively involved in subsequent work with the family, other than to hold a watching brief. As a supplement to the *British Journal of Clinical and Social Psychiatry*, June 1985 Vol. 3 No. 2, M. G. T. Chapman and A. C. Woodmansey wrote a paper entitled 'Policy on Child Abuse' (*see* Bibliography). In it, they made several criticisms of procedures, focusing in particular upon case conferences and registers. They felt that the only significant function of conferences is to 'allay the anxieties of professional workers (and their realistic fear of being scapegoated)'.

They felt that the decisions which conferences are supposed to make are too complex, and require too much specialist knowledge, to be entrusted to a multi-professional grouping of people, some of whom may possess the necessary skills required, others of whom may not.

I sympathise very much with this point of view. The pervasive ethos often seems to be, 'If in doubt, have a conference', as if, by some mystical and unfathomable means, the process itself will tackle the problem. As Chapman and Woodmansey point out, there is no substitute for professional competence. With regard to registers, Chapman and Woodmansey have some particularly scathing things to say:

'After the initial case conference, the child's name tends to be put on a register. The function of each of these two procedures seems to be to justify the other: for there appears to be no evidence that they have been accompanied by a reduction in the number of victims.'

A common criticism of the practice of registration is the stress this can create in both practitioners and clients. Most procedures involve some kind of commitment to visit the family in question on a regular basis. This frequency of visiting may be wholly appropriate, and is often no more frequent than the amount of contact would be without registration, but it may be increased and intensified due to the fact that the particular child is on the register. This can create more stress in the family, make them feel as if they are 'under the spotlight', and this can sometimes increase the risk of further abuse (bearing in mind the links which exist between stress and abuse). Similarly, being responsible for a case which has been the subject of inter-agency meetings, and which is going to be reviewed in the near future, can make the workers feel as if they are in the spotlight. This may make them over-reactive and less able to formulate a balanced response to situations as they arise.

Procedures can militate against the taking of risk. Workers are anxious about the possible consequences for them should a mistake in judgement lead to public condemnation. Whilst some may feel that this is a good thing, it must always be remembered that social work, particularly in the field of child protection, is about risk-taking. Over-cautiousness can lead to as many detrimental effects for children as can spontaneous, badly thought-out decisions. It can lead to a worker being too reluctant to place a child back in its family or too reluctant to take the necessary steps to remove a child from a dangerous environment. In short, a procedural approach to problem solving can mean that no decisions of any note are ever made, and can lead to experienced workers being reluctant and afraid to exercise professional judgement.

In my experience, procedures can lead to the development of a significant rift between practitioner and manager level within departments. From a managerial point of view, it is desirable to lay down policies and regulations with regard to the way in which staff in the department will work. That is an essential role for managers in any organisation. In theory, the procedures are supposed to improve the work of the practitioner. From the point of view of the practitioner, procedures from head office or central government can be very useful, can make staff feel supported within a framework of written guidance. However, when things go wrong, there can be a shift in the inter-relationship between procedure, management and practitioner. Management can use the existence of procedure to absolve itself from any responsibility, as can government departments. It is at these times of crisis that social workers can be criticised for any approach which deviates from a slavish adherence to procedure. This has been demonstrated time and time again in the course of public inquiries into child deaths. Practitioners are well aware of the advantages and disadvantages which procedure documents confer.

This issue is even more starkly demonstrated with the use of practice guidelines. These are documents which can be issued to social work staff from a variety of sources. They can be produced within the department, can be issued by pressure groups, professional organisations and government departments. Their status is advisory, but this status seems to shift when a serious mistake comes to light. Workers can then find themselves criticised for not taking on board the guidance contained in documents which suddenly seem to have lost their advisory nature, and have been transformed into legally binding contracts.

Summary

The procedural framework, then, has been built up over the years in order to help individual agencies to work more soundly in the field of child protection. The major thrust of the procedures has been to increase the level of communication and co-operation between agencies, but they also seem to create some problems for social workers. Procedures and commonly shared ways of working are a vital element in the attempt to protect children – however, they must never be allowed to stifle the exercise of individual professional judgement, nor should they be used to add to the pressure felt by workers and clients involved in this inevitably stressful area of work.

8 The Rights of Parents and Children

INTRODUCTION

The nature of legislation and procedure which has developed in the field of child protection within the last twenty years is complex. The Children Bill in particular indicates an increasing awareness on the part of the legislators of the potential for abusing statutory powers. A developing sensitivity to the need to take into account the wishes and feelings of all interested parties, before taking significant decisions in child protection cases, is clearly evidenced by some of the proposals in the Bill.

This attempt to balance the need for effective powers against their capacity for abuse is the latest manifestation of a much more general problem in social work, one that is by no means confined to the area of child protection. How much weight should be given to the rights of parents to bring up their children how they wish? What should happen if the wishes of the parents conflict with those of the child? In the last resort, how important is it that children remain with their natural families?

RIGHTS AND RESPONSIBILITIES

There is a distinction to be made between rights and responsibilities, and the Children Bill attempts to shift the debate away from the rights of parents, towards parental responsibility (*see* Chapter 6). The developing ethos appears to be one in which adult carers of children must provide a level of basic care below which their rights can be challenged. The power to control and shape the lives of vulnerable members of society (in this case children) carries with it a responsibility to discharge that duty adequately. There can be no inviolate right on the part of an adult to bring up a child in any manner the adult sees fit. However, the problems begin when we try to define the line between 'adequate' and 'inadequate' parenting (*see* Chapter 1).

It seems to me that children are the ones who have rights. In the main, they are not free agents, and are dependent upon those who care for them for many, if not all of their needs. It is improper to consider youngsters as being in possession of responsibilities in relation to self-protection. Children have a right not to be abused. I would argue that they also have a right to a happy childhood, but for a variety of reasons (not necessarily connected to the failings of their parents), this is not always possible. They have a right to experience love and affection within a safe and consistent environment. When these rights are seriously and persistently violated, social work and other agencies intervene.

Social workers have a legal duty to intervene in certain situations, and a variety of legal powers are provided in order that this duty can be fulfilled. The evolution and demise of the place of safety order (*see* Chapter 6), some have argued, is an example of the way in which the balance between rights and responsibilities can be misjudged. To a certain extent, the popular view of the balance between the privacy of family life and the powers of state intervention depends upon the background to the most recent child abuse crisis to receive media attention. The death of a child returned to his or her natural parents from long-term foster care probably shifts the balance of popular opinion away from the rights of parents. On the other hand, the Cleveland situation in 1987 certainly focused the attention of the public upon the need for the greater protection of family life. These are rather crude generalisations, but they serve to illustrate the point that, in recent years at least, our views about state intervention in family life have often been in a state of flux. The recent trends and developments in professional thinking around the issue of the importance of family life are outlined below.

PERMANENCY PLANNING

The debate about the rights of parents has flourished most vociferously in the field of fostering and adoption. The debate focused around a concept called 'permanency planning'. This concept recognises the need to make plans for children in order to encourage their upbringing in a stable and predictable environment. During the course of the early 1970s, the problems which can occur for children who are in long-term foster placements, whose situation is allowed to drift along without being formalised by a process of legal adoption, began to be recognised. Some professionals began to argue that, without a permanent resolution by way of rehabilitation home or adoption, children suffered through a lack of legal and social status. Research studies began to show that if decisions about the permanent future are not made within the first few months of a placement in care, the chances of the child being able to develop to its full potential were limited. The child was likely to be destined for a disruptive care history, and its childhood years would probably be marked by numerous moves from one foster placement and/or institution to another.

This debate was fuelled by the publication of a book by Goldstein, Freud and Solnit called *Beyond the Best Interests of the Child* (*see* Bibliography). Central to this work was the view that children could not be expected to relate realistically to two sets of parental figures, natural and substitute. Children needed permanence, and, once removed from home, children ought to be quickly rehabilitated, or be adopted. This was around the time of the Colwell inquiry (*see* Chapter 7). A feature of this case was the decision to place Maria Colwell back with her mother after a foster placement of long standing, influenced by the alleged strength of the blood tie. Some commentators have also argued that the 'planning for permanence' movement was encouraged due to a political shift in some quarters away from state expenditure to support families, to a doctrine which stressed the need for people to stand on their own feet. In other words, if parents aren't fit to

185

to care for their children, then the children ought to be removed.

Permanency planning does recognise the importance of the biological tie, and stresses the need to support children in their own families wherever possible. However, it questions the inviolable nature of the biological tie which had hitherto enjoyed the unquestioning support of large sections of society. Permanency planning implies that the rights of children override those of their parents, who in some circumstances must forfeit their claims in the interests of the welfare of the child.

The Children Act 1975 was a piece of legislation which, amongst other things, concentrated on issues of adoption. It gave local authorities more power to assume parental rights over some children, and made the process of adoption somewhat easier. Social workers were given more control over the lives of children in their care and, in an attempt to bolster the security of children in substitute homes, the Act enabled parental ties to be severed more simply. The Act also made permanency a very central issue of child care policy.

Opponents of this legislation argued that the case that children could develop adequately with only one set of parents was not proven, that vulnerable families were likely to receive less by way of help to enable them to keep their children, and that the Act concentrated on removing children not at risk. At this time, the pendulum seemed to have swung away from parental rights, to those of local authorities and substitute carers. Permanence and removal dominated prevention and rehabilitation.

Latterly, the debate seems to have shifted more towards a greater recognition of the dangers of vesting too much power in the hands of the local authority, and a variety of pressure groups have very ably spoken out for the rights both of parents and of children. A parliamentary committee published The Short Report in 1984, which helped to bring the question of prevention back to the fore. In the opinion of this report, prevention was being blocked because agencies gave it low priority in terms of organisational commitment and resource allocation. The report also recognised the fact that it was difficult to justify expenditure on incompetent families, the effectiveness of which is uncertain.

This report urged the development of flexible preventive services such as child minders, short-term and daily fostering (to give parents and children the occasional break), and other allied services. The report also advocated the scrapping of parental rights resolutions, the establishment of family courts and a higher priority being given to the rehabilitation home of children in care. Subsequent reviews of child care law, culminating, in part at least, in the Children Bill, have taken on many of these proposals.

THE IMPACT OF CLEVELAND

The story of the Cleveland affair has been thoroughly analysed by many commentators (with varying degrees of insight), and it is linked to the debate about the relative rights of those involved in child abuse. There has been the development of a general debate concerning rights and responsibilities, and this is central in terms of its impact upon the process of child protection. Events in Cleveland demonstrate this clear connection in a variety of ways.

Whether justified or not, there was significant criticism of the way in which children in Cleveland were removed from the care of their parents, very quickly, usually by way of a place of safety order. Were some children removed too soon? Were the grounds for concern sufficient to warrant the overriding of the rights which the parents had to care for their children? These issues have been examined during the discussion about place of safety orders and proposals for their replacement (*see* Chapter 6). However, this is an example of the way in which the general debate about the balance to be struck between the rights of all parties involved in providing care for children is of specific relevance in child protection.

Once removed from home, the contact which some children were allowed to their parents also caused disquiet in some quarters. There were criticisms that access was severely limited, or that arrangements were made which hampered the ability of the parents to have any meaningful contact with their children.

As work with individual children progressed, doubts began to be expressed about the extent to which parents and children were able to contribute to the formulation of plans for the future. All of these issues, and more besides, were highlighted in Cleveland in 1987 and were the subject of comment by the subsequent inquiry. In relation to suspected child abuse in general, and intra-familial sexual abuse in particular, these subjects are extremely complex. They must not simply be seen in terms of groups of professionals blindly failing to acknowledge the balance of rights which must be taken into account when decisions have to be made.

For example, in some cases it may be perfectly justifiable severely to curtail the contact between a child and its parents if one or both parents are the alleged abusers. There may be the need to create this separation so that the child feels safe enough to give a full account of the abuse. But for how long can limited contact be enforced in order to assist disclosure when little or no information is forthcoming? There comes a time when a judgement must be made between the need to obtain uncontaminated information and the potential damage which may result from a break in the parent-child relationship.

The Cleveland crisis added impetus to the general debate about rights and responsibilities, further shifting the popular consensus in favour of a greater sensitivity towards the rights of parents.

RIGHTS AND RESPONSIBILITIES –
A PERSONAL VIEW

The debate about rights and responsibilities has developed through the past twenty years, culminating in the Cleveland affair in 1987. It seems to me that a balance is being created between two extremes, namely the inviolate nature of family life, and the removal of children at risk of abuse. It seems perfectly possible for child protection workers to carry out their task being mindful of the needs of parents and children, without compromising their primary function which is protection.

There are situations in which swift protective action needs to be taken, but these occasions are now usually occurring only after all other alternatives have been explored, and are certainly not undertaken as a thoughtless, automatic response to all situations of risk. The law as it relates to children has, over the past twenty years, begun to clarify the balance between rights and responsibilities for parents, children and child protection workers alike. In general, the safety and welfare of the child is of paramount importance, and social workers will usually receive legal support for action taken on this basis – even when, as sometimes must happen, the initial management of the case infringes upon the rights of some of those who may be involved.

Social workers receive support from within their agencies, and usually from the law, when they can show that their actions resulted from a careful consideration of the facts which were available at the time. Those whose rights have been curtailed will often accept decisions if the basis for them is openly and honestly communicated. Many problems seem to emanate from a reluctance to share the decision-making process with parents in particular. Clear and honest communication will not always result in consensus, but it will often help aggrieved parties to understand why a certain course of action has been taken.

THE ROLE OF PARENTS AND CHILDREN IN THE PROCEDURES

The general debate surrounding the relative rights and responsibilities of those involved in child protection goes on. It is worthwhile at this point to explain in more depth the relationship between child protection procedures and individual

2

189

rights, concentrating on the following: initial investigations, medical examinations, child protection case conferences, child protection registers and reviews.

Initial Investigations

If a social worker receives a referral from a third party to the effect that a child is being abused by its parents, ought the worker be allowed to conduct an initial investigation which may involve an interview with the child, without the permission of the child's parents or guardians? This is an extremely complex and difficult problem. On the one hand it may well be important to see the child quickly, away from the family home, in order to gather as much uncontaminated information as possible, prior to confronting the alleged abusers with the material. On the other hand, is it reasonable for children to be seen by strangers, whether social workers or police officers, without the prior agreement of the parents?

In a case of intra-familial sexual abuse, there may be a number of reasons why it is preferable to follow up an initial referral quickly, and without the consent of the parents. The child may be intimidated if it feels that its parents are going to be immediately informed. The child may feel more relaxed about talking about the abuse before its parents (one of whom is the alleged abuser) have been informed. The improved quality of the initial statement is likely to prove more effective when the alleged abuser is interviewed. If the abuser is given little or no time to prepare an alibi, this may also increase the likelihood that the truth is discovered. There is also the understandable tendency of children to retract allegations fairly early in a case, and so it may prove necessary to act relatively quickly in response to an initial referral.

Counter to these views is the argument that contact between a child protection agency and a child ought not to proceed without the consent of the parents. The following example will illustrate the problem. A ten-year-old girl begins to disclose to a teacher at school that her father is molesting her. She is frightened of what he would do if he found out she was telling anyone. The teacher contacts the police and social services, who arrange to send a social worker and a police officer to the school to take a statement. When they phone the head teacher, they are told that they cannot conduct such an interview on the school premises without obtaining prior permission from the parents. The child feels safe at school, and is unlikely to be prepared to be interviewed elsewhere. In such circumstances, what ought to happen? Contacting the parents may produce an unhelpful response. They may refuse permission (especially if they are suspected of committing the abuse). If this is so, it may be that a legal solution would have to be found in order to separate the child from home, which may have all manner of detrimental results. Although the parents may give permission, this may so inhibit the child that she no longer feels able to talk. The abuser would be alerted to the investigation and would possibly have time to manufacture a false alibi. If a combination of factors weakened the likelihood of establishing the truth, we may be guilty of doing nothing other than increasing the risk of re-abuse for the child or making it highly unlikely that she would tell anyone in future.

Situations such as these often represent those times when all agencies must be prepared to put the welfare of the child first, before defending the rights of parents. One must always strive to seek solutions which take all sides into account. This cannot always be done. My point is that, when a decision is taken to curtail parental rights, in order to heighten the prospects of promoting the welfare of the child, a social worker must be able to justify why the action was taken, in the first instance to the parents themselves and subsequently, if the need arises, to the courts. In this way, a person can be mindful of the responsibility to protect children, whilst at the same time acknowledging the dangers of abusing such powers as the law confers.

Obviously, the younger the child, the more important it becomes to weigh these issues carefully. Older children are often at a level of comprehension which allows them to participate fully in decisions which are taken. There may exist cases where the child's wishes will override those of its parent, where conflicts of interest develop, for example, if a child agrees to an interview with the police but the parents object. Where the child is young, or is unable to give any sort of reliable informed consent, there is a need to be careful, to weigh the issues with care, and justify the decision taken on the basis of what is deemed to be in the child's best interests.

Medical Examination

The role played within child protection by medical examinations provides yet another focus for discussion about the rights of parents, children, and child protection agencies. As in the case of the initial interview, a social worker must be careful before subjecting children to medicals (other than where it is felt necessary to provide medical treatment) for which parents haven't given their consent. Consent to a thorough examination may well be implied if a parent allows the child to be seen by a doctor. In the case of physical and/or sexual abuse, a thorough medical examination is often desirable. In such circumstances, the legal situation is currently confusing (*see* Chapter 6). Often, children will be able to provide their own consent to examination, but at present a doctor is probably acting against the spirit of the law, and of established procedure, if he conducts an examination for the purposes of obtaining evidence of abuse, and the informed consent of the parent or child is not forthcoming. In cases where it is felt necessary to conduct an examination for purposes other than to determine the need for urgent treatment, and it is not possible to obtain consent, the law must be used in order to shift the legal responsibility for the child away from the parents to another individual or agency.

If handled correctly and openly, it will only be in a few cases that problems concerning medical examinations will arise. Often, if the importance of a detailed examination is fully explained to parents and children, consent will be forthcoming. The withholding of consent by a parent who also happens to be the suspected abuser could also turn out to be useful evidence which may be put before a court at some future date. I feel that it is fair to say that the publicity engendered by the Cleveland affair in 1987 created widespread and exaggerated fears about the protocol involved in organising medical examinations. It has not been my experience that consent is normally withheld. Nor is it my experience that children and young people are being subjected to unnecessary examinations. There are exceptions, of course, and Cleveland may have helped in alerting us all to be more circumspect in our handling of these delicate matters. They invariably arise at the outset of a case, when anxiety levels are high on all sides, so mistakes can very easily be made. (Please note that, in juxtaposing Cleveland alongside problems concerning medical examinations, I do not wish to give the impression that I am criticising events which subsequently became the subject of public inquiry. I merely note here that these issues were highlighted by innumerable commentators on the Cleveland affair, and caused all agencies to re-examine their own working practices.)

Case Conferences

The child protection case conference (*see* Chapter 7) is a crucial element in the professional management of child abuse. There is, however, no measure of agreement amongst those involved in the protection of children about the involvement of parents and children at a case conference. It is certainly the case that the attendance of parents is something which the Department of Health is encouraging social service departments to consider favourably. The Cleveland inquiry also suggests that it is advisable for parents to be there unless their attendance is likely to hamper the tasks of the conference. Some local authorities have parents present at most, if not all case conferences, and have done so for some considerable time.

I have had no direct personal experience of parental attendance, and as such feel unable to form an opinion. There is a developing awareness of the need to work with parents, and to make them a part of the decision-making process, and it is certainly within the spirit of this ideal for parents (and children, if they are deemed to be of a level of understanding rendering them capable of making a contribution) to be invited to case conferences. The presence of parents may help to focus the meetings on to issues of fact, and to limit the extent to which some participants are allowed a free rein to over-interpret alleged signs and symptoms of abuse. Although it is for the chairman of the conference to help the meeting apportion weight to individual contributions, it may be that parental attendance would significantly assist in the process by which material discussed in the meeting is factual and relevant.

Opponents of parental attendance use the following arguments to support the claim that parents should not be invited. They say that the conference is primarily a professionals' meeting which must sometimes balance a variety of opinions. The attendance of parents would restrict the professional basis of the discussion and may inhibit relevant opinion and uncorroborated statements (which may also be relevant) from being discussed. Parental attendance may restrict the sharing of confidential information by the medical profession and others. It may be that one or both parents (and children, if they are present) might hear significant information about their partners or family members for the first time. If this is true, then a formal case conference is surely not the place for this information to be released. Another argument concerns the distress which the material may cause to parents, and the inability of some parents, faced with a group of professional people, adequately to represent themselves (some have argued for legal representation for parents at conferences). Another point concerns the role of the local authority legal section. A lawyer is often present at case conferences in order to advise members on legal matters (grounds for care proceedings, wardship, emergency action, and so on). It has been argued by opponents of parental participation that it would be unrealistic for the lawyer representing the local authority to be expected to discuss potential weaknesses of a course of action in the presence of parents against whom the authority may at some future date need to prove a case in court.

Parental attendance is a controversial issue, and it is for the reader to make up his or her own mind on it. I am clear that it is wrong to compromise by having parents present for part of the meeting, indicative of tokenism of the worst kind. We ought to make up our minds on the issue, using as the basis for the decision the interests of children, and either have parents present or not.

However each area chooses to act on this topic, it is important to allow parents some input to the meeting. If they are not present, it must be the responsibility of the conference to make itself aware of the views of parents and children and, wherever possible, to communicate as honestly as possible the result of the meeting, giving a full explanation of the basis for reaching a particular decision.

Reviews

The arguments against full parental participation in the process of reviewing a child protection case (after a case conference) are less strong than those put forward against their initial involvement. Reviews are less likely to involve the sharing of new, possibly controversial and untested information. Ideally, those involved in the case will have been able to form a reasonable working relationship with the child and its family, and for these reasons participation in the review may prove to be less fraught with difficulties. Having said this, it remains the case that parents are not automatically involved in reviews, and this is an issue upon which a great many groups and individuals have been commenting for some time. There is a sense in which talk is cheap. A greater involvement of parents in the decision-making process relating to child protection procedures is being urged upon local authorities from a variety of sources and for many different reasons. We must become more accessible to the general public, our systems must become more open to scrutiny in so far as this does not hamper child protection responsibilities. Only by acting upon our good intentions will the public become more supportive of the job we are trying to do on their behalf.

Child Protection Registers

Should parents always know that their child's name is on the register? Should we keep lists of dangerous adults? These questions again raise a number of interesting issues with regard to the balance of rights and responsibilities. It is now accepted practice that, unless there are very good contra-indications, parents will be told of registration and what the resultant implications are. As I have mentioned earlier, situations will occasionally arise where it is felt likely that to inform parents will heighten the future risk to the child. In such cases, it would be justifiable not to inform the parents in the interests of the welfare of their child.

A number of people have questioned the usefulness of retaining lists of abused children. Surely it would make more sense to keep lists of adults who are felt to be a risk to the welfare of youngsters? As we have seen, Schedule 1 offenders are often monitored, as far as procedure will allow, but even this system is seriously flawed. We often fail to hear about those convicted of Schedule 1 crimes who do not receive custodial sentences. After a few changes of address many of these people are out of the monitoring system. Consider, also, the following scenario. A man physically and sexually abuses his sons and daughters. There is no significant evidence upon which to obtain a criminal conviction, but care orders are made on all the children. The man leaves the home, and his wife divorces him. He is now a free agent. He isn't a notified offender, although, on the balance of probability, he was guilty of serious child abuse. Ought agencies be allowed to keep details on him, in order to be alert to future situations where he may be involved in another household with children? He isn't a convicted criminal. He has no record. He is a free man. Would we be guilty of infringeing his rights if we were to attempt to monitor his dealings with children in the future? How far should we be able to go, in terms of

196

monitoring allegedly dangerous adults, in the interests of child protection?

There are no simple answers to any of these questions. My opinion is that, providing a child protection agency is able to demonstrate that its records are accurate, relevant and securely kept, anything which may assist in the future protection of children is acceptable – even if this may mean the recording of unresolved but strong suspicions against an individual adult. Others addressing this problem from an alternative viewpoint will have a different perspective, and will perhaps wish to re-affirm the importance of the belief that people are innocent until proven guilty. Also, there is a growing and entirely understandable mistrust of agency records in general, which seem to become ever more intrusive, and open to misuse.

Legislation now provides guidelines for the retention of many personal records, particularly if those records are kept in a computerised system. In recent years, there have been developments to strengthen the rights of individuals to have access to material which is kept about them by departments such as social services. These changes in legislation and procedure (the precise details of which are beyond the scope of this book) have all helped in the past few years to move towards the establishment of an uneasy balance between the rights of individuals and the responsibilities of agencies.

SUMMARY

In the field of child protection there must always be a consciousness of the need to take into account the views and wishes of all concerned. From the point of view of social work, the welfare of the child remains the guiding principle as the worker attempts to intervene in complex situations which require a balanced and objective view. On occasions, this principle will mean that the rights of other people, especially actual or potential abusers, will be compromised. An honest approach, which attempts to explain the reasoning behind

197

decisions with which parents or others disagree, will usually enable a constructive working relationship to be established and maintained. Attempts to deviate from the truth, or to be economical with it in a vain attempt to please everybody, will ultimately fail, and will make the likelihood of trust developing between client and worker extremely remote. This is then likely to have serious implications for the future, and may prove harmful to the child.

Individuals can usually accept a contradictory view if it is explained to them, and this can only be done if significant decisions are taken after careful thought. The developments in child care law which appear to invest children with rights and their carers with responsibilities, represent an ethos which ought further to clarify the precarious balancing act which often results from a child protection case.

9 Investigation and Initial Assessment

In this chapter I will examine some features of the initial contact between clients and social workers when child abuse is reported. Because the nature of the work involves collaboration between a variety of different agencies, some aspects of the roles of the police and medical practitioners will also be considered. I will establish themes, common to most initial investigations, highlighting the inherent difficulties of this area of work. Some ways in which social workers assess cases of abuse will be explored, as will the impact upon both clients and professionals of this early contact.

REFERRALS

Social workers can receive referrals about cases of child abuse from a wide variety of sources. Children can make self-referrals, but this is the exception rather than the rule. More usual is the referral which is received from some third party. Depending upon the particular circumstances of the case, this person can be a relative, a friend, a school teacher, or a neighbour. Once allegations have been made which indicate that a child or young person may be being abused (*see* Chapter 6), the local authority social services department has a legal obligation to make enquiries. Most local authority internal procedures place a responsibility on their social work staff to investigate all referrals of abuse as a matter of priority.

The growing awareness of the existence of child abuse, coupled with the obligation to enquire into referrals which are received as a matter of some urgency, places social work staff in an unenviable role. They often have to make quick judgements about allegations of abuse based upon information which may be incomplete, confused and suspicious. Anonymous referrals are often received from people claiming to be neighbours or relatives of a family. Some of these referrals are malicious in nature, and are designed to cause trouble. Malicious referrals are not common, but they do occur occasionally.

Initial information is often confused and incomplete. If it is a self-referral, the client may be suffering from shock and anger related to a recent episode of abuse. This may influence the quality of the information disclosed. If the client is young, he or she may well not possess a vocabulary with which to describe the situation. The client may be an infant, whose verbal skills are very poor or non-existent, but whose appearance and behaviour is strongly indicative of abuse. Those who refer themselves are also compelled to come to terms with anxiety about the implications of the referral, such as, 'Will Daddy go to prison?' 'Will I go to prison?' 'Will my friends find out?' 'Will anyone believe me?' 'Will Daddy hit me again?'. The impact of these issues on clients is significant. In relation to self-referrals in particular, and to the participation by the client in an investigation in general, there are many pressures, fears and anxieties which can colour the quality of the initial information. Social workers must always be aware of these pressures, and ought never to minimise their capacity to appear as very powerful and authoritarian figures, and a key source of stress for vulnerable clients

Not all referrals present difficulties. Occasionally, a child who has been physically assaulted will present at school, at the doctor's surgery or the local hospital in such a way that there is very little doubt that abuse has occurred. The alleged abuser will admit immediately that they have inflicted physical injury to the child and will accept responsibility for it. These cases tend not to be the majority. More usual is a situation in which a child's behaviour or the uncorroborated suspicions of an adult, lead those professional agencies involved in child care to be uncertain as to the abuse. It is at this point that an initial investigation must take place, in order to make some judgements about the extent to which the child is at risk.

All referrals ought to be taken very seriously, including anonymous ones, although it is difficult to visit a family following an anonymous telephone call, as you are uncertain about the validity of the referral, and unsure about the reception which may be awaiting. Families about whom referrals are made have a right to know that they have been reported; to deny the public the right to make a complaint, in confidence, about potentially dangerous situations for children, is to limit the degree to which suspicious cases come to the attention of social workers. Consider the following case.

Mrs X telephones the office. She refuses to give her name but says she lives near a family called Adams who have two small children both aged under 5. She says that the children are often left unattended in the evenings, are often to be heard being shouted at and beaten by their father, and that the elder of the two children has a definite hand-print on the side of his head. You check your records in the office and note that there have been three previous anonymous calls over the past year, all of which were found to be exaggerated. On each occasion the Adams family were visited and the children appeared fit and well. Do you visit? In such circumstances, whilst there may be quite legitimate doubts about the validity of the referral, there would be no doubt that a home visit would be made.

Let us suppose that you visit the family during the course of the evening finding both Mr and Mrs Adams at home. You explain the nature of the visit. Mr Adams becomes quite irate and is convinced that the anonymous caller is his next door neighbour with whom he has recently had a row about an unrelated matter. You are told that the children are upstairs in bed. Would you insist upon seeing them? What if the parents refused to let you see them? There are legal means by which the children could be seen in such a case (*see* Chapter 6). Would you invoke the law? Again there would, in my view, be little doubt that the children ought to be seen.

This kind of referral often places social workers in invidious situations, where they have to make quick judgements about what action they will take, attempting to balance alleged risks to children, the rights of parents and the validity or otherwise of the information. Whilst in no way attempting to excuse badly conducted initial investigations, it is easy to see how errors of judgement are made, which on rare occasions can have grave consequences.

Most social work departments have a system which involves staff either taking turns to spend time in the office dealing with initial enquiries, or working full-time for an 'Intake' team, that is, a team which specialises in dealing with short-term work, initial assessments, and so on. Agencies will have internal procedures which guide staff as to actions to be taken at this crucial point in the work. There are some basic requirements of all staff who are involved in the initial stages of work. They must be very good listeners, be able to note accurately any information they receive, and be able to differentiate between fact and opinion. They must have a clear understanding of the legal framework within which they operate, and be able to translate procedure into practice whilst working under stress, often quickly and with limited information.

THE INVESTIGATION OF CHILD ABUSE

At the time when a referral suggestive of child abuse is received by an agency, it is usually the case that some preliminary discussions take place before any action is taken. As has already been suggested, the agencies most closely involved at this stage will normally be social services, the police and health professionals. There has been a great deal of recent attention paid to the ways in which these agencies co-ordinate their actions at the beginning of a child abuse case. Some instances have been publicised of agencies making very quick judgements about what action ought to be taken without reference to professional colleagues from other disciplines. Working under stress, perhaps without the required professional support and guidance, mistakes can be made, and action can be taken which compounds what may already be a difficult situation for the child and its family.

The need for carefully considered responses to referrals, based upon adequate and informed liaison between agencies, has to be balanced against circumstances which often require speedy intervention to protect children. As is usually the case, this balancing act is performed by frontline workers whom it is all too easy to criticise when things go wrong, and when there is the illuminating benefit of hindsight.

Ideally, then, some initial discussion between agencies will take place before any action is taken, particularly when the referral appears to be a substantive one. What are the roles of the three key agencies at this point?

The *social services*, as we have seen, have a responsibility to investigate allegations in order effectively to protect the child. They need to make judgements about the likelihood that abuse has occurred, the extent to which the child has suffered harm as a result of this abuse, and about the likelihood of abuse recurring if no action is taken to protect the child. Initially, physical safety of the child is the overriding focus of intervention and there is a range of emergency measures available in order to help social workers protect children. Social workers are likely to be involved in interviewing suspected victims, collecting information about the background of the situation and, depending upon the circumstances, may well be visiting alleged offenders in order to seek clarification about the abuse.

The *police* have a duty to investigate crime. In that regard their function differs from that of a local authority social worker. However, as most allegations of abuse usually involve illegal acts, the police are often involved, along with social workers, at the point when a referral has been made. A great deal of effort has been made in recent years, on the part of both the police and the social services departments, to work together more effectively at the investigative stage of a child abuse case, to make the process more comfortable and less harrowing for the child. A key feature of this collaboration has been a growing concern about the number of times children have had to repeat their version of events, to different professionals. Joint investigations between police and social workers are now much more common than in the past.

Health workers (GPs, hospital doctors or consultant paediatricians) are obviously concerned primarily with the physical signs and symptoms of abuse. Having said that, too blinkered a view when assessing a case of child abuse can be dangerous. Most medical practitioners will take into account a much wider view of the child than physical health before feeling able to give opinions as to the likelihood that abuse has taken place. Collaboration between all the agencies who may be initially involved is required in order to pool together different perspectives prior to being able to make decisions in other than emergency situations. The role of inter-agency procedures is vital in this regard (*see* Chapter 7).

Case Example

What is the process when a referral is made? Let us suppose that a child complains to his teacher that his father beat him on the bare buttocks with a dog lead. The child is seven years old and seems frightened to go home. His teacher has seen several large weals on the child's buttocks. A referral is made by the head teacher to the social worker at 2 p.m. The social worker, who happens to be on intake duty in the office, makes a careful note of the referral and says to the school that he will visit as soon as he has checked the department's records. He makes the checks and finds that the child and his family are not known. He telephones the health visitor who tells him that the family used to receive visits in the past, but there was never any concern about the welfare of the three children. The police are contacted. Procedure here will vary depending upon local policy. Many areas would encourage the social worker to visit and assess the validity and extent of the abuse prior to contacting the police. They also know nothing about the family pertinent to the alleged incident, but ask to be informed should abuse prove to be strongly suspected. So, the social worker, armed with very little information, visits the school and, in the presence of his teacher, sees the boy. The child becomes agitated and upset and says his father hits him regularly with his hand, a walking stick and the dog's lead.

The boy agrees to accompany the social work home to talk with his parents. In the car, the boy says his two elder sisters never get hit, and that no one likes him at home. Both parents are at home. They deny that the boy has been hit and say he is making the story up. They say he banged his bottom on the edge of the bath the previous night by accident. The social worker persuades the boy's mother to accompany her son and the social worker to the hospital where the boy is examined by a paediatrician. He has several severe marks on his back and buttocks of various colours and shapes, suggestive of abuse with a variety of implements over a period of time. His mother breaks down and cries, telling the doctor that her husband has just lost his job and is under tremendous stress. He lashes out at his son from time to time.

The social worker takes a very distraught mother and child to the office where he contacts the police, who arrange to interview the child and his mother with the social worker. (Note that this repetition might have been avoided if the police had been involved from the start.) After having taken statements from the boy and his mother, the police interview the father, who eventually admits the abuse. He is detained overnight at the police station but plans are to release him on bail the following morning. If you are the social worker in the case, what would you do about the following issues:

1.   Would you allow the boy to remain at home?
2.   Would you want to interview the elder children and have them examined?
3.   Would you wish the father to be prosecuted (knowing that it is likely to increase the stress within the family which has contributed to the abuse)?
4.   The little boy is heartbroken, feeling that he is responsible for sending his father to prison. What would you say to him?
5.   What would you tell the other children?

This is a relatively straightforward case, but it contains within it issues which require fairly rapid attention on the part of the social workers and others who may be involved. In order to gather sufficient information upon which to base decisions about the need to take urgent action to protect children, appropriate interviews with the child, and with those adults who may be implicated in the alleged abuse, must take place. There is a need to limit the number of interviews which should be conducted, and to minimise the stress involved as far as possible.

Interviewing Children

Initial interviews with children who are suspected of having been abused are a critical stage in the effective management of a case. The social worker is often faced with allegations which are not supported by any corroborative medical or witness evidence. This is especially true of sexual abuse. The need to obtain clear, factual information is therefore always very important.

The social worker must always begin with an open-minded view of the case. This is vitally important, because the child must be encouraged to feel that he or she is being taken seriously. They may have tried to tell before, and been ignored. They may feel anxious that they will be unsupported, and have lived for a considerable time in an environment which has taught them to be very wary of adults. They require a supportive response which allows them to feel able to trust the adult/s who are conducting the interviews.

Often, the child has not actually said that they are being abused. Under such circumstances the child may well feel particularly threatened by being questioned about things which may not be true, or which the child had chosen not to disclose. Other than in overt cases of child abuse, it is often vital to allow initial investigation to proceed at a pace which takes into account the wishes and feelings of the child. This may mean that the child is retained in a potentially abusing environment, but there is often little to be gained by coercing

206

children into making comments about things which they find stressful, and about which they are very upset.

The age of the child is of particular importance in relation to the way in which the initial interviews are to be conducted.

Pre-School Children

Very young children are dependent upon adults for their needs. They have great difficulty in coming to terms with the fact that adults in whom they have put their trust have let them down. They are probably confused and upset. Often they will be unable to put their feelings into words. They may be at an age where speech has yet to develop. Observation of these children is obviously a key feature of initial contact, as behaviour may be the only means by which they are able effectively to communicate the fact that they are unhappy and frightened.

Interviews should be relatively brief and direct. Children should, wherever possible, be seen in an environment within which they feel safe and secure. Often they may benefit from having parents present (if they are not implicated in the abuse). This will be discussed in more depth later. Youngsters must never be forced to make any disclosures of abuse, or to explain situations which they do not want to discuss. It is often possible to communicate better with small children in non-verbal ways, through play, art, and by the use of a variety of games and toys.

In relation to sexual abuse in particular, the use of anatomically correct dolls has received a great deal of publicity in recent years. These dolls are made with sexual organs realistically reproduced. They have holes in their bottoms, tongues which come out, and are designed to help young children to explain a variety of sexual abuse about which they may not have developed the appropriate vocabulary, or about which they may be embarrassed to talk. Although they can often be helpful in clarifying what took place, they can also be quite dangerous. Children may be frightened by them, they are sometimes used by people who have not received appropriate training, and they occasionally leave me wondering whether their design and novelty value for children is a factor which, in itself, contributes to what the child might actually say.

It is vital, no matter what the age of the child, to assure them that they are not in trouble, and are not responsible for what may have happened to them. Initial interviews will often prove to be inconclusive, and at such times, agencies will be left with agonising decisions about the need for urgent protective action.

Six- to Thirteen-Year-Old Children

These children are much more aware about the moral issues involved in child abuse. They usually know that abuse is wrong. They often still feel responsible, and may minimise, or deny, what has been taking place. Often, they are acutely self-conscious and there is a need to consider the sex of those people who may interview them, particularly if sexual abuse is an issue.

Here, the social worker needs more time to make a relationship than with younger children, and they often require much more reassurance about what might happen to them if they tell. If possible, children within this age range need to be more involved in the decision-making process. They need to feel that they are important and are listened to.

Children over Thirteen

Adolescents are often involved in issues of control and autonomy with adults, and in particular their parents. They can often have intense reactions to situations, and tend to take life seriously. They may often find it difficult to admit that they are frightened and hurt, and may not easily seek help. They may also display overt emotional or behavioural problems which are a response to their victimisation.

With this age group, it is vital to spend some time trying to establish a reasonable working relationship. The social worker needs to be honest and direct, and avoid talking around the subject. He or she has to be aware of the victim's own reactions to the alleged abuse, and adjust his or her own reactions accordingly. Becoming involved in arguments with this age group is likely to be very counter-productive. It is important to enlist the victim's support in an uncritical and honest manner. Treating clients as equals, with openness and frankness, is usually the most productive way of approaching initial contacts with potential adolescent victims.

MEDICAL EXAMINATIONS

There are a variety of tasks which need to be completed during the course of the early stages of a child abuse case, including information gathering, protecting the child, and assisting those involved to cope with the stress and strains put on them by the intervention of the agencies concerned. The medical examination is a vital component.

No doubt as a result of the publicity surrounding events in Cleveland, the role of the medical examination in child abuse has been the subject of much controversy. Medicals should never be viewed as an automatic response to every situation. One always requires good reasons before subjecting a child to what may be seen as a form of further abuse. In cases of overt and serious physical injury, a medical examination is crucial. However, a social worker is treading on increasingly thin ice if he or she uses medical examinations to attempt to uncover abuse for which there is only a slim suspicion.

If a child hints that they may be being physically abused a pre-emptive medical examination, for which neither the child nor its parents have given consent, may contribute to all kinds of animosity and mistrust. In some cases, it may be advisable to retain a watching brief and perhaps see the child in a normal context, for example, a swimming lesson or gym lesson at school, before deciding to take any action.

The role of medical professionals in relation to the detection of some forms of abuse, particularly neglect and failure to thrive, is important. The validity and timing of medical examinations in all but the most extreme of cases always requires thought. Even for serious forms of abuse, the impact which an unsympathetic medical examination may have indicates the need to proceed with caution. For example, if a young child accuses her father of forcing her to have anal intercourse with him, the impact on the child of being intimately examined, perhaps by a male doctor, in the middle of the anxieties which disclosure creates, could be devastating. All the professional agencies involved are more aware of these issues now than in the past, and are usually ready to balance the need to take action to collect information against the general welfare of the child.

The venue of medical examinations, who does them, the technique, and their timing are all important considerations. A more humane and sympathetic approach is constantly being evolved. Often, these changes for the better have occurred in response to occasions when cases have been mishandled.

Interviewing Alleged Abusers

Let us suppose that an initial interview with the child has been conducted, a decision has been taken not to arrange for an immediate medical, and the other agencies have been liaised with appropriately. At this point, discussing the results of the preliminary inquiries with the alleged abuser may have to be considered. Often this will be a member of the child's immediate family, perhaps the child's parent/s.

Neglected children, and many emotionally abused children, are only viewed as such after periods of observations, during which time efforts are made to minimise the problems which seem to contribute to the abuse. On the other hand, social workers and others often have to see adults in relation to a specific incident. This could be an unexplained injury to a child, or a partial disclosure from the child of abuse.

These initial contacts are especially stressful when they involve the parents of the child. The social worker may be faced with a mixture of anger, shock, denial and threat. It may be that only one parent is implicated, in which case, some difficult decisions have to be made about the way in which interviews are to be conducted. Should you talk to both parents at once, or the alleged offender, or the non-abusing parent? If it appears that a crime has been committed, the police will have to be involved. Should you involve the police from the start, and risk the possibility that their time will be wasted (and the potential stigmatisation to the family of being the subject of a police investigation), or is it best to visit and speak with alleged offenders in order to clarify the facts *before* contacting the police? This can have unfortunate consequences if it helps to alert abusers to the prospects of an investigation, allowing them time to fabricate their explanations.

In this field of work, difficult questions are constantly being posed and answers failing to be provided. Each case is different. As agencies become more aware of the crucial role which inter-agency co-operation plays, particularly in the investigative stages of a case, so these issues are more likely to be addressed before any one agency takes pre-emptive action. The guiding principle, as ever, is the welfare of the child.

ASSESSMENT OF RISK

How can an initial assessment of risk be made? Again, in all but the most severe cases, the evidence must be weighed, such as it is, and an assessment made about the validity of the referral, and about the likelihood of repetition. Sometimes, there must be a decision as to whether the child should remain at home (if home is where the abuse has been taking place), or be separated for a time during which a more comprehensive assessment can be made. How can abuse be substantiated, and how are decisions about emergency action arrived at?

Having received the referral, interviewed the child and the alleged abusers, liaised with other agencies, and possibly having had the child medically examined, the social worker will be faced with information which may be confused, uncorroborated, and conflicting. The following points are of importance when assessing the next step to be taken.

The Nature and Severity of the Abuse

Various forms of abuse, which are easy to detect, and for which there are no other possible explanations, present fewer difficulties for social workers when they come to assess the extent of immediate risk. For example, a social worker is likely to distinguish between an incident of over-chastisement which left a hand-print on the child's legs, and a child who has been burned several times on the palms of its hands with cigarettes.

The Nature of the Referral

If parents quickly realise that they have done something wrong and report the incident, asking for help, then the prognosis for the child may be better than in those cases where the disclosure of abuse is couched in secrecy, confusion and anger.

The Accounts of the Abuse

A clear statement about the abuse is often not available. In relation to physical abuse, the social worker must be more wary of those situations in which the story doesn't match the injury, or where the accounts given by those involved vary.

The Wishes, Feelings and Behaviour of the Child

The demeanour of any children involved in the case must be observed closely. What is the relationship like between child and parents? Is the child fearful? Does the child look to its parents for support? Are there significant differences between the way in which the child behaves inside and outside the home which might indicate anxiety and unhappiness? What does the child say it wants?

History of Abuse

Were the parents abused as children? Have previous referrals been received about the family? We have seen that there may be a link between generations of ill-treatment, and this is a strong indicator that the situation requires very careful consideration.

Family Stress

Marital discord, divorce, isolation and debt are all factors which contribute to the stresses which families can experience. The detection of stress within families about whom there has been a referral of abuse heightens concern for the child's safety.

Temperament

Are the parents volatile, or placid? Do they appear to be prone to outbursts of temper? Perhaps they have very rigid expectations of the child and are unable to comprehend the basic needs which all children have in terms of warmth, food, love and attention. If this is so, the social worker is faced with decisions about the degree to which intervention might modify the parents' attitudes and behaviour, whilst being aware that the child may suffer further abuse during this process.

In order to make a decision about the validity of the referral, the extent of the abuse, and the future risks to the child, the above factors must all be taken into consideration. If the environment within which the child is living does not appear to be safe, decisions then have to be taken about removing the child or, in some cases, persuading the source of the risk of abuse to leave.

IN CARE OR NOT

The impact of abuse on children is great. Social workers are well aware of the possible negative effects on children who are already abused of being removed from their families and placed with strangers, either in residential children's homes or with foster parents. Increasingly, when it is felt that removal from home is the only safe option, alternatives other than a placement in care are considered. Grandparents, other relatives or family friends may be able to provide accommodation for a child at the point of crisis, which allows a more in-depth assessment to be undertaken and which limits the dangers of a total family separation. However, the pressures on the child at the time when action is taken are immense. They often feel responsible for the abuse. They are liable to retract original statements, and may be put under pressures, overt and covert, by extended family members, to deny what was originally said. The abusing parents may still be seen as a threat by a child who is living with relatives. For these reasons, whilst family placements should always be considered as an option, great care needs to be taken.

The decision to remove a child is often taken quickly, by professional staff who are themselves under stress. Mistakes are made. If you were a social worker, and had to decide upon removal of a child, how would you approach the task? If you allowed the child to stay at home, and it received further serious abuse, how would you feel? If you removed the child hastily into care, where it became very upset and anxious about being separated from home, and its parents became 'labelled' in the community as abusers, but the decision subsequently turned out to be wrong, how would you then feel? Having been involved in both situations, I can say that there is little to distinguish between the degrees of guilt and responsibility which are felt. The best that social workers can do, and the most that society can legitimately expect of them, is to make sure that whatever decision is taken is based upon a careful consideration of all the facts available at the time. The decision must be lawful, and it must be taken on the basis of what is considered to be in the best interests of the child.

In my experience, parents and children will be understanding of decisions which are taken if they have been put fully in the picture, if their views and wishes have been sought and noted, and if every effort is made to maintain meaningful communication between all those affected by the situation. Abuse of various kinds is often about secrecy, mistrust and poor communication. If the agencies empowered to protect children work in such a way as to replicate these problems, they are guilty of abuse themselves.

WHEN THINGS GO WRONG

The following story is quoted in order to illustrate the problems which can arise when the initial contacts between client and professional go wrong, or are not handled particularly sympathetically. The account was given to me by an ex-client, who has kindly allowed me to reproduce it, and her views highlight much of what has already been said in this chapter.

At the time when she wrote her material, she was recovering from the most traumatic time of her life. She had disclosed to her mother that she had been sexually abused by her father for the previous nine years, beginning when she was about seven. Her father admitted the offences, which included having sexual intercourse with his daughter on several occasions. At the time when she wrote the following, she was sixteen years of age.

'With reference to my own experience, the interviews last far too long (9.00 p.m. – 1.00 a.m.). During this time a statement had to be taken which was handled quite well by a policewoman, but I think statements ought to be taken by more than one person (two?) so that the victim doesn't have to repeat themselves to several different strangers. In my view it would be a good idea to have a tape recording made of the whole interview/statement. Also I think giving a statement would be easier to give at the victim's own home or place of their choice. e.g. home? school? out of doors? a close relative or friend's home?

'Personally I found it a comfort and ease to have my parent (mother) with me during the statement but in all cases I think the victim should be given the choice of whether or not to have the parents present – the parent could also be involved? or the parent may know already?

'During the time spent at the police station a medical took place which was degrading and totally pointless as there was absolutely no question at all of an assault having taken place recently. I think medicals should be given *only* if it is *certain* that evidence could be found. Also the victim should have the choice of the doctors sex – male/female.

'After the police interviews, statements and medicals were over with, a social worker came. At first I was put off by the idea of "someone else asking the same questions over again" but when our social worker came it was a man, which I thought was going to make things difficult – it didn't – but I think I should have had the choice of male or female. The social worker was easier to talk to than the police and gave my family a lot more information than the police, who promised they would. Our social worker comes once a week, which I think is quite sufficient, but I know that if I need or want him I can contact him at any time.

'I didn't think that my family GP should have been involved as I did not ask to see him. I disagreed with him asking and advising me to see a psychiatrist. This made me feel like someone who was going crazy and needed help. I did not!

'I think the police were in the wrong to ask women from the Rape Crisis Centre to come and see me. The police could have just given me the Centre's address and number, then I could contact them myself. If I felt that I wanted to talk to someone I would have sent for them.

'Finally, I was appalled and upset by the sentence of three years which I felt, being the victim, was inadequate for the harm it had caused both mentally and physically. I was asked by the police and by the social worker if I would stand up in court if need be. I told both that I would if it would help with the sentencing. The police made no further contact concerning the court case at all. I think that I should have been asked if I would like to defend my case. I would have.

'Also I don't think it fair that my mother should have to pay for an injunction order at the time of the person's release as she was told by the police, she would have to do. To tell the truth, I regret, I think, the whole business of telling someone – it was a waste of time as the outcome was hardly worth it for me. Although it may prevent the same person from doing anything similar to a different person.'

16-year-old school girl.

Her words have not been edited or altered in any way. She was describing the way in which she felt about what happened to her in a very practical sense, and was particularly concerned with the impact which the various professionals had on her life. There are many issues which arise out of her comments.

Control Children and young people who are abused by adults are, in a very deep-seated way, stripped of all vestiges of control. In the case of my young client, she had little or no control over her own body-space, which was violated by an adult member of her family who was in a position of power and authority over her. It is for this reason that it is vital to allow victims to be actively involved in decisions which are taken when the abuse comes to light, so as to begin at the very earliest stage possible the process by which control and autonomy can be restored.

This client was upset about being referred, without her knowledge or consent, to social services and Rape Crisis.

Investigation This case highlights a bad example of initial investigation. The disclosure seems to have been handled rather inflexibly by the police, who processed the information

217

in a regimented fashion without reference to the needs of the client and her mother.

Imagine the state of confusion which the girl must have been feeling on the evening in question. She was taken to the police station and interviewed over a four-hour period which included a medical examination. It would be difficult to accept that under such circumstances anyone would be in a position to produce accurate statements. No opportunity to add to the original statements was offered, even though the client remembered other points later.

Medical examination Again, her comments are very real criticisms of bad practice. For a girl who is the complainant in a sex abuse case involving a man to be subjected to an intimate medical examination by a male doctor at the point of disclosure, will hardly help her to relax. Whilst her views on the likelihood of evidence being found are open to question, her comments indicate her feeling that she was not involved in the process, and that her treatment constituted a form of further abuse.

Parental involvement This client was lucky in that the non-abusing parent was supportive and caring. She was believed, and was not put under any pressure to retract her statements. This is not always so. The balance between the rights of parents and the need to protect the child is often a very difficult one to achieve.

Communication After abuse has come to light, there is often a lengthy wait until the case is eventually processed in the courts, if this is felt to be appropriate. My client complained of not having been given sufficient information during this time. We must all be sensitive to the needs of victims in the aftermath of a disclosure. This, once again, relates to questions of power and control. If you tell someone a secret, you often feel frightened about what the consequences might be. Victims of child abuse will often feel anxious about the outcome of their disclosure. One way in which this can be ameliorated is for good communication to take place during the time immediately following the disclosure, in order to help the victim, and other people who will be affected by the abuse coming to light.

Damaged goods syndrome   Some victims of abuse feel to a great extent that they were responsible, that they have been singled out for ill-treatment because they are damaged, and deserve to be treated badly. This client was most upset at having been advised by her family GP, no doubt with the best of intentions, to seek psychiatric help. As she says, this made her feel as if she was ill. This also re-emphasises the need to allow clients to be part of the process of decision-making which follows disclosure of abuse.

Sentencing   Again, we hear a plea for clients to be more involved in the decisions which are taken on their behalf. In this case, her father pleaded guilty to the charges, and the police felt that there was no need for her to give any evidence. Interestingly, we often feel that we must always avoid, wherever possible, the need for young victims to be subjected to court proceedings. I would dispute the validity of this view. For some clients, the experience of court can be therapeutic, in spite of the dangers of cross-examination by defence counsel and the rather unnerving atmosphere which formal courtroom settings create. Some children benefit from being believed by the system (as represented by the courts). They can experience a sense of relief and vindication. As to whether they also achieve a feeling that justice is being done will depend on their attitude to the final outcome. My client felt positively harmed by what she described as a lenient sentence.

Her final words are very sad. Having gone through the process, and having been dealt with by a whole range of professionals from different agencies, all of whom were doing their best for her, she felt ultimately let down, and regretted having told what was happening to her. It is because this

219

sentiment is echoed by a significant number of those who go through similar experiences that we must constantly seek ways of improving our responses to clients at the initial, and most crucial, stages of work.

ASPECTS OF INITIAL THERAPY

To distinguish initial investigation from assessment and treatment is artificially to compartmentalise a process throughout which there are no clear divisions. Thoughtful and sympathetic early intervention can have therapeutic benefits for children and adults involved in child abuse. It is, therefore, important to begin to establish some of the following themes during the initial phases of intervention which can be expanded upon later in the process.

Trust It is vital that those professionals involved in initial intervention with clients who may have been abused are able to form a trusting relationship. In the case of the young girl who was abused by her father, her initial treatment was likely to obstruct the extent to which she would be prepared to trust the worker/s involved in the aftermath of the abuse. There are those clients who benefit greatly from some form of treatment, when the initial crisis has passed (*see* Chapter 10). In order to benefit from any treatment undertaken, there has got to be some basis for trust. If clients are not involved enough in the decision-making process, or if professionals promise things which they can't achieve, then it is difficult to recoup that breach of trust at a later stage.

For example, there are times when clients will wish to talk to social workers, and others, in confidence. As we have seen, social work staff operate within a legal and procedural framework, which does not allow a completely free hand. Social workers are not always able to guarantee confidentiality to clients where abuse is concerned.

Similarly, social workers are not always able to give guarantees that children will be safe. Our case analysis

220

showed that the client was exposed to some degree of 'system abuse', where her treatment at the hands of the professionals involved amounted, in her opinion, to a form of further abuse. We are unable to give unequivocal statements that we will ensure children are protected from re-abuse. We sometimes make mistakes. We sometimes are unable to take effective protective action because of a lack of evidence.

Who is the client?   In a case of intra-familial abuse, there are likely to be a variety of individuals who are deeply affected. The child/children, the abuser(s) and the non-abusing parent, and other children in the household. At the time when the abuse begins to come to light, all of these people are, to varying degrees, likely to require help. Social workers can easily become sucked into the web of emotional confusion which is often a feature of abusing families. Clearly, at the early stages of investigation at least, the children are the clients. Their interests are the first consideration, even if this means that the needs of others go unmet.

Children who are involved in situations where they are being abused within their own homes are likely to respond warily to workers who they feel are unwilling or unable to give individual attention to them.

Structure   As we have seen during our examination of case histories, a great many abusing families are confused, have unclear systems of communication and live in a network which is forever shifting. One of the most important things which can be done during early contact with such families is to bring some structure to bear. This can be introduced by a system of regular visiting, so that clients know in advance when they are going to be seen. This can prove to be one of the most therapeutically beneficial aspects of social work intervention. It can help clients learn to exercise self-discipline, so that they experience at least one relationship which is conducted within clearly understood boundaries, and which is adhered to by the worker.

Similarly, setting limits to the length of each contact with the client can have positive effects, in introducing structure to an environment which may be, in some respects, lacking in controls. Time-limited sessions also allow the client to be more circumspect about what they choose to say. As we have seen, it is important to allow victims to be in control, as much as is possible. Open-ended sessions can be seen as coercive and threatening.

Communication Of vital importance during the early stages of a case is the need to encourage productive channels of communication between all those involved. If the alleged abuser is retained in police custody, or if the victim is removed from home and placed with relatives or in care, this can prove difficult. It may be that early contact between the victim and family is not appropriate. Perhaps the child is too fearful of re-abuse. Perhaps the adults involved have extremely negative feelings about the child, so much so that contact could prove destructive.

Most children benefit from being able to communicate with their families, even if they have been badly abused. It is often difficult to contemplate, but almost all abused children retain a very strong bond with the parents who abuse them. They desperately want the abuse to stop, but this doesn't mean they don't love their parents. In order that the nature of the abuse can be clarified, the responsibility for the abuse must be set in its proper context. In recognition of the fact that it is unlikely that all contacts with the abusing parent are negative, access between children and abusers (especially if the abusers happen to be the child's carers) is usually beneficial.

The social worker must take into account the wishes and feelings of the child and adults, and weigh the evidence in relation to potential damaging effects before making decisions, but it is usually the case that children will suffer if no contact is organised. Even if, for whatever reason, direct contact is inappropriate, phone calls and letters can serve to retain whatever positives might exist in the relationship between abused and abuser.

Even if the child remains at home, there are likely to be important communication issues which need to be urgently addressed. All those involved within the household are likely to have great difficulty in expressing their feelings about the abuse. They will need help to facilitate this process. It seems that we all have a tendency to keep our feelings to ourselves. We often are able to talk about things that have happened to us in a descriptive way, but find it more difficult to put our feelings about events and other people into words. This tendency, in relation to a situation of child abuse, about which most family members will have a range of feelings, can often be an initial stumbling block to the therapeutic process.

I also think that we are, in general, more at ease when being critical about other people than when we are being positive. In order immediately to move away from a view that an abusing relationship is all bad, workers will often need to spend time encouraging those involved to look at the positive, as well as the negative aspects of the inter-relationships involved.

In order to test out my theory that we seem more able to talk negatively about people than to say complimentary things, perhaps you could spend five minutes doing the following: in relation to someone you know well, either a family member or a friend, make two lists comprising ten good points and ten bad points. My guess is that the positive list would be harder to do, especially if the lists were limited to aspects of the person's character, rather than descriptions of their habits and appearance. The point is that feelings are hard to communicate. Work with families involved in abuse is often about helping feelings to be shared, so as to improve the levels of natural respect and understanding between family members who have either lost, or never had, the capacity to inter-relate in other than a damaging and abusive way.

EFFECTS ON PROFESSIONALS

The possible effects of abuse on both victims and those who ill-treat them are serious. They can also be damaging for those professionals who work either exclusively or extensively with child abuse cases, particularly in the early stages of the work when they are more likely to be faced with points of crisis.

Up to a point, stress may tend to enhance a person's capacity to work well. However, too much stress can lead to generalised ill health, an inability to think issues through carefully, and a decreased capacity to take responsive action. I do not feel able to comment on whether social work carries with it more stress than other jobs. I do feel, though, that social workers are from time to time faced with decisions which and have far-reaching consequences for the lives of other people, and to that extent, the potential effects of stress may be particularly important. Stress is linked to the nature of the job. Dealing with people in crisis, and making decisions which may involve eliciting anger in some and trauma in others, can have a wearying effect. The possible consequences for clients and social workers themselves if serious mistakes are made are an obvious source of stress.

Supervision has a major part to play in helping professionals cope with the stress of the work. It is important to be able to talk with other colleagues about the work with which you are involved, and to receive guidance and support in times of difficulty. These all help to maintain staff at a sufficiently high level of functioning for them to cope, and work for the benefit, rather than to the detriment, of their clients. The environment in which staff must work is also a contributory factor to the production of stress. Cramped and inadequate accommodation with poor facilities for interviewing does little to assist in the task. Too heavy a caseload will also limit the general effectiveness of staff. A high turnover of social workers in those areas of the country which have particularly vulnerable populations does not encourage the development of enhanced practice.

Training for staff can, in my view, also produce stress and professional frustration. Social workers and others are becoming increasingly aware of the need to respond in a sophisticated manner to child abuse. Just as the level of public awareness is increasing, so are social workers, police, health professionals, and so on, learning more and more about the impact of abuse on clients and modifying their responses accordingly. However, if the rate of understanding, heightened by training, outstrips the resources which are available with which to practice new techniques, frustration and stress will be the inevitable consequences. A social worker with little training and no insight into the work may cope personally with a caseload of fifty. A well-trained and committed worker may struggle at times with a caseload of half that number, because he has a greater awareness of what could be achieved, given adequate time and space.

CONCLUSIONS

The initial phase of a case is crucial, therefore, to the future resolution of the issues involved. Whilst there are times when emergency action to protect children is essential, we are now becoming much more aware that most cases benefit from a calm, reasoned approach, during which adequate liaison with other agencies for the purpose of collecting relevant information is the most productive way in which to proceed. The interests of the child are always uppermost in the minds of those who must investigate cases of child abuse. There is no magic formula available to help us make assessments of risk and that is why, from time to time, serious errors of judgement will be made. I both hope and believe that, in the future, such errors will increasingly relate to genuine mistakes made with the interests of the child paramount, rather than to an absence of informed judgement and proper planning.

10 Treatment Issues in Child Abuse

Whilst many people are able to deal adequately with periods of abuse in their childhood, and grow up to lead a contented and fulfilled life, there are others who become extremely debilitated by their experiences. The case for treatment has been established, and the different aspects of it need to be examined.

WHO REQUIRES TREATMENT?

It is my view that all children and their families who have been involved in substantial abuse would benefit from some form of treatment. However, unless there is agreement between all parties that treatment will take place, or a legal relationship between the child and the statutory agencies, then the prospects of any meaningful work being undertaken are severely limited. It is also dangerous to use 'severity of abuse' as the criteria for deciding upon the need for treatment. The extent to which children are damaged by abuse depends on a whole range of factors, only one of which is the actual severity of the abuse.

Children may behave in such a way as to give extremely clear indications indeed that there is a need to address issues concerning the abuse which has taken place. My fear is that the potential long-term benefits of treatment are denied to whole groups of clients, whose reticence and ambivalence in the aftermath of abuse are misinterpreted by those conducting preliminary investigations as an indication that they are coping well. My evidence for saying this is based only upon the experiences I have had of dealing with the children of adults who themselves were abused in childhood, many of whom have said that their treatment needs were ignored or dismissed. This has two important implications. Firstly, the fact that treatment was not offered to some of these people may subsequently have contributed to the eventual abuse of their own children. Secondly, if their children do go into treatment, some parents may have a tendency to block the possible effectiveness of treatment, feeling that their child may be receiving attention which they were denied.

Ideally, all cases of abuse, whether severe or not, would be properly assessed at the time they came to light with a view to making a decision about the need for treatment. However, social workers are often left in a position where they must prioritise their work between many competing demands upon their time. Some cases are assessed well. Others are not. Some clients, for a variety of reasons, are unable to enter into a voluntary contract with those who would be able to provide treatment. Also, we have seen how it is that the majority of abuse never comes to light. For all of these reasons, large numbers of abused children, and those who abuse them, never receive any help.

WHEN DOES TREATMENT BEGIN?

There are those who compartmentalise the process of client/worker interaction into distinct phases of work. They see investigation, assessment and treatment as being mutually exclusive tasks, with very different aims and objectives. Indeed, I have attempted to distinguish between early intervention and long-term treatment. However, this is to oversimplify a process which is far more complex. There are several aspects of the initial intervention in a case which, if dealt with correctly, can have significant long-term thera-peutic benefits for the client (*see* Chapter 9). Similarly, although assessment is often singled out as being a discrete task, my view is that the process is a continuous one. Social workers and others who are working with an abusing family will be reassessing the case throughout the period of their involvement.

In many abuse cases, it is useful to distinguish between the initial intervention/information-gathering period, and any therapy or treatment which is subsequently offered. By the time that any treatment programmes are set up, both the workers in the case and the family will have a reasonable grasp of the nature of the abuse which has been uncovered. Although there may be a great deal of denial involved, and the client may from time to time retract from, or add to, the initial disclosure, there is likely to be some degree of understanding about what has been alleged. Any criminal proceedings will be being processed, and the child will have been placed in an environment, whether home or elsewhere, which seems to afford a reasonable amount of protection from abuse. I do not wish to imply here that everyone will agree that the child has been abused, or that the child is correctly placed. These could remain as key treatment issues which may never be resolved to everyone's satisfaction. The process of introducing a carefully considered package of treatment must, to some degree, depend upon some of the immediately pressing considerations having been dealt with.

For example, it is difficult to engage an abuser in meaningful treatment if he is in prison awaiting trial, the result of which may be a custodial sentence or not. It certainly hampers prospects for family meetings if one or more key family members are being detained elsewhere. If those involved in providing treatment are uncertain as to the nature of the abuse that has allegedly taken place, this can also severely limit the degree to which any therapeutic intervention will be either appropriate or valid.

Often there arrives a time in cases of alleged abuse when a plateau is reached, beyond which it is impossible to travel in terms of simply accumulating more and more information, or when the effect of waiting for other events such as criminal or civil proceedings to take their course allows the child and its family to slowly drift back into old patterns of abuse. The family could also develop entrenched positions with regard to blame and responsibility which delayed treatment will find very difficult to break down.

WHO SHOULD PROVIDE TREATMENT?

There is a large group of people, both professional and otherwise, who may well be involved in the treatment of child abuse. These could include any combination of the following: social worker/NSPCC worker/residential child care officer, psychologist, psychiatrist, probation officer, foster parent, parent, health professional (for example doctor or health visitor), private counsellor, and voluntary organisations (child care action groups, Rape Crisis Centre, and so on).

Whilst there are no rules available which would indicate who should provide treatment in any particular case, the following are a number of issues which would need to be considered before determining how an individual case would be dealt with.

Wishes and feelings of clients Many clients, whether children or adults, express strong feelings about having contact with people whose role it is to provide treatment. Treatment will involve the discussion of personal details which are painful to clients, and which can often cause embarrassment, strong feelings of anger, despair and guilt. Whatever the techniques used by the therapist in an attempt to retain these feelings in a workable context, the intrusion of an outsider into a family group which, by its very nature may be isolated and bedevilled with secrets, is a threatening experience for most people to contemplate.

Children and adults may display a preference for a therapist of a specific gender or age. Some abusers resent being seen by workers who have no children of their own. 'How can you know what it's like bringing up kids if you've never had any?'

Whilst these, and other issues are to be borne in mind when trying to meet the needs of clients, the professional is always working within limitations in terms of the availability of resources. In my view, the therapist needs to be aware of potential areas of conflict, and be prepared to discuss them. This may be therapeutically productive. For example, if a male sexual offender objects to being seen by a female worker, this may be usefully discussed in terms of the client's fear of women and his need to control relationships, both of which may be key issues which led to the sexual abuse in the first place.

The wishes and feelings of clients must always be acknowledged and, if conflict proves too extreme, accommodated. However, the social worker needs to be aware of being manipulated by abusing adults into providing help on their terms. Therefore, the ability to use difficulties which arise out of the reaction to the therapist and/or therapy for positive ends must be developed and encouraged.

Should the therapist have been involved in initial work?
This is a common dilemma for social workers in allocating cases. There is one school of thought which suggests that a potential therapeutic relationship can be so damaged by the process of initial intervention that the persons who were involved at the time when the case was first investigated ought not to be involved in the treatment which may follow. Initial investigation may involve the use of authority, the application of the law and enforcing decisions to which family members object, such as the removal of a child into care. It is argued that these issues subsequently inhibit the development of a working relationship within which treatment can take place. Others feel that this is not the case, and that clients can benefit greatly from the continuity which is provided by being dealt with by the same people throughout. A relationship of trust can quickly emerge when the case worker is able to demonstrate clarity of thought and a determination to help throughout the initial crisis period.

My view is that it is often better to separate out, as far as possible, initial intervention from treatment, in terms of staff involved. I think that early contacts can be traumatic and confusing, and it is difficult for both client and worker readily to accept that the person who came to do initial interviews with the police or otherwise, who organised medical examinations, and who took emergency protective action is now calling under a different guise altogether. Some attempts to separate out these interlinking functions can also help to limit the overpowering effect on workers which child abuse work can have. The setting up of effective treatment requires considerable thought and planning. It is often difficult for workers who have been heavily involved in cases at the point of crisis to take a step back from the turmoil which is often a feature of abusing families. However professional, workers can develop quickly-formed first impressions of families which can be difficult to shake off, even in the face of significant evidence from the family that their early judgements were ill founded. This can subsequently prove to be damaging for objective long-term treatment.

The decision to involve different people in cases at different times has implications for resources. Certainly within social services, I have been aware of decisions about who should provide treatment in these cases being based upon the availability of social work staff with the training, confidence and competence to do the work, rather than upon the needs of the clients. It could well be argued that the resources should always be there to provide the best for clients caught up in abusing situations. In reality that is not always the case.

WHO IS THE CLIENT?

In a case of intra-familial child abuse, it is not always easy to determine who the client is. Obviously, the social worker's initial contacts are based around the need to promote the safety and welfare of the abused child, but when they begin to consider longer-term treatment, it becomes more difficult to be clear about where the major focus of the work lies.

There are a great many factors which can contribute to the production of abuse, and each family member is likely to have

231

unmet needs which must be addressed. There are also a wide variety of factors external to the family which can significantly increase the likelihood that abuse will take place. Should the therapist concentrate upon relieving the socio-economic stresses to which a family may be subjected, or ought they to work with the victim, the abuser, the non-abusing parent, brothers and sisters of the victim or the family as a whole? Again, there are no universally accepted rules which govern the way in which these questions are answered. Each case is unique, and the focus of the work will depend upon the issues which have emerged as the main factors contributing to the abuse following a process of assessment.

With a complex case of abuse, in which a variety of family members are victims, where there are significant marital problems and a history of abuse in the parents' childhood which have remained unresolved, it becomes an extremely daunting prospect for one person to be responsible for doing all the work. Workers can become overloaded with information and have little time available to think about the effectiveness of their approach. They can become deflected from agreed treatment plans by crises which can develop within the family during the course of their involvement, and in some cases may begin to replicate the confusion and helplessness which is a feature of many of the families they are trying to assist. Victims of abuse may become wary of therapists whom they share with others, notably the abuser. They may, understandably, be unwilling to trust someone who is not working with them alone. The same can be true of other needy people in the family network, of which there are likely to be several. Therefore, just as there needs to be great care taken about separating out initial from longer-term work, so there must be careful consideration of the advantages and disadvantages of allocating workers to different sections of the family network during the treatment of the case.

These issues are complex, and are often affected by factors other than an assessment of the needs of the client. It is all too easy to concentrate solely on the victim, and to ignore, or minimise, the influence of other key people, notably the

232

abuser. This is because we often feel more comfortable working with victims than with offenders, and are less likely to feel overwhelmed by the multiplicity of issues with which we can be presented, if we engage in work with other family members. In intra-familial abuse, to ignore the needs of the whole family membership, with the possible exception of the victim, is to do little to prevent the abuse from happening again.

SOME TREATMENT TARGETS

Treatment must be targeted upon the possible effects of abuse on victims (*see* Chapter 4), and depend upon the results of a comprehensive assessment in each case. However, child abuse can have grave implications for other people as well as the victim. Abuse generally indicates the need for treatment of the abuser, and there are others (such as the non-abusing parent and non-abused children) in the household who are likely to have been affected sufficiently to require some degree of therapy. There are possible treatment targets for all these groups, and for the family as a whole.

The Abuser

Denial This is an extremely common feature of many abusers. They become locked into a pattern of denial so strong that they often begin to believe that they are really not to blame. This pattern of denial must be addressed quickly in order that the treatment of the other people involved (principally the victim) can progress. However, the denial can be very pervasive, used as it is in order to ward off feelings of guilt and the fear of possible consequences. Many abusers will return from prison, having been convicted of a variety of offences against children, and will deny that they ever did anything wrong. A more subtle form of denial is to shift the blame on to someone or something else, for example, 'I was drunk and don't remember what I did', 'God told me to do it',

'If he had behaved I wouldn't have fractured his skull'. Overcoming denial is a major aim in therapy with abusers.

Guilt Some abusers will admit to their responsibility, and can become totally debilitated by the overwhelming feelings of guilt. This is especially true of those adults who injure a child during a fit of temper, and who in all other particulars may be model parents. For such adults, the realisation of what they have done may be quite devastating, and the feelings of shame and guilt which result are likely to be central targets for treatment.

Self-awareness Adults who significantly abuse children, either by acts of commission or omission, are likely to have serious problems, indicated by the behaviour in which they indulge. For example, sexual abusers require treatment directed at their sexual behaviour. Those who physically assault children require therapy which focuses upon their violent behaviour. Whilst these points may seem to be obvious, the nature of child abuse is so complex that therapists can sometimes fail to address these central issues, being easily deflected on to some of the many other potential targets of work. The need for abusers to be helped to examine their abusive behaviour is crucial, if a realistic attempt to modify their relationships with children is to be made.

Control Underpinning much of the behaviour of abusers are issues of control and power. Sexual abuse, physical abuse and wilful neglect may all contain elements relating to a deep-seated need to exercise control and power over others. Perhaps adults who are unable to achieve levels of desired control with other adults find children more susceptible to their wishes. It may be that some adults themselves feel powerless and insignificant (lack of status, low income, poor self-image, and so on), and react by creating a self-fulfilling fantasy in which they wield power and authority, with children being on the receiving end. The exact source of the

need to feel control over others is another important therapeutic target.

Unresolved past issues   In Chapter 5 it was suggested that
a significant minority of abusers were themselves abused as
children, and some of the case histories which were examined
in Chapter 3 illustrated this point. That being so, it is always
necessary, during the course of treatment, to look at aspects of
the abuser's own experiences of being parented. This enables
us to examine whether or not unresolved issues from the past
are being replayed in the present.

Parenting skills   Some youngsters are neglected, emotionally
and physically abused, as a direct consequence of a lack of
knowledge on the part of the parent about how to bring up
children. It is an impossible task to determine the boundaries
between adequate and inadequate parenting. We all have a
view, which is likely to differ in varying degrees from the
opinions of others. However, some parents lack very basic
information about the need to protect, feed and clothe their
children adequately. Significant numbers of parents un-
wittingly abuse their children emotionally because they are
unaware of the need to display love and affection towards
their children. These issues often present a baseline for
treatment, in that practical parenting skills must be developed
before any progress in other areas becomes possible.

Positive experiences   Therapeutic work with those involved
in child abuse, whether abusers, victims or other family
members, can sometimes create an atmosphere in which only
the negative aspects of the situation are discussed. This can
often be misleading. Along with the abuse, other, more
positive features of family life will be present. These need to be
acknowledged and, if possible, developed by the family with
the help of the therapist.

It may be that the abuser is so locked in to a pattern of
behaviour as to be devoid of 'normal' positive experiences. If
so, the treatment task is to begin to help the abuser to develop

other more socially-accepted patterns of behaviour. This may well lessen the desire to abuse, and will help to build up a more positive self-image, which may in turn contribute to increased self-control.

The Non-Abusing Parent

In cases of intra-familial abuse, it is often a source of surprise that the non-abusing parent either didn't know that the abuse was taking place, or was unable to prevent it. In many instances, this is so. Some children are sexually victimised for years without other members of the household being aware of the fact. Just as victims of various forms of abuse are persuaded not to report by threats of violence, so are non-abusing parents sometimes coerced into remaining silent. It may be that they are physically threatened, or that they fear the consequences for the future of the family if they tell anyone. This can create a series of treatment issues for this group of people, many of whose needs are often neglected in the therapeutic process.

Confusion After the discovery of abuse, the non-abusing parent may be flooded by a mixture of competing feelings. They may feel anger towards their abusing partner, anger towards the victim for admitting that the abuse has occurred, and guilt. This feeling of guilt may relate to concern that they failed to stop the abuse, or were unaware that it was happening.

Failure to protect This may be a real issue, depending upon the circumstances of the case. Some commentators feel that this is always a factor to be taken into account. My feeling is that, having experienced some cases in which there was no possibility of the non-abusing parent being able to protect the child, each case must be judged on its merits. Too rapid a judgement about the complicity of the non-abusing parent in the abuse sometimes serves to shift the focus of responsibility away from the abuser. This must not be allowed to happen.

236

Relationship with the victim   In some cases of abuse, in particular sexual abuse, there may be difficulties in communication between the victim and the non-abusing parent. These may either have prevented the victim from seeking help or may have limited the degree to which the non-abusing adult was prepared to follow up any indications of abuse about which they were aware.

Parenting skills and unresolved past issues   Just as for the abuser, these factors may be important considerations in therapy for the non-abuser. Perhaps a parent failed to respond to the overt abuse of a child by the other parent due to a lack of insight into the needs of children. It may be that an adult was so severely abused as a child that he or she is now oblivious to the potential damage which a similar form of abuse can cause to children.

It is important to note that there are many cases of abuse of all types where responsibility must be shared equally by all adults in the household. The systematic neglect or emotional abuse of a child will rarely be achieved without at least the tacit acceptance of all adults having close contact with the child. It may also be the case that the child was abused by someone other than a member of the household, for example, an aunt, uncle or babysitter. In my experience, these cases still create treatment issues for the parents of the child, in relation to aspects of guilt, blame, anger and possibly failure to protect. I am simplifying the scenario in such a way as to exclude extra-familial abuse, but I would not wish to mislead the reader into thinking that child abuse is only practised by parents on their own children.

Brothers and Sisters

Just as in the case of a non-abusing parent, the brothers and sisters of a victimised child are often a neglected group in terms of treatment. However, if one or more children in a family group have escaped the abuse which has been inflicted

237

upon another, there may well be difficulties which require attention in therapy.

Anger This may be directed at a variety of people. Obviously it may be aimed at the abusers. However, it could also be directed at the victim for telling about the abuse and perhaps, as a consequence, for causing the family unit to be disrupted. It may be vented at the non-abusing parent for failing to protect the victim.

Guilt There may be understandable feelings of guilt associated with a failure to protect another family member from harm. There may also be feelings of guilt about why one child rather than another was abused. For example, if one child in a family is being singled out for physical abuse (as sometimes happens), the other children may subsequently feel responsible for appearing to allow their brother or sister to receive the abuse instead of them – 'Whilst my Dad was assaulting my sister, he wasn't hurting me'.

Neglect After abuse has been discovered, it may be that a great deal of work is undertaken by the therapist with the victim and the parents. Other children in the household may react adversely to being left out of this process, especially if the therapy leads the parents to focus an increased amount of positive attention on the victim.

Denial Again, this is potentially a key treatment issue for this group, just as it is for all the others involved. The children who haven't been abused may tend to minimise the harm done in order to protect the abuser. They may actively victimise the abused child, to coerce a change in the story which threatens the continuation of the present family dynamics.

The Family Group

Each member of a family in which abuse is taking place has a different perspective on the issues involved. It is also important to appreciate that the treatment which is offered following abuse takes into account the need to explore its causes and effects with the family as a whole, and with particular members of the family in different combinations. The effectiveness of individual treatment can easily be diminished if its gains are not somehow brought to the family as a whole, and if the family, as a distinct unit, is not encouraged to examine aspects of the way in which it functions, in order both to understand why it was that abuse occurred, and to explore means by which its future recurrence can be minimised.

Two key issues for 'family' treatment are trust and communication, both of which will often relate equally to the individual groupings we have just discussed, and also to the victim.

Trust   The betrayal of trust is a central feature in all cases of child abuse, and will require urgent attention by the therapist, both in individual sessions with all concerned and in work with the family as a whole. The victim's trust in the abuser/s has been violated. The adults may be mistrustful of each other, and this distrust is likely to reflect upon relationships between other family members. The therapist will be a threatening intrusion for some or all of the family members, and the barriers created by a general lack of trust will usually hamper the development of a therapeutic relationship.

Communication   Many abusing families do not communicate with each other. Individual's needs are often not met because the means by which they become known are distorted or blocked by the lack of proper channels of communication. It may be that parents are immature, or too wrapped up in their own problems to see the needs of the family as a whole. It could be that power and control within the family is unevenly distributed to the extent that powerless family members are unable to communicate their needs to others. A whole range of sub-groups can develop within families, which may serve to exclude some members, making them feel that they are not important enough to have opinions. If communication is seen to be a problem, the examination of inter-relationships within the family unit, in an attempt to untangle the sources of the problem, will be a principal aim of treatment.

Isolation We have seen earlier in the book how some families exclude themselves or are excluded from the community in which they live. This may often be a deliberate attempt to prevent the discovery of the abuse, or it may be as a result of the nature of the family, and be a factor which contributes to the eventual commission of abuse. In treatment, attempts must be made to explore this aspect of family life, with a view to enhancing the confidence of the family unit, to help it to reach out to any supportive networks which may be available in the locality. Many experts feel that a good indication of the success of treatment is the extent to which the family as a whole, and individual members of it, are able to develop links outside the home, make new friends and participate in activities with other people.

COMMON THERAPEUTIC METHODS

Individual Treatment for the Victim

After dealing with immediate problems, such as making the child safe, and eliminating or significantly minimising the degree to which the child is at risk of further significant abuse in the near future, the professional must then begin the process of helping the victim to come to terms with the abuse, and with the factors which may have contributed to it.

The goal of therapy with individual clients who may have been abused is to enable them to trust in the therapeutic relationship, and to help them to express their feelings about their experiences, both positive and negative. We have already seen some of the barriers which are likely to exist within the relationship which the therapist has with the child. These obstacles cannot be ignored, and must be dealt with in treatment. Consistency is a key factor in the process, as the child will gain from time-limited sessions at regular intervals.

Whatever technique is used in individual work with children, the aim is to facilitate communication. The means by which this is approached must depend upon the age of the child and its particular abilities. For example, it will be of very little use talking to a five-year-old child from the other side of a desk in a social worker's office. This is to make the mistake of imposing an adult world on to that of a child and may, for sexually abused children in particular, simply reinforce the extent to which they have been used by adults as miniature grown-ups. Young children communicate through play, and if the therapist wishes to engage in meaningful dialogue with youngsters, some form of play therapy must be undertaken. The use of dolls, painting, story books, puppets and drama requires a degree of skill and interpretative ability on the part of the adult involved, but it can often help children to release strong feelings about their experiences which otherwise might remain locked within.

As an example of this, a colleague of mine was working with an eight-year-old who had been physically and sexually abused by her father over a number of years. She was unable to describe in words her feelings towards her parents. My colleague encouraged her to make small plasticine puppets during periods of play therapy which were used to act out little domestic scenes. These scenes started off being totally imaginary, until on one occasion the girl decided to make a puppet which she called 'Daddy'. This doll came in for some severe physical treatment from the other dolls during the domestic scenes, which became gradually more and more associated with the girl's real-life family. After each session the 'Daddy' puppet was locked away in a tin box and very carefully the box was locked inside a desk drawer at the insistence of the girl. Her behaviour became calmer over a period of time during which she began to talk a little about her feelings for her father. She eventually threw the dolls away.

In this case, the therapist was able to develop a relationship of trust with the child and, by using a medium with which the

241

child felt comfortable, was able to help the girl to find expression to some of her feelings about what had been done to her. This example is interesting in that it illustrates an important feature in the relationship between a therapist and a child abuse victim, namely the issue of autonomy. Their experience has often been one of complete subservience to the wishes and whims of the adults with whom they live. A key aim for treatment is to begin to allow the child to establish some control over its life, and this can be developed productively within the structure of the therapeutic process, by fulfilling victims' needs to be involved as far as is practical in decisions which are taken about them. They must be encouraged to assert their wishes and feelings upon those around them. Not only will this go some way towards healing the hurt which the abuse may have caused, it will help to make the child less susceptible to re-victimisation in future, because self-assertive children are less obvious targets to potential abusers.

Many abused children will not have experienced the opportunity to participate in a relationship with an adult where their feelings are respected, and where their opinions are listened to. Some children will have been denied any opportunity to indulge in imaginative play, and, as a result, may be very slow to engage in the therapeutic process. Helping the child to develop means of expression, and the provision of a framework within which communication can happen, are aims for treatment which transcend the experience of abuse, in terms of being significant gains for the victim in all facets of their life.

Work which was undertaken during the initial investigative stage requires development and consolidation during treatment. The reality of the abuse, particularly in relation to responsibility for its commission, must always be a feature of therapy, in order to help the victim to create a realistic interpretation of events. Positive elements in the child's life must be acknowledged, along with the abuse, so as to avoid an over-concentration on negative factors, and to discourage the child from seeing him or herself purely as an abuse victim.

242

Individual Treatment for the Abuser

The barriers which can interfere with meaningful therapy for abusers are severe. We have already discussed some of these, including denial, guilt and lack of communication. For those who abuse children physically and/or sexually, the motivation to engage in treatment may be so weak as to make it meaningless. There are those who argue that any treatment for offenders which doesn't occur within a framework of legal sanctions (go into treatment or go to prison) will fail.

Individual therapy with the abuser must have at its core the need to place the responsibility for the abuse firmly with the abuser. In some cases this may not be immediately self-evident. For example, a father may well have been driven to assault his son physically due to the boy's persistent bad behaviour. However, the factors which might have contributed to the commission of the abuse must not be allowed to detract from the responsibility that the adult always has, to respond in an appropriate, non-abusive way to the needs of children. Over time, discussions about the nature of the responsibility for the abuse may lead to demonstrations of genuine remorse and feelings of guilt. On the other hand, these feelings can often be feigned in an attempt to defend against the intrusions of the therapeutic process.

Abusers need to be helped to understand the potential and actual harm which abuse can cause for children, in order that the situation is not minimised. Some abusers who were themselves victims in childhood can be unaware of the impact which abuse can have. A very basic educative input as part of the treatment process focusing upon the needs of children, both material and emotional, is often of great benefit.

The development of self-awareness, based upon an evaluation of both the past and the present, may help some abusers to understand why they behave in the way they do. For some, this can be an extremely threatening and painful process, particularly if the past contains elements of great sadness which have been suppressed for many years. Helping some clients to write down a simple life story can be a way of beginning to assist in the development of personal insight. It can reinforce a sense of self which may well have been distorted and warped through the years by some sort of constant denial.

Helping adults to learn effective and socially acceptable methods of child care can also be a crucial factor in treatment. This may often involve the therapist in observing the offender and the victim together, pointing out situations of stress and discussing more appropriate means of dealing with them, such as send a son to bed early, instead of hitting him with a stick or threatening to leave him.

Just as is the case with the victim, it will be counterproductive to concentrate solely upon the negative aspects of the life of an abusing adult. As we have seen, many abusers have few normal social outlets, friends or hobbies. Eventually, the encouragement of a more varied and less isolated perspective will help the abuser to feel a greater sense of self-respect, and this may in turn minimise the risk of future abuse.

We have seen how it is that many abusers feel the need to play out issues of control, through the victimisation of children. This desire for control may be tested out within the treatment process. The abuser must not be allowed to achieve control, but ought to be encouraged to explore the reasons why this need for power and control is projected on to children.

Group Work for Victims

The use of group therapy in the treatment of victims of child abuse has some advantages over individual treatment for some clients. It is normal for adolescents to be influenced to a significant extent by their friends and by people of their own age, often more so than by their parents. For most adolescents, this apparent shift in relationships is part of the normal process of developing into an independent adult. At the time when young teenagers are beginning to doubt and question the authority of their parents, all adults can become a source of antagonism for them. They prefer to confide in their school friends, rather than to bring their problems home. In terms of abused youngsters of this age group, the strength that can be derived from their contact with young people of similar ages can be a productive therapeutic tool.

A small group of youngsters, brought together by one or two therapists who have the appropriate skills necessary to work with groups, can help to enhance work which may be going on in individual sessions. Some victims are actively isolated from their community by their abusers, and may gain enormously from the confidence that comes from becoming a member of a group. It may benefit victims to be aware of the fact that they are not alone, that they will not be shunned by other people because of what has happened, and that they, just like the other members in the group, are normal people who have been involved in abnormal events. If the group comprises a mixture of personalities in different stages of therapy, reticent youngsters may be encouraged to share experiences by more confident members of the group in a more natural way than could ever be achieved in individual sessions with their therapist.

Such groups can together examine a variety of practical issues which might help to minimise a recurrence of the abuse. Self-assertiveness training, and an examination of options available should abuse recur are tasks which groups of victims might usefully explore together. Also, the creation of a local network, where victims expand the numbers of their associates, could increase the possible alternatives open to those who continue to be victims.

The introduction of a youngster to a group of abuse victims requires a great deal of thought and sensitive planning. If the young person is not adequately prepared or ready for the experience, the process itself may be too threatening and abusive. Victims can offer empathy and understanding to other abused children in a way which is not possible for the therapist to achieve. If carefully handled, such groups can be extremely therapeutic. Therapists must be aware, however, of the enormous power which groups can create, and this power

245

can have the capacity for good and for ill, in relation both to clients and therapists.

Group Work for Abusers

In-depth therapy for abusers is not commonly available throughout the UK. There are a small number of projects available, run both by the statutory agencies and private therapists, which are beginning to examine this significant gap in the services being provided, but much of this work is at an experimental stage. The use of group work for abusers is a well-tested technique in the USA, but cannot be said to be common practice in the UK. Putting offenders in groups for the purpose of treatment may have a number of positive effects, not the least of which is the cost-effectiveness of the treatment.

If an abuser is introduced into a group with others who may be at various stages of the treatment process, the pressure which the group might bring to bear on the new arrival not to minimise what he or she has done can be helpful. A part of that same process is a tendency on the part of some offenders to minimise their offence in terms of the effect it had on the victim. Confronting this person with other offenders, some of whom have already worked through this denial and who can recognise their behaviour in that of the new arrival, may be a means by which this particular and significant barrier to treatment is dealt with more effectively than by individual counselling.

Some offenders become consumed by guilt and anguish about their behaviour. This damages further a fragile self-image which may have contributed to the abuse in the first place. As with the victim, abusers may gain from experiencing contact with others who may have been involved in similar activities. It will help them to feel less isolated, and could begin the process by which some degree of self-respect (and self-control) is reconstituted.

Some basic child care skills training can be introduced into group sessions which will benefit from the contributions of all group members. They must be encouraged to share experiences as part of the collective learning process. Significant numbers of abusers lack understanding about the needs of children, and continue to minimise the potential damage which their abuse is creating.

For both victims and abusers, group treatment must complement any individual therapy which is taking place. It is a recipe for disaster if a number of treatment methods are pulling clients in different directions. A network of communication between all the different treatment strands must be established, in order that isues not appropriate to one forum can be dealt with in another. This ensures that individual needs are met.

FAMILY WORK

In most cases of child abuse, the family unit remains a critical factor in relation to the outcome for all those involved. Whether affected deeply or only peripherally, all members of the family group will have a part to play in organising the future. Whether the plans are that the family remains together or not in the aftermath of abuse, it is wrong to ignore the importance of this group. The need to involve family members in some collective treatment holds true, whatever other work is being undertaken. In order to judge the degree to which a child is at risk in the future, some observation of the family dynamics is necessary. There may be issues within the family which have significantly contributed to the abuse. These must be dealt with by way of family treatment, alongside ongoing work with a variety of its constituent parts.

Family sessions can help to reassert responsibility for the abuse, allowing the victim to hear from the adult abuser that it was not the child's fault. This can help to diminish feelings of guilt that the child may have, and can assist the family as a whole to begin to view the abuse in a realistic way. It frees them to talk about an issue which may have been a taboo subject for so long.

247

Taking video recordings of family sessions can help individuals to understand their strengths and weaknesses. If, for example, the adult male is overbearing, speaking for other family members, using tones of voice and threatening body language to suppress the views of others, being able to see himself in action can be a salutary experience. A key feature of family work is to encourage the development of clearly-perceived communication systems within the group. Are all the family members good listeners? Do they encourage each other to express their feelings and wishes? The achievement of better communication and an open, honest approach to problems is likely to go a long way towards improving the quality of life for both the individual members and the family group as a whole.

Some practical aspects of home life can also be dealt with in family sessions. For example, in the case of a physically abusing household, family meetings can explore the issue of behaviour and discipline. What things upset the parents most? How do they punish the children? How can the behaviour of the children by more appropriately modified? Some sexual offenders who are being rehabilitated into the home may also benefit from the establishment of basic rules and regulations at key times in the family routine, bathtime and bedtime in particular. Does Daddy bathe the children? Are the children allowed in their parents' bedroom? What kind of touching is acceptable, and what is not? What signs should family members watch out for if abuse is recurring, and what do they do about it? However awkward and unpalatable some of these tasks may be, they all serve as a means of prevention, which in the long run is to everyone's benefit.

The family must not be allowed to sink into an emotional abyss by being labelled as 'abusing'. Throughout therapy, positive aspects of the family must be acknowledged and encouraged. What does the family like to do together? Why don't they do it more often? What does each family member like most about the family? Positive elements always coexist with the less favourable traits of these families, and must be promoted, not ignored.

PROBLEMS WITH TREATMENT

In cases where particularly serious abuse comes to light, it is often impossible for the family to remain together. The alleged abuser may be in police custody or in prison, or the children of the household are removed into the care of the local authority, or are required to live with friends or relatives. In such circumstances, it is often difficult to plan an integrated treatment package. Feelings about removal from home, and the prospects for an eventual return, are likely to occupy a central place in the thoughts of victims and offenders alike, which can limit the degree to which issues related to the abuse itself are dealt with. Allied to this problem is the time it sometimes takes for cases to be processed in the courts, whether through criminal or civil proceedings. It can often be many months after the discovery of abuse before a case is finally dealt with by the courts. This time-lag can create a situation of uncertainty which hinders the establishment of a suitable treatment plan to which all relevant parties are committed.

There are often large numbers of individuals who have an influence upon the views of victims, abusers and their families. Members of the extended family, such as grandparents, aunts, uncles, cousins, and so on, may all be influential in shaping the responses of members of the family most closely involved in the abuse. It is inconceivable that a combination of therapists, using a variety of treatment techniques, could hope to effect change in the views of everyone having knowledge about the case. Nor could those involved in treatment be kept away from the well-meaning intentions of others. Pressures can be brought to bear, particularly upon the victim, to retract allegations, or to minimise the abuse, so as to limit the disruption to family life. In reality, these pressures must be accepted by the therapist, who must attempt to reinforce reality and objectivity with those for whom treatment has been designed.

The pressure which abusers can place upon victims to deny or minimise the abuse, by way of the actual or implied threat of violence and/or re-abuse, may often severely limit the degree to which treatment can be pursued. The strength of the denial within some offenders is often immeasurable, and this remains one of the major obstacles to treatment. The issue of denial can create unexpected complications for families from time to time. For example, consider the case of a ten-year-old girl who discloses that her father is having sexual intercourse with her. Due to lack of corroborative evidence, and a denial on the part of her father, she is removed from home and placed in a children's home. She immediately begins to retract her statement, saying that she told at the beginning to try and get Dad into trouble. Over time, if this situation persists, complications can develop. We expect denial and retraction in some cases. How long do we refuse to accept it as the truth? What if the child's original story was false? In some way, denial is viewed as further evidence that abuse has occurred. If our message is offenders is 'Tell us the truth and we will try to help you', what do we do if the 'truth' which they tell doesn't equate with what we want to hear? These problems are very real and must be taken into account. The significance of a thorough investigation prior to the development of a treatment plan in each case cannot be stressed too strongly.

Treatment designed to enhance self-awareness and better communication, whilst not taking into account practical difficulties which may be a central source of family malfunction, is likely to be of minimal use. The link between economic deprivation and child abuse is important. Any therapist attempting to engage in work with people who feel completely entrapped by their material circumstances, who fails to consider ways in which the situation can be alleviated, is likely to have little long-term impact. A great deal of family treatment is expected to take place with families who operate under the most appalling financial and social constraints. It may be that we expect too much of treatment with this client group.

Similarly, treatment designed to promote insight, without the prior provision of adequate practical child care skills, is likely to be of limited use. This is particularly so, in families whose abuse of their children relates more to practical inadequacy than to more deep-seated psychological problems.

ASSESSING OUTCOMES

A source of frustration for social workers and other professionals in the child protection field is the problem of judging how influential treatment has been in the long-term. When a person has been working with a family for a long time, and is able to see progress, in that the abuse seems to have stopped and the family members appear happier and more contented, how much of this progress is due to treatment and how much is due to the passage of time? For families who are engaged in serious and protracted forms of abuse, the passage of time seems to have no healing properties at all. The influence of treatment remains an extremely elusive concept.

The professionals must develop a clear perception of the major problems which were present at the time treatment started, and develop strategies for working on them, keeping the whole process under review. They must also work with clearly understood goals and objectives in mind, so that significant change can be adequately monitored. In terms of victims in particular, the goals of treatment must centre around the desire to limit or eradicate the abuse, and to promote normal development. There may be families who do not respond to treatment, as a result of chronic psychological problems, or a complete refusal to acknowledge the abuse. Many abusers will have developed such a strong association with their abusive behaviour, or may be so intellectually limited as to make it unrealistic for treatment of any type to modify their behaviour to any extent.

It would be wrong to assume that treatment has failed if the result is a decision that a particular individual or family is not to be trusted with the care of the children in future. Similarly, if a marriage breaks up as a result of the discovery of abuse or if a child finds himself or herself in long-term care, efforts which have been made in treatment to help those involved to communicate, to learn about themselves and to express their feelings have not necessarily been wasted. Although treatment in such cases has not led to a resumption of the old family system, it may well have helped the process by which long-term decisions have been reached, and have been of benefit to the future development and adjustment of the people involved. This will enable them to lead more fulfilled lives, a little more in control of their feelings about the abuse than might otherwise have been possible.

When one looks at a family whose members have been in treatment for some time, with a view to assessing the degree of progress which has been made, there are a number of key indicators to study.

Family members must understand the abuse, and where responsibility for it lies. This includes the victim, the abuser, and all other involved people. There must be a surety that feelings of guilt and blame, as well as denial and anger, have been tempered by a realistic acceptance of the truth.

The children of the household must be able to be more self-assertive. This will give an indication of the growth in confidence of the children, and their ability to take action to protect themselves in future.

Family members should listen to each other. This will prove that communication has been improved, and family members are more able to share problems in the knowledge that they will be listened to. This makes the prospect of collusive and secretive abuse less likely to develop, and minimises the formation of family sub-groups which exclude other members.

The non-abusing parent is more confident. In those cases where one adult partner has been either unaware of the abusive activities of the other, or felt unable to do anything about it, an increased awareness of responsibility and the need to actively protect children should have developed. The non-abusing parent is now confident that they would both detect or be told of the abuse and would know what to do about it.

The parental relationship has improved. In those cases where there have been problems, relationship issues have been discussed openly and acknowledged, on both sides. Some evidence that the relationship is more rewarding and equal is desirable.

Relationship boundaries have been established. The family relates to each other appropriately. Parents no longer have unrealistic expectations of the children. And there has been the introduction of a routine, encompassing standards of behaviour and sanctions which are understood and accepted, from the point of view of both adults and children.

Adult/child relationships are better. These relationships are less fraught and anxiety-provoking than perhaps used to be the case. Parents and children derive appropriate pleasure and satisfaction from the relationship, and are able to talk about positive and negative feelings towards other family members openly without undue fear of reprisals.

There is an acceptance of progress. The professionals as well as the clients feel happy about the case. This might sound banal, but it is a fact that there is often very little of substance on which to base positive reactions, except a feeling that things are improving. If these feelings are shared by others, then this is often a sign that progress has been made.

HOW LONG DOES TREATMENT LAST?

There is no way of knowing how long a client, or a family, will be in treatment. This must depend upon the extent of the problems which the abuse has caused, and on the ability of the clients and the therapists to be involved in productive work. Long-term treatment, of two years and more, can begin to be detrimental to clients, who can develop an unhealthy dependence upon a therapist. There is a danger in such cases for the professional to enjoy the feeling of being needed, retaining the case for their benefit rather than that of the client. A clear set of objectives, and a method of intervention which is periodically reviewed, coupled with regular supervision and consultation with professional colleagues, can help to keep the professional relationship in context. It will also alert those involved to the time when treatment can end.

TERMINATION

A client who has grown to trust a therapist, who has helped them work through some painful and confusing issues, and who may have helped them to feel better about themselves, is likely to find the idea of termination of the professional relationship difficult. For a time, this may lead to a regression to earlier, mal-adaptive behaviours. Victims may feel further victimised, they may feel that trust has once more been broken. Abusers may feel anger and guilt, and a sense of isolation may ensue. These temporary regressions are to be expected and will require discussion. Their temporary nature will become self-evident if the timing has been correct.

In social work, some terminations occur due to other, less client-centred reasons. People may leave jobs, and teams may feel under pressure to limit the extent to which they engage in long-term therapy in favour of more immediate crisis-intervention work. On such occasions, the potential damage done to clients can be extensive and is often underestimated.

11 Future Developments

Some areas of child protection are likely to be the focus of increasing debate in the future. In many ways, it is fair to say that a concerted response to the problem of child abuse has begun to take shape only recently. It is a facet of human behaviour about which we have only become conscious in relatively modern times. As our limited knowledge expands, so our response to the problem becomes more sophisticated. This developmental process has gathered pace during the last two decades. It has been given impetus by the publicity which some tragic and particularly horrific cases attract, and also as a result of the growing numbers of professionals who work in the field of child protection.

The abuse of children is now a phenomenon which occupies an increasingly important place on the national agenda. More knowledge of the subject can help in the development of procedures to confront the problem. It can also create tensions and stresses, as we attempt to take into account our growing awareness, being mindful of the limited resources with which we have to work. A number of areas are particularly significant in relation to the future of child protection work, and these need to be examined realistically.

THE ORGANISATION OF SOCIAL WORK

Many social workers who work within local authority social services departments are trained to practise generic social work. That is to say, they work with the whole range of client groups, from children and juvenile offenders, to the mentally and physically handicapped and the elderly. Child protection is a task which requires particular skills and knowledge. The work is complex, and extremely stressful. It is unrealistic to

255

suppose that every trained worker will be adequately equipped to deal effectively with cases of child protection.

In the 1980s, social work organisations have begun to develop more specialist responses to a variety of client groups. This has certainly been the case in child protection, where numbers of departments now have child protection teams whose staff work more or less exclusively in that field, and receive post-qualifying training aimed at developing their skills in the particular area. The voluntary/private sector has often been at the forefront in establishing pioneering new projects in specialist areas. The move towards greater specialisation in local authority social services will probably pick up pace over the next few years, as it seems unrealistic to expect individuals to provide general services to all types of clients. Social workers have their strengths and weaknesses. They often display a greater enthusiasm for, and commitment to one client group than another. The more we learn about a subject, the more sophisticated becomes the response, and this is true of all aspects of social work. In time, it will become difficult to justify the maintenance of generic social work. Rather, there will be workers who provide a referral point, who are trained to provide general advice, or a response in emergency situations, but whose main function will be to refer clients on to more specialist teams depending upon the type of case.

Whilst there is evidence of this happening at present, and I am confident that this approach will develop, there are some problems associated with it. The issue of child abuse is not one which can be understood in splendid isolation. Families within which abuse is occurring are likely to be experiencing a whole range of problems, many of which will be factors contributing to the ill-treatment of children. The need to adopt a holistic response to situations of abuse must not be compromised by the growth of ever more specialist units. Whilst more and more social workers will probably find themselves working in a specialist setting in the future, the need for their basic training to provide them with a general grounding in the whole range of social work tasks will remain strong. This training will prevent the response they give to their clients from becoming limited and constrained by too blinkered an approach.

INTER-AGENCY CO-OPERATION

Allied to the move towards greater specialisation is the likelihood that some elements of our response to child abuse will become integrated across current professional boundaries. Guidelines and procedures have, over the years, encouraged closer co-operation (particularly at the investigative stage of cases of child abuse) between social services, the police and the health authorities. There will probably come a time when investigative and assessment units, comprising professionals from the three key agencies, will work much more closely together. This concept will perhaps be developed to a point where numbers of professionals from different agencies work under the same roof, with a brief to respond to the early stages of a child protection case – it is becoming increasingly evident that co-operation is required to a degree which cannot be guaranteed simply by working to a set of procedures.

Genuine co-operation depends a great deal upon the working relationships which are developed between practitioners in different agencies. As our response to child abuse develops, some aspects of case management will probably be dealt with by a genuinely co-operative team of professionals from different agencies, working from a multi-agency unit. I am not advocating an erosion of the distinctions between the tasks of different professionals involved in child protection. I think that we need to closely examine those parts of child protection which do require collaboration, and enter fully into co-working in those areas. Some aspects of the initial investigation fall into that category. There are a whole range of other tasks, relating to assessment, and especially treatment, for which social work ought to retain its unique role.

PREVENTION

It is in the area of prevention that significant progress needs to be made in the next few years. It is becoming evident that, without a large input of new resources both in terms of training, support and manpower, the growing numbers of cases of abuse which are coming to light are making current stretched resources increasingly inadequate. It is important that we continue to develop a response which attempts to prevent abuse from happening in the first place, as well as striving to improve the provision of services to cases which are referred.

The education of parents and children, both in schools and through the media, is commendable, but inadequate. By no means wishing to mislead the public into a crisis response to the subject, I do none the less support an increase in those educative programmes which attempt to help children in particular to protect themselves. Children must be made aware of the need to assert some degree of control over what they allow adults to do to them. They must be taught what to do if they find themselves in an abusing relationship. Similarly, adults need to receive more considered information about the nature of the problem, so that they can be on the lookout for abuse both in their own families and within their communities. Hopefully, this will encourage them to make referrals with the confidence that they will be dealt with professionally and in a considered way, which puts the interests of the child first.

More contentiously, it may be the case that if our society were to move away from a simple punitive model for dealing with abusers to one which focused more on the need to provide abusers with treatment for what is a serious problem, more actual or would-be offenders may come forward for help. However, associated with this point is the general debate about the origins of abuse. In some cases, it may be appropriate to consider much more seriously research findings linking abuse to economic and social deprivation. A failure to acknowledge this would lead some to say that the single most important issue relating to prevention is ignored. My view is that social work is ill equipped to do anything about this issue, other than to point out to the policy-makers that the links appear to be there. The frustration felt about working with some clients whose problems are not self-created, and who are consequently able to do little about them, must be accepted as part of the job.

I also feel that we need to conduct much more research into the relationship between abuse and the media, in its widest sense. Pornography is a particularly obvious example of this alleged link. Does exposure to pornographic material, which may contain elements of violence and under-age sex, make some people more likely to abuse children? I have heard arguments for and against. There are those who talk about individual choice. Surely, they claim, a person is not forced to watch a pornographic film, read a particular magazine or book? For most adults this is true of course. It is not true for children, some of whom are exposed either accidentally or deliberately to these materials. Nor is free choice being exercised for children if they are abused as a consequence of the influence upon the offender of exposure to pornography. If there is a link, it may well be justifiable as a further preventive measure to think of ways of limiting or eradicating the flourishing trade in pornography.

There is a serious problem regarding prevention with which social workers are only too aware. How is it possible effectively to measure the success of a preventive programme? All too often, social workers and other child protection professionals become sucked into a working environment in which they spend most of their time responding to cases of abuse. There is little time left for prevention. As resources are squeezed, preventive initiatives are often among the first to be dropped, in favour of the more immediate, easier to understand task of dealing with actual abuse. How would it be possible for social work agencies to limit their involvement in cases of notified abuse in favour of spending time helping families to avoid abuse in the first place? If a social worker is working in a preventive capacity with a family, and no abuse takes place, is this as a result of their intervention skills or would there have been no abuse if they had never been involved?

We are slowly collecting a body of knowledge about why abuse happens. We ought to begin to target imaginative prevention programmes within certain sections of the community, guided by this growing knowledge. Abuse of children will never be eradicated, but in the long term, taking into account some of the horrendous effects of severe abuse, prevention is certainly better than cure.

TREATMENT OF ABUSERS

This is a subject about which I feel particularly strongly, and it is related closely to the debate about treatment. Understandably enough, much of our effort when abuse is discovered is aimed at helping the victim. Abusers, in my experience, often receive scant consideration. Some of them are prosecuted and many receive custodial sentences. Many of them never get to court, and persist in minimising or denying the abuse. I have met abusers who have repeatedly ill-treated children in a number of ways, regardless of whether they have been prosecuted or not.

Research findings would tend to support the view that they are often likely to re-offend if they do not receive intensive treatment. The extent to which we currently offer treatment to abusers is patchy. It is not an area of work about which many people feel confident or in which many are experienced. In my view, this represents a very serious gap in the service we provide. The key to protecting children is to limit the likelihood that their abusers will hurt them. My concern is that, as yet, only very limited attempts have been made to link treatment up with the criminal justice system. Many attempts to offer treatment to abusers, to help them to see the damaging effects of their behaviour, and to examine the reasons why they behave in the way they do, occur without any firm legal boundaries. Voluntary agreements to enter into therapy which challenges them critically to explore their behaviour may often fail. I have heard a number of therapists from the USA who have been convinced that therapy will only be effective if entered into as part of an agreement made in the courts.

It is my hope for the future that we will see an increasing activity around proper offender treatment programmes, and an acknowledgement by the courts that it may often be better, in terms of future prevention, to consign defendants to periods of treatment rather than incarceration. Increasing the numbers of abusers who are brought before the courts will depend upon the developing public awareness of the size of the problem, and more professional initial investigative techniques.

CHILDREN IN COURT

I have discussed, albeit briefly, the impact upon children of an appearance in court (*see* Chapter 6), and some recent developments aimed at allowing their evidence to be submitted in a way which maximises accuracy and minimises trauma. The more effective the court process is, in relation to child witnesses, the greater the likelihood that abusers will be convicted. We must be wary about achieving a balance between the rights of adult defendants and child witnesses. Many would claim that at present the balance is weighted too much in favour of the adult.

It remains to be seen whether the introduction of video technology into the court room, both in terms of relaying live evidence from another room, and of replaying earlier interviews with children, will improve the legal process. The possible relaxation of the rules of evidence, in regard to uncorroborated evidence in sexual abuse cases, may also prove to increase the numbers of cases successfully prosecuted in the courts. Referring to my comments about treatment of abusers, I hope that the result of these proposals is that increasing numbers of abusers are successfully encouraged to enter into therapeutic contracts, within the boundaries of an order made in the court. This is better than allowing the prison population to grow, in the knowledge that many ex-convicts soon repeat their abuse on other unfortunate victims.

A NATIONAL REGISTER

Locally administered child protection registers are often difficult to compare, from area to area. In spite of every effort to manage the transfer of information effectively when a registered child moves from one area to another, mistakes are still made. In the future, a national register will hopefully be set up which will make the transfer of information more effective, and will help to provide a much more effective database with which to consider the allocation of resources to better effect. I would also like to see the establishment of a national register of dangerous adults, so that some attempt is made to monitor the movements of adults about which there are major concerns. In many ways, in spite of its implications in terms of human rights, such a register would make more sense to me as an aid to prevention than our current register of children. The current systems which we operate in an attempt to monitor the movements of known Schedule 1 offenders is flawed. This issue requires urgent consideration.

SOCIAL WORK IN A
MULTI-CULTURAL SOCIETY

It is established how difficult it is to define child abuse. Whilst we may have little trouble in describing the extremes of behaviour, we begin to encounter major problems as we strive for consensus about what constitutes abusing behaviour which isn't extreme. In a society which comprises a mixture of cultural groupings, each of which may have its own ideas as to what constitutes that elusive term 'good enough parenting', this consensus becomes more difficult to determine.

In order to reflect the reality of the society in which we live, social work must recruit staff from a diversity of ethnic backgrounds. As in many other professions, this goal appears to be hard to achieve. In part, the reason for this may be to do with the perception which some ethnic minority groupings have of social work. Racism is an extremely pervasive form of abuse in the UK, and this is no doubt a factor which contributes heavily to the under-representation of some sections of our society in the social work field.

There is a general lack of understanding of the impact of these issues. In the course of their practice, most social workers tend to deal with each case on its merits, adopting similar criteria when assessing the need for action, whatever the ethnic background of the clients. If this is bad practice, then it is in part evidence of a general lack of both education and research in this area. I sincerely hope that social workers are helped to be more aware of the need to understand abuse as it relates to minority groups. I feel that a good first step in this direction is to be more honest about the existence of racism in the workplace and within our communities, and to be much more proactive about recruiting people into social work from within minority groups.

SOCIAL WORK AND THE PUBLIC

I may seem critical of the way in which social work is sometimes portrayed in the press. I hope that I have balanced this by acknowledging that social workers who do a complex and risky job sometimes get it wrong, and that there are times when they deserve criticism.

The relationship which social workers have with the public is probably not good. I think that most of us would feel this to be the case. If this is true, it has worrying implications for the future of child protection services. We need the confidence and active co-operation of the public in order to discharge our duties effectively. The profession of social work itself is, in part, to blame for any misunderstanding of its role. I do not feel that we are active enough in promoting what we do. We are adopting an ever more defensive and guarded stance, when I feel that we should be much more vocal in acknowledging our strengths as well as our weaknesses. In the future, I would hope that, as a profession, we could become more assertive about what the public can expect from us. We should be honest about the limitations of our role, and help people to understand more clearly the constraints under which we are working.

Some aspects of child protection are being opened up to public participation in ways which were not considered appropriate a few·years ago. The invitation of parents to case conferences, and access to records, are two examples of this shift. This should be built upon in the future, in order that the misunderstandings which often take place in the wake of a reported crisis are less likely to happen. The challenge for social workers is that openness means increased scrutiny and accountability. We must develop our own sense of professional worth before we can hope to convey it to the general public.

In the field of child protection in particular, social work has been facing a crisis of confidence which, to a large extent, found expression during 1987 in Cleveland. It is my firmly held opinion that social workers would be assured of the support of the general public if only the latter were provided with more information about the social work role, and about the resources with which it has to be carried out.

CONCLUSION

As I come to the end of this book, I am acutely aware of its limitations. Its scope was far too broad to allow for detailed discussion of most issues. I have therefore found myself heavily editing its contents, making some aspects which I have discussed appear much too over-simplified. I hope that I have given a realistic overview of some of the major issues, and that it might encourage more detailed study of some aspects of the subject.

There is very little which can be said about the subject of child abuse which is absolute fact. Even medical findings, and some aspects of the law are open to individual interpretation. The social work profession is a relatively new one, and the professional response to child abuse is, in many respects, in its infancy. A balanced picture of some of the major areas of current debate is very difficult to give mainly because there is much about which I have no definite opinion. A healthy scepticism about dogmatic attitudes would be the sensible view to hold relative to the current state of our knowledge of child abuse, its origins, and how to deal with it.

I hope that this book hasn't completely destroyed anyone's faith in human nature. Child abuse is, as far as we know, not an activity in which the majority participate. Most children enjoy a happy, carefree childhood, with adults who derive their pleasure from watching youngsters develop into healthy independent young people. It is my hope that in the coming years, this majority of the population will steadily grow, as an increasingly informed partnership between the public and child protection agencies makes the abuse of children an unusual event.

Bibliography

Baker, A. and Duncan, S., 'Child Sexual Abuse: A Study of Prevalence in Great Britain', *Child Abuse and Neglect* Vol. 9, pp 457–467, Pergamon Press (1985)

Bevan, H.K., *The Law Relating to Children*, Butterworth (1973)

Blom-Cooper, L., *A Child ·in Mind*. The report of the commission of inquiry into the circumstances surrounding the death of Kimberley Carlile, London Borough of Greenwich (1987)

Bolton, F.G. and S.R., *Working with Violent Families*, Sage Publications (1987)

Bremner, R.H., *Children and Youth in America: A Documentary History* Vol. II 1866–1933, Harvard University Press (1971)

Butler-Sloss, E., *Report of the Inquiry into Child Abuse in Cleveland 1987*, HMSO (1988)

Campbell, B., *Unofficial Secrets. Child Sexual Abuse: The Cleveland Case*, Virago (1988)

Chapman, M.G.T. and Woodmansey, A.C., 'Policy on Child Abuse' (SCP Report No. 13), *British Journal of Clinical and Social Psychiatry*, Vol. 3, No. 2 (June 1985)

Conte, J.R. and Shore, D. (Eds), *Social Work and Child Sexual Abuse*, Haworth (1982)

Cook, J.V. and Bowles, R.T., *Child Abuse. Commission and Omission*, Butterworth (1980)

Dale, P., *Dangerous Families*, Tavistock (1986)

Department of Health, *Survey of Children and Young Persons on Child Protection Registers, year ending 31st March 1988, England*, Personal Social Services, Local Authority Statistics (May 1989)

Department of Health and Social Security, *Non-Accidental Injury to Children*, HMSO (1974)

Department of Health and Social Security, *Child Abuse: Central Register Systems* (1980)

Department of Health and Social Security and the Welsh Office, *Working Together*, HMSO (1988) —

Dingwall, R., Eekelaar, J. and Murray T., *The Protection of Children. State Intervention and Family Life*, Blackwell (1983)

Ebeling, N.B. and Hill, D.A. (Eds), *Child Abuse: Intervention and Treatment*, Publishing Sciences Group (1975)

Finkelhor, D., *Sexually Victimised Children*, Free Press (1979)

Fineklhor, D., *Child Sexual Abuse. New Theory and Research*, Free Press (1984)

Gill, D., *Illegitimacy, Sexuality and the Status of Women*, Blackwell (1977)

Giovannoni, J. and Becerra, R., *Defining Child Abuse*, Free Press (1979)

Goldstein, Freud and Solnit, *Beyond the Best Interests of the Child*, Free Press (1973)

Goodman, L., *Clarke, Hall and Morrison's Law Relating to Children and Young Persons*, Butterworth (1972, 8th Edition)

Hallett, C. and Stevenson, O., *Child Abuse: Aspects of Interprofessional Co-operation*, Allen and Unwin (1980)

Holman, R., *Putting Families First. Prevention and Child Care*, Macmillan Education (1988)

Jones, D.N. (Ed), *Understanding Child Abuse*, Macmillan Education (1982, 2nd Edition)

Kempe, C.H. et al, 'The Battered Child Syndrome', *Journal of the American Medical Association*, No. 191 (1962)

Kempe, C.H. and Helfer, R., *Helping the Handicapped Child and His Family*, J.B. Lippincott (1972)

Kempe, C.H. and R.S., *Child Abuse*, Fontana (1978)

Leeding, A.E., *Child Care Manual for Social Workers*, Butterworth (1980, 4th Edition)

Light, R.J., 'Abused and Neglected Children in America: A study of alternative policies', *Harvard Educational Review*, No. 43

Maluccio, A.N., Fein, E. and Olmstead, K.A., *Permanency Planning for Children. Concepts and Methods*, Tavistock (1986)

Mayhall and Norgard, *Child Abuse and Neglect, Sharing Responsibilities*, Wiley and Sons (1983)

Pelton, L.H. (Ed), *The Social Context of Child Abuse and Neglect*, Human Sciences Press (1981)

Pringle, M.K., *The Needs of Children*, Hutchinson (1974)

Sedley, S. et al, *Whose Child?* The report of the public inquiry into the death of Tyra Henry, London Borough of Lambeth (1982)

Sgroi, S., *Handbook of Clinical Intervention in Child Sexual Abuse*, Lexington Books (1982)

Steele, B., 'Violence within the Family', in *Child Abuse and Neglect. The Family and the Community* (Helfer, R.E. and Kempe, C.H., Eds), Ballinger (1976)

Walker, C.E., Banner, B.L. and Kaufman, K.L., *The Physically and Sexually Abused Child. Evaluation and Treatment*, Pergamon Press (1988)

West, D.J. (Ed), *Sexual Victimisation*, Gower (1985)

Wooley, P.V. and Evans, W.A., 'The Significance of the Skeletal Lesion in Infants resembling those of Traumatic Origin', *Journal of the American Medical Association*, No. 158, 7 (1955)

Zander, M., *Social Workers, their Clients and the Law*, Sweet and Maxwell (1981)

Index

abuse (*see* child abuse)
abuser, treatment issues 243–4, 260–1
access 153
anal abuse 96–7
anatomical dolls 207–8
area child protection committees 170–1
assessment of risk 211–13

Baker, A. and Duncan, S. 53–4
Bergh, Henry 37
blood disorders 90
bonding 125–6
bone injuries 92–3
brittle bones 93
bruises 89–90
buggery 96–7
burns 93–4

Caffey, John 40
care orders 155–7
Carlile, Kimberley 100, 164
case conferences 175–8
centile charts 99–100
Chapman, M.G.T. and Woodmansey,
   A.C. 180
child abuse,
   behavioural effects 101–12
   physical effects 89–101
   statistics 48–52
child assessment orders 154
Child Care Act 1980 147
child protection registers 172–5
Children Act 1948 39
Children Act 1975 186
Children and Young Persons Act 1933
   144, 150
Children and Young Persons Act 1969
   149
childrens' departments 39
childrens' rights 189–97
civil law 142
Cleveland crisis 44, 94–5, 141, 150,
   187–8

Colwell, Maria 45–6, 169–70
communication 126
consent to medical examination 192
cot deaths 94
criminal law 142
criminal offences 144–6
Curtis committee 39
cycle of abuse 117–19

death, by child abuse 48–9
definitions of abuse,
   emotional abuse 30–1
   failure to thrive 27
   neglect 24–7
   physical abuse 21–4
   problems 14–20
   sexual abuse 27–9
delinquency 106
denial 233–4, 258
depression 103

Ellen, Mary 36–7
emergency protection orders 151–3
emotional abuse 100
   awareness of 47–8
   causes 124–9
   definitions 30–1
ethnic issues 262–3

failure to thrive 27, 31, 99–100
family work 247–8
feminism 46, 131
Freud, Sigmund 43–5

greenstick fractures 92
groupwork,
   for victims 244–6
   for abusers 246–7
guardian *ad litem* 158–9
guilt 234, 238

head injuries 91–92
health workers 204

Henry, Tyra   91–2
high risk children   138–40
homosexuality   110
Houghton committee   169
hymenal opening   95

immature parents   127
inappropriate maturity   104
incest   146
inflexibility   120
initial assessment, in or out of care
   214–15
initial treatment,
   communication   222–3
   effect on professionals   223–5
   structure   221–2
   trust   220–1
   who is the client   221
inter-agency co-operation,
   administrative problems   163–5
   future developments   257
   personal problems   167–9
   professional problems   165–7
internal injuries   94
intolerance   119
interviewing,
   abusers   210–11
   adolescents   208–9
   pre-school   207
   six- to thirteen-year-olds   208
investigation of abuse,
   duties of local authorities   148
   when things go wrong   215–20

Kempe, Henry   45
key worker   177

lack of trust   101
large families   128
learning difficulties   106–7
local authorities,
   duty to investigate   148
   duty to promote children's welfare
      147–8

manipulative personality   105–6
marital discord   122
masculinity   131
media   13

medical examinations,
   consent   192–3
   investigations   209–10
mental illness   131
multi-cultural issues   262–3

national register   262
neglect   97–100
   causes   124–9
   definitions   24–6
non-abused children in family   237–8
NSPCC   38

O'Neill, Dennis   39
over-alertness   103
over-protectiveness   31

parental rights,
   case conferences   193–5
   initial investigation   190–2
   medical examination   192–3
   registers   196–7
   reviews   195–6
parenting skills   235–7
passivity   103
past unresolved   133–4
permanency planning   185–7
physical abuse,
   causes   119–24
   definitions   21–24
   effects   89–94
place of safety orders   149–51
   problems   150–51
poor self-image   102–3
police,
   emergency procedures   154–5
   role in investigation   203–4
pregnancy   97
prematurity   140
pressure marks   90
prevention   258–60
Prevention of Cruelty Act 1889   38
procedures,
   administration   163–5
   co-operation between agencies   162–3
   developments   169–72
   help or hindrance   178–82
   problems   165–9
   role of   162